Gates of the Wind

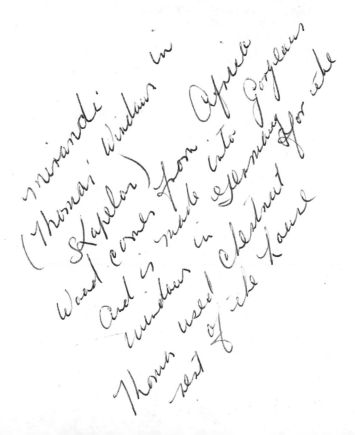

Miandi in
(Thomai Window in
Skapelos) Africa
Wood comes from into Gorgeans
And is made glowing for the
window in Germany
Thomai used Chestnut
rest of the house

EFSTATHIADIS GROUP S.A.

88, Drakontos str.
104 42 Athens
Tel.: 210 5195 800
Fax: 210 5195 900
GREECE

ISBN 960 226 089 0

Gates of the Wind

MICHAEL CARROLL

EFSTATHIADIS GROUP

Contents

Illustrations

* *Photograph by Irina Hale*
† *Photograph by David Gaun*

To
Evangelos Hannas
Δήμαρχον Σκοπέλου
Vangeli
'Admiral of the Northern Sporades'
and
'Best in the Balkans'

North to the Sporades

It looked as if the man was carved from the same grey rock on which he stood. Head lowered, his face in shadow, he held the trident poised at arm's length, the bright iron of the prongs glittering above the blue-green water at his feet. He stood there an age while the sun lowered itself in the sky, approaching the bare red mountain-top. I watched the sun and the fisherman and the surface of the water below him, until suddenly the trident flashed and fell, and the man crouched as if he had snapped free from the rock; and as the trident soared up again, scooped from the sea, I saw the water cascade in a rainbow trail from the octopus spitted at its point, the long tentacles writhing like a ragged flag over his head.

They shouted across to me later, the man who had speared the octopus, and his companion. They had a fire on the rocks, and as I rowed ashore in the dinghy, bringing my own contribution of tinned food and a flask of ouzo, the flames threw a leaping circle of light upon their hunched figures and hollowed faces, lighting the rocks above them and the crimson-painted bows of their boat below.

The wind had dropped a little. We sat round the fire after we had eaten, smoking while we offered ourselves to that mutual interrogation that passes for conversation among people on the sea who meet briefly in harbour or bay before moving on about their business. Who are you? Where do you come from? Where are you going? Banalities, but peculiarly satisfying: as if after so much time in a boat alone, with only the distant and changing shapes of mountain and cape by which to place himself, there grows in a man the need to voice his own identity, to affirm himself in relation to others; and when this speaking-out of names is over, then that further, humanly vital dimension is recaptured: he is whole again, restored, and ready to put out once more into those always strange sea-spaces that wait beyond the high entrances of every bay.

I had not spoken to anyone for five days. I had sailed up from Aigina, by Sunion and the Petali Islands, arriving in time to be caught there while the wind piled the sea through the straits, barring my way. I had already made one attempt to go north, and had been blown back. The two fishermen had left their village a week ago, fishing unsuccessfully down the east coast of Evvia until the *meltémi*, that north wind of summer, Etesian trade-wind of the ancients, had blown up – though a month early – and sent them scurrying south through the Cavo Doro, the straits between Evvia and Andros, and pushed them sideways into this deserted but sheltered little cove, set as it were between the toes of the Evvian mountains, that bare horny foot planted in the sea, dividing the Aegean north from south.

The lonely bay was becoming a place of decision, a dividing line, for me also: I had been waiting there, wind-bound, for two days and nights. The place was called Anemopýles, the Gates of the Wind. The gates were closed against me, the bolts shot home.

I could have been wrong about the name. Certainly the fisherman who had speared the octopus thought so. 'Anemopýles?' He shook his head. 'The Northern Sporades are called the gates of the wind.' He gestured northward, and raised his hand, fingers outspread. He touched each finger in turn, frowning as he recalled the names of the islands, one by one. 'Skiathos. Skopelos. Alonnisos. Kyra Panayia. Iura.' And then he put his mouth close to his extended hand and blew through his open fingers with a great hissing noise, and laughed. '*Aftá einai* – those are the gates of the wind.'

'*Katálava.*' I could see what he meant: on the chart the Sporades were spread out in a curved line, set like gate-posts across the Western Aegean; but the prospect did not seem very encouraging, for it was to those islands that I was intending to sail.

'Tomorrow?'

The taller of the two wiped his mouth with the back of his hand and glanced up appraisingly at the stars. '*Meltémi*. But in the evening, perhaps, it will stop.'

The probability of the *meltémi* dropping at sunset is a commonplace of Aegean sea-lore, but in the last few days the wind had blown day and night without ceasing. I made a decision: I would leave it to the wind, as, after all, I had done so often before. If it didn't stop in the evening then I would change my course, go south with the sea to

Milos where I had never been, or Crete, or Rhodes. I would give up the Sporades. Let the wind decide.

Next morning I waited while the wind screamed through the rigging. By afternoon it seemed to be blowing less strongly. I could see the two fishermen bestirring themselves with their nets and gear, and tensely as always before the possibility of a night passage, and still only half believing, I began to make my own preparations.

An hour before sunset the caique left. The men hailed me as they passed. 'Go now!'

The bay was empty; the wind had died to a sigh. Everything was still. I began to haul in the anchor chain. The slow grate of its iron links echoed from the hills.

*   *   *   *

It had begun, I suppose, about seven years before, with journeys to Greece as an undergraduate, to the Peloponnese, Crete, the Ionian Islands; and later, on the way east, and beginning to be a writer – one long journey through Persia to India – a visit to Mount Athos. That last, to the Holy Mountain, was of special significance, for on a morning in early September, chugging across a blue silk scarf of water in a local caique towards the Mountain's port of entry, was suddenly born an idea that even then seemed to contain the germ of a whole way of life. It was, simply enough, to get a boat, just big enough to live on, and sail the island-studded waters of the Aegean.

It was not until three years later that the boat was launched in the shadow of Cornish hills, and late that same summer, after three months' leisurely sailing, nosed her way out of the Corinth Canal into the Aegean Sea.

Astarte is clinker-built of mahogany, oak-beamed, and basically of a sturdy Cornish fishing-boat design; she measures thirty-two feet by ten. There is no cockpit so that her deck slopes at one level from bows to stern, where a carved balustrade surrounds a seat and the tiller, this deck and rail being a common feature among caiques of the North Aegean. In sailing language she is called a cutter, which means she has three sails: jib and staysail before the mast, and a mainsail, gaff-rigged and 'loose-footed', which means there is no boom; her sails are coloured a dark red-rust, or wine. A 20-b.h.p. diesel takes her through windless waters at about six knots. Below there is a roomy main cabin and forecastle, with the usual fittings. With her long bowsprit, clipper bow and transom stern she looks as much like a caique as a yacht, which was just as I had intended, except that she is painted white with dark blue coamings. A great friend of mine who is a sculptor carved her a figure-head, an image of the Phoenician goddess Astarte, for whom the boat is named, ancient and potent deity of the moon, of fertility and the sea, ancestress of the Greek Aphrodite.

I had been told that I was an escapist and a romantic; the same could be said of anyone with a boat. I loved the Greece I knew, her climate and her people, the kind of free life that could be had with a boat among the islands. I did not want to get involved, to be tied down, anywhere, even in Greece; and with a boat this was easy – if I didn't like a place I had only to start the motor or hoist a sail, pull up the anchor and move on.

But I had been discovering, slowly enough, that living on a boat was in itself a full-time occupation; the mere effort and time required to keep afloat and alive, simple self-preservation, left remarkably little of either time or energy for anything else. The books I had planned to write as *Astarte* ploughed between the islands had failed to materialize; any writing I did was always when I was safely and firmly on land, and being one of those unfortunates who is never content with what he has, I found I was looking for something more: a place to come back to after every voyage, a kind of base.

Perhaps it was more, even, than that. I was beginning to sense that this freedom that I boasted, this uninvolvement, held the seeds of its own imprisonment. Here I was, always an outsider, looking in for a moment, moving on, unconnected. I felt the lack of something – other people, a place to belong to, and, not caring to admit it too explicitly, found myself always searching for what I called the 'perfect natural harbour', a safe anchorage in all seasons and all weathers. It must be beautiful; there must be fresh water, and trees, and no one else living there, and yet it should not be too far from some island town or village.

I was sometimes afraid that I would never find such perfection; that no one place could fulfil all these conditions. Often I had come upon a bay that possessed one or even more of the three essential characteristics, but which inevitably lacked another. After two years I was able to eliminate certain areas from the search: the Dode-

canese were too remote, the Cyclades too dry and barren. . . .
Perhaps I would never know what I was really looking for until I had
found it.

The year before Khios and Samos had filled my imagination. I
had gone north inside the Evvian channel, emerged by Cape Arte-
mision and sailed too quickly through that little known group of
islands called the Northern Sporades – putting in only at the main
harbours, hurrying to cross the Aegean where I was convinced I
would find my anchorage. In Khios and Samos, as far as my search
was concerned, I was disappointed; but that winter in England,
waiting for the spring again, there kept floating across my memory
the shapes of those islands that I had passed by so hurriedly, the
Sporades: broad mountain tops rising high into the brilliant Greek
sky, slopes green with pine forests, speckled white with villages; and
again I remembered them as I had left them, as they dropped slowly
astern, purple shadows humped on the horizon, imbued as sometimes
such places are with a mystery and a promise that seemed to gesture
to me personally, and wait only for my return.

The straits of the Cavo Doro, between Evvia and Andros, are
notorious as much for current as for wind; also in those narrows are
gathered the threads of shipping routes from Sabnika and Istanbul
to Piraeus and the western Mediterranean. In place of the *meltémi* a
light westerly hardly ruffled the starlit swell, just filling the staysail
that I hoisted more for the conspicuousness it might lend me than
for any addition in power. There was no moon. Because of *Atarte*'s
own motor I could not hear the engines of the big ships using the
straits that night, the tankers and cargo vessels, steamers and passenger liners; but I could see their lights, glittering from miles away,
and I watched them apprehensively as they grew brighter bearing
down on me simultaneously from ahead and astern: the tankers'
array of mast lights, the liners' tiers of illuminated portholes, strings
of deck lights, like enormous candled birthday cakes drifting through
the night. I kept my course, with every light full on, torch flashing
on the red sail. Only once did a ship have to change direction
for me, though it did so rather later than I would have liked, and I
stood and saw the cigarette-end glow of the sailor leaning over the
rails at the stern, and as *Astarte* bucked and bobbed in the ship's
bow waves I relieved my feelings by shouting something after

him, a cry lost, perhaps just as well, in the thunder of powerful engines, in the hiss of phosphorescent turmoil churned up by giant screws.

A slow dawn lit the grey shoulders of Skyros lifting above the horizon far to the north. Skyros lies apart, some forty miles to the south of the main group of the Sporades. With sunrise I began to identify the capes and offshore islands as unwillingly they separated one from the other as I approached, and with the first shafts of the sun came the first gusts of the *meltémi*, roughening to white the sea ahead of me, and on the fingers of the wind the scent of Aegean hills. The wind sharpened the light of that early morning, the barren peaks of Skyros shone with borrowed gold. The island as it rose higher towards me seemed like a censer swinging in a huge blue-domed basilica of sky, smoking not incense but the rich dry odours of mountain summer herbs. Intoxicated with thyme and spray, heading for the shelter of those deep inlets that I knew awaited me, I was overcome by one of those wild surges of happiness – shouted speeches to wind and sea, snatches of incoherent song, leaped about the deck – knowing that soon would come the rattle of anchor chain in four fathoms upon a clear sea floor, and sleep. . . . After all, I had arrived.

That afternoon when I awoke towers of cumulus were building in the north, and I moved round to Linaria, the only port of Skyros, on the west coast of the island. Night came with a storm of wind and rain. I sat in a taverna by the quay in the company of two young men who insisted on treating me to supper while the water collected in pools on the stone floor, and we watched through the shaking windows purple and white light flashing on sea and hills and on the drenched caiques straining at their anchors.

One of my hosts was about to leave for his national service. His pale, finely boned features hardly seemed promising material for the Greek army. 'When I'm finished I'll go on a big ship,' he said. 'I want to see the world. Nothing ever happens on this island.' Later under the influence of our third kilo of wine he confided in me that really he wanted to be a poet. I asked him if he had written much and he looked surprised. 'Here, in Skyros? There's nothing to write about. Besides here I have no time.'

The other one was of a broader build. He worked as crew on the great caique I had noticed moored next to *Astarte*, the *Ayios Nikolaos*,

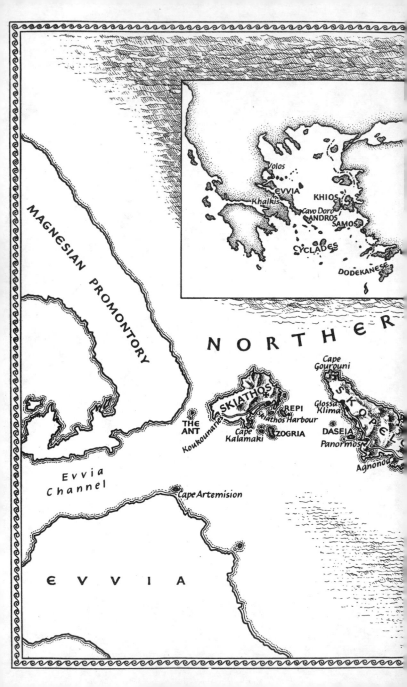

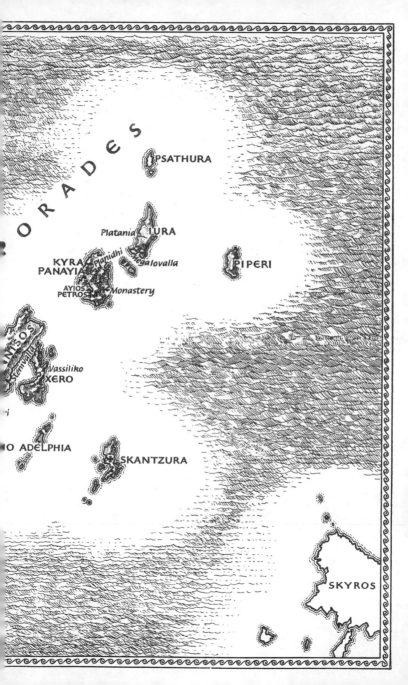

built in Egypt and with an Arabic inscription scrolled in gold upon her tall prow. 'Tomorrow morning will be fine,' he said. 'If you must leave, leave early.'

I followed his advice and at dawn was under way, a fair south-easterly filling the sails. Long before midday the Sporades had raised their heads in line above the horizon, and the wind had turned stronger, with big seas breaking in foam about the stern. I had planned to head first for Skiathos, the most westward of the Sporades chain, but Skiathos was good shelter in every wind but this one. I decided now to put into a bay on the west coast of Skopelos, clearly marked on my chart. The name of the bay was Panormos.

I remembered the name well. I was with a friend the previous autumn when we moored for a single day in Skopelos harbour, and had noticed a Greek standing by the gang-plank, looking over *Astarte* with critical appraisal. He was small and lean, and like many Greeks of that build, perfectly proportioned. His eyes were brown and very bright and he had a beaked nose. The top of his head was quite bald. I asked him on board, and we began to talk. His name was Evángelos Hannás.

In Greek 'Evangelos' is usually shortened to 'Vangeli', and it was as Vangeli that I knew him. He spoke English quite well and told us he also was a ship-owner, pointing with a smile to a beautiful caique about the same length as *Astarte* moored close by. He had named her *Makhi*, after his six-year-old elder daughter. It turned out that Vangeli had been the last mayor of Skopelos and was a man of some standing in the island, though from his easy manners and quick friendliness I would not have guessed it. I had thought he was about forty, in spite of his bald head and deeply lined face, but I had under-estimated his age by nearly ten years.

Vangeli was somebody hard to forget. With some people, I find, it always takes time for their personalities to come as it were into focus. With Vangeli the focus was clear and sharp, and immediate. Having met him, even for a moment, I could sense his vitality, the energy bursting out of him. He stood apart from other islanders, as if really he was a man from the cities, constantly, even nervously, alive. And yet he was an islander, and his family had always lived on Skopelos. He told us something of his past – after the war an accountant in a firm in Volos, and then when the constraint became intolerable, breaking out to sea, owner and captain of a large trading caique, sailing the Aegean with his cargoes – anything that was profitable, oranges to cement – from Rhodes to the Peloponnese, Crete to Kavalla. He still spoke of the *Ayios Dimitrios* which he exchanged for *Makhi*, a much smaller boat, some years before when he became mayor, as of an old, lost friend.

On that first meeting he invited us back to his house. He was alone just then, he said. He had some land over in the west of the island, at a place called Panormos, and his wife and family had gone there to stay and pick the olives. He lit a fire under the great geyser in his bathroom and gave us hot baths, cooked us a memorable omelette, a Hannás speciality as he modestly described it, and that evening spent much time drawing us diagrams of the best anchorages in the islands for which we were leaving next morning. He also gave us good advice about fishing, offered polite explanations as to why we had so far been so extraordinarily unsuccessful, and supervised the purchase of simpler but more effective equipment as well as giving us some of his own, and gave us instructions as to depth, bait and a hundred other things.

'Perhaps you will come again to Skopelos next year?'

'Perhaps,' I said as we tried to thank him for his hospitality.

'Do not forget Panormos,' he said. 'The best harbour – in the Balkans!' (At the time I wondered at this strange geography: Skopelos was hardly in the Balkans. Later I came to know that whenever Vangeli wished to describe something out of the ordinary, beyond compare – such as Panormos harbour, or his own skill at cooking, anything in fact that he deemed superlative – he came out with this phrase: '*best in the Balkans!*') 'Safe? Even when the sea is very wavy and too much wind, you can sleep there and be afraid of nothing.'

There is an island guarding the entrance to Panormos Bay called Daseiá, which means 'wooded'. As I brought down the sails and turned in with the motor I wondered if the harbour was as good as Vangeli had said. A broad bay lay scooped out of the pine-forested mountains; at the far end a long swathe of ivory-coloured beach fronted on a valley rich with olive trees, cypresses and poplar, sloping back into green hills upon whose distant ridges gleamed the white of a few scattered cottages. I was so busy examining an old caique drawn up on the beach to the north, that it was with a shock of surprise that I turned suddenly to the south and saw the real anchorage unfolding before me, a long inlet winding deep into pine-dark hills, a bay within a bay, Panormos the 'all-harbour'.

I stepped ashore not long before sunset, tying the dinghy to the ruin of an old jetty that ran out from beneath a large crumbling barn, whitewashed and roofed with old style rust-coloured Byzantine tiles. Its bulging walls seemed to hang over the edge of the water, and stacks of firewood leaned against them; by the jetty stood a number of tall tin barrels filled to the brim with resin. Farther along the shore, opposite where I had anchored, a dilapidated little cottage still had an air of occupation about it. A goat was tied up by the door, beside a makeshift oven built in the rocks, and from the lower branches of a carob tree cheeses in goat bladders were hanging in the warm air to dry. I followed the path back along the side of the inlet towards the main bay and the valley that rose from it. Vangeli had said he had a house at Panormos. I hoped he would remember me.

Someone had been planting cypresses on the little promontories this side of the cove. Olive trees grew above the rocks by the water side, between almond trees and patches of red earth. The jingle of mule-bells, and the sound of women's voices reached me through the trees. I stood back against a low cliff to let them pass, two men in ragged work clothes and bound rope shoes with axes on their shoulders, three women in gay voluminous dresses and bright shawls. A curly-headed child rode the donkey at the end of the little procession.

I asked them where I could find the house of Evàngelos Hannàs, and they gave me directions: it was not far. They worked for Vangeli, the men told me. They came from Alonnisos, the island farther to the east, bringing their wives and children and a few possessions, to live here during the summer, working on the pines as foresters and collectors of resin. Just now they were finishing work for the day, and they pointed to the curved earthenware jars, slender necked and filled with spring water, that were tied on each side of the mules. Would I like a drink?

Someone was shouting from the hills as I walked on, a long drawn-out cry that sounded like '*four-nell-o*!' I climbed the winding mule-track between rocks and young firs and bushes thick with red berries and was about to emerge upon a broad track cut out of the hillside high above the anchorage, when an immense explosion rocked the earth shooting a column of dust into the blue air. I crouched as a shower of earth and pebbles descended on me from the sky. The second explosion caught me midway between the path and an over-hang of rock below the track, but by the third I was comfortably sitting with my back against stone, listening to the rapid series of concussions while my breathing returned to near normal.

Allowing a reasonable interval after the last, I came out, cautiously, on to the levelled hillside. A lorry, driven by a young man dressed in clothes resembling military uniform, drew up beside me and two workmen jumped out of the back. They watched me with astonish-ment as I shook out my shirt.

'Didn't you hear us shout "*fournello*"?' one of them said with marked irritation. 'You might have got killed!'

His companion, more sympathetically, advanced to help me dust myself. 'We're building a road, you understand – from Skopelos all the way to Glossa.' He jerked his thumb towards the driver. 'The army.' They waved cheerfully as they drove off. 'Vangeli? Just up there – you'll see the house in a minute.'

It was only ten minutes' climb. The house was one I had noticed sailing in, nestling high up on the south side of the main valley half hidden by giant pines, a two-storey building, tiled, but not very big. An old woman with a gentle face and grey hair tied in a bun sat sewing in the shade of the trees by a low white parapet and rose with surprise as I walked up to her. She led me round to the other side where an open wood-fired kitchen gave on to a terrace carpeted with pine-needles. Against the wall, half asleep, sat an old man, who mumbled a polite but startled greeting and continued to look at me with amazement and, I thought, some suspicion. Perhaps it was rather extraordinary, now I came to think of it: a foreigner arriving suddenly and unannounced, as it seemed out of the sea, in this remote corner of the island.

But if they were curious they did their best not to show it. The old woman sat me down, and called inside. In a moment an attractive woman with thick dark hair, whom I guessed to be in her late thirties, came out wiping her hands on her apron. Her name was Alexandra, and she was Vangeli's wife. I sat under the pines while they plied me with ice-cold water, which I was in great need of then, *loukoumi* – Turkish Delight, ouzo and finally coffee. No, unfortunately Vangeli was not in Panormos at the moment; he was in Skopelos village, some two and a half hours' walk over the hills. But they would send a message. There was no need to do that, I replied; I would leave for Skiathos in the morning, and after a week would go to Skopelos and meet him there. I left after some time, refreshed and delighted with the kindness of my reception.

Down by the shore of the cove again the resin-collectors and their families gathered round me with presents of milk still warm from the goats, and green apples. The men stood in the sea washing themselves after their day's work, and the little girl romped and splashed behind them, lifting her red petticoat as she danced ankle deep in the shallows. Their reflections trembled on the windless water. The rocky peninsula that protects the anchorage was already in deep shadow. The sunset flared behind the pines.

I lay on deck and smoked while the night turned a wheel of stars across the sky. The resin-collectors slept early: I had seen their fire and the oil lamp extinguished long ago. The silence was so deep I could hear from across the water the goats shifting their feet and the sound of a fish jumping was loud enough to startle. The sea was locked out, hidden from sight. It was a lake, an inland lake high in the mountains, a tarn edged with black pines mirrored in shining black water. Why was there no village here, no flourishing port busy with boats, markets and the voices of men and women? What could have happened? I remembered the ruins of occasional cottages round the bay, so few and so small. *Pan-ormos*, 'all-harbour'. An ancient word, Homer used it: 'always fit for mooring in'. Whatever had been here, and I was sure there had been something, seemed to have gone without trace. A thousand, two thousand years ago? Surely there must be signs, marks on stone, signals from the past; and if they existed I would find them. But there would be no answer in this water-silence, nor in the pattern of stars overhead – none, at least, that would satisfy me for longer than this night. If I had been told, that first time I slept in Panormos, that already I had taken a first step in a new direction, I would not have believed it; nor that my old wariness of involvement, in spite of itself, was about to be defeated, nor that these islands I had come back to would this time not let me go.

The sound of oars woke me early, and a voice hailing *Astarte*, vaguely familiar and with a strong foreign accent. By the time I had stumbled on deck the boat was alongside and Vangeli's face grinned at me over the taffrail. We shook hands.

'I have brought you some fish. Barbounia, the very best to eat! Take them. They sent me a message, and I came from Skopelos this morning early.'

We drank coffee down in the cabin. 'So you go to Skiathos now – and after to Skopelos? Good, I wait for you there. Do not be late coming!'

I promised him I wouldn't. We went on deck. 'It is better to go now, before the wind,' Vangeli warned, sniffing the morning air. I hadn't finished my coffee, and I said so. Vangeli brushed aside this objection with the scorn it deserved. "*Meltémi!*" He was already at the anchor. As I found out, Vangeli was seldom wrong about the weather; and it was because of this, and because of his wide experience of boats and the sea that I was later to dub him 'Admiral of the Northern Sporades.'

'*Kaló taxidi* – good journey! I wait for you in Skopelos.'

Astarte gathered motion, cleaving the sun-blue waters of the bay. I watched him row swiftly back to the shore, his lean wiry body bending over the oars. He turned and waved.

2

Skiathos

Skiathos village is built on two hills, at the head of a broad bay ringed to the south with islands. The smaller of the two harbours, with a line of cafés, tavernas and shops that open on to a quay where boats and caiques moor, is shadowed in late afternoon by steep cliffs upon which topples a pyramid of white houses mounting into the sky. An island called Bourtsi, now joined to the harbour-front by a short causeway, separates the harbour from a second, bigger bay, a deep inlet where ships may anchor. Here the sea shelves into a curve of sand and a lagoon that is almost marsh, beyond which the olive groves, another sea of green and silver, slope back into the hills.

They call Skiathos the 'green island', and though most of the Northern Sporades might qualify for such a description, especially if the traveller is coming from the south and the eroded barren beauty of the Cyclades, it is true that Skiathos gives such a welcome, overwhelming impression of fertility that it seems like a miracle. During summer when the prevailing winds blow regularly from the north, the south coast of the island is perfectly sheltered: a long line of beaches, interrupted occasionally by pine-covered promontories, face over a calm blue sea the distant mountains of Evvia.

The degree of clarity with which one can see the Evvian mountains is the most accepted method of forecasting the weather from the harbour. One of the first friends I made on the island was a man skilled in just this art. His name was Myrodis, a Skiathite who had spent many years of his life in America and preferred to be known simply as Gus. Gus claimed, with reason, a considerable knowledge of local sea-lore, and when I first saw him, a tall, grey-haired, thin man with a stoop, high cheekbones over sunken cheeks, and a pair of rimless spectacles, often broken, resting on the bridge of his nose, he was in charge of a yacht owned by a German who had left it there for the winter under Gus's care. With this yacht Gus was accustomed to make long voyages single-handed under sail, to Salonika and back, and to Piraeus. There was a long tradition of sailing in his family, Gus told me. His father, in the days when no motor was heard between the islands, and sails were the only means of propulsion for boats big and small, was a caique owner and captain of some local fame. His greatest feat was to sail his boat back from Salonika – a hundred miles away, with a great storm behind him – covering the distance safely in some unimaginable few hours. From then on he was known in Skiathos as *pouláki*, the little bird, and in the islands where nicknames are common and are even passed down from father to son, Gus told me rather proudly that he too was sometimes referred to as *pouláki* by some of the older people who still remembered.

Besides teaching me how to tell the weather in Skiathos, Gus felt it was his duty to point out also many of the sea dangers, sunken rocks and shoals that abound about the coast of the island, and took me once to Koukounaries, a bay advertised now in Athens and elsewhere as the 'most beautiful in Greece'.

Last year Gus had owned and managed a little brushwood-roofed taverna or café, set up on the beach under the trees for the bathers, many of whom camped in the woods during the hottest months. Gus had handed over the taverna to another man, a cheerful swarthy little fellow called Leonidas, and now we were paying the place a visit partly to see how the new owner was preparing for the season. He seemed to be nearly ready, had set up with rough carpentry two counters at right angles to each other, and installed a paraffin stove on which he immediately set about cooking us fresh fish and eggs, offering us excellent bottles of Greek beer to get on with, while we were joined by two fishermen who had drawn up their boat on the sand, and an old man who walked with a stick and introduced himself as Barba Nikola Armamento.

Barba Nikola, I was informed, was the *demioúrgos* of Koukounaries. He had 'opened up' this corner of Skiathos, killing off all the snakes – some of which apparently were enormous – that used to flourish on the shores of the lake behind the pines, planting olives and fruit trees, even making by the tread of his mules a rough path that today was being busily transformed into the main island road. The idea of any part of Skiathos needing a pioneer to explore it and 'open it up' seemed quite extraordinary to me, but then even the briefest glance at Barba Nikola is enough to convince one that here was an extraordinary man. Small, bald-headed, his face alone was arresting enough, with its prominent hooked nose and pendulous lower lip, bright eyes always in motion under thick protruding brows. He has a reputation for being both a poet and a wit. That evening as we ate under the oil-lamp hanging from a pine-branch, and the wine was raised in glasses to the new moon, and to my return to the Sporades, he began to speak in a series of rhymed couplets, answering everything from a request to pass the salt to an inquiry as to his age in this manner. I agreed to return to Koukounaries another time, and Barba: Nikola promised to entertain me in his cottage in the hills. He is going to read me some of his poems, and I am to translate them into English and 'send them abroad'. As he put it, modestly enough, 'You never know, perhaps I shall become famous.'

An event of that afternoon that gave Barba Nikola an opportunity to exercise his wit was the strange sight of a boat being rowed across the bay by a priest. There would not have been much to remark upon in the ordinary way, but this priest happened to be naked except for a pair of scarlet bathing shorts. To a foreigner perhaps there might be nothing astonishing even in this, but in Greece a priest is never seen wearing anything less than his full dress of long black robe and tall funnel-shaped hat. There are moments when he is permitted to divest himself of his hat, but to expose his body to public view – even, I suspect, to his own personal view – is simply unthinkable. There was a ripple of excited and disapproving comment as we gaped at the apparition rowing past, the long black hair bobbing on the priest's pale back. 'There won't be so many at his church on Sunday, after this,' said Gus, shaking his head. But to me, pagan and foreigner in one, it seemed only a good omen – the emancipation of the black-robed brotherhood, perhaps the admission at last of an older creed, health and the sun.

The sounds of music and singing – unusual for mid-afternoon – met us at the quayside on our return. Under the trees at the bottom of the steps three musicians surrounded by a group of young men sat and played. They were leaving today for the mainland and the start of their two-year period of National Service.

I sat and had coffee with Panayioti, a cheerful and kindly young man with a chubby rather childlike face, and gentle round brown eyes. He chuckled as he beat time to the music. 'Do you know the words?'

I confessed I did not, and he told me that they sang about a brave, handsome young *pallikári* leaving for battle, leaving behind him a beautiful girl whom he promises to marry.

'And does he?' I asked.

'Does he what?'

'Come back and marry her — ?'

Panayioti looked at me pityingly 'Of course he doesn't. He gets killed by the Turks. Then the girl drowns herself.' He beat the table happily to the rhythm. It was true my question had been a silly one. Greek songs do not have happy endings.

Panayioti stopped his tapping. 'As a matter of fact I'm thinking of getting married myself.' He looked at me sideways and grinned sheepishly. 'What do you think of that?'

'Why not?' I replied airily. Being a bachelor on a Greek island, except perhaps during the tourist season, has very little to recommend it. 'Who is the lucky girl?'

'I don't know yet.' He looked suddenly at a loss, and even, I thought, rather frightened. Frightened not because he wouldn't be able to find the right girl to marry, but because once he started looking for a girl he was almost certain to find one – in which case it would be only logical to marry her.

'Don't worry,' I said, with an air of well-assimilated experience. 'It has its compensations.'

Panayioti nodded slowly. So he had heard. It was difficult not to like Panayioti. At the moment he was a sort of unofficial aide-de-camp to a wealthy and charming Anglo-Greek couple, Paul and Terry Crosfield who were buying some land near Cape Kalamaki on the south coast of the island. Panayioti knew everyone on Skiathos and was able to help arrange everything, getting the right papers from the notary, hiring a boat and other useful things of that kind.

He was always ready to help me in any way he could. One of the odd things about Panayioti was that in fact he was a person of unusual influence and power on the island. This was simply because one of his sisters was a personal maid to a senior Minister in the government. In a country where an overgrown bureaucracy renders every appeal of the individual so lengthy and complicated that it is hardly worthwhile setting in motion, such a voice of the fountainhead of power appeared to be invaluable. On Skiathos people are always polite to Panayioti.

The musicians had risen, and still playing frantically, set off with the soldiers of the future arm in arm behind them on a tour of the back streets. I asked Panayioti if this usually happened when a batch of young men left for the army or for the wars, and he said it had always been like this. I would see more in the evening, when the *Kyknos* came in.

He was right. About six o'clock when everyone in Skiathos comes down to the harbour and either takes a seat at the tables spilling out on to the quay, or wanders with friends up and down before the line of caiques rocking at their moorings, the group of young men, swollen by others of their contemporaries come to see them off, reappeared and marched noisily up and down in front of the cafés.

They boarded a small caique that was ready waiting for them, and for the next hour motored in and out of the two bays, in company with their more privileged friends, as well as the musicians — the sound of music and singing echoing across the water.

The deep blast of a ship's siren signalled the approach from Skopelos of the *Kyknos*, the steamer that plies three times a week between Volos and the Sporades, and as the long white shape slid between the outer islands into Skiathos bay, the last stage of the farewell began. White handkerchiefs appeared fluttering from the caique, the singing reached a crescendo of brave abandon, and the boat veered wildly across the water until, summoned by a peremptory and impatient hoot from the *Kyknos*, the party boarded her, and the big ship passed out of sight behind Kalamaki Cape.

Although the farewell had taken place at a time specially designed for the maximum publicity, in front of the biggest audience that the island could command, hardly any of the crowd strolling at the water's side or sipping coffee or ouzo at the café tables had taken the slightest notice of the departure of this flower of their youth. Only a few peasant women, snuffling tearfully by the water-steps and probably the boys' mothers, had returned the waving of handkerchiefs and now, huddled together for sympathy, moved slowly away.

*   *   *   *

October to the end of May is the season of the trawlers, the *anemó-trata*. After the beginning of June they are forbidden to fish. It was the last day of their working year, and I stood watching with the others at the quayside while three of them came in together, churning round the headlands from the south.

Perhaps the most romantic of all caiques, these, with their broad *karavóscaro* sterns and raking prows, blunt masts draped with huge russet nets hauled up on the blocks to dry, decks dripping with sluiced seawater, knee deep in fish, cluttered with all the worn machinery of their trade – winches, chain, coils of rope thick as a man's neck . . . and to see them coming in was always something of a drama, approaching the harbour at sunset at full speed, with a dozen or more men aboard, their faces blackened with wind and sun, filthily dressed, hanging like apes or pirates from the shrouds.

There was some cremony, too, of the most simple kind that evening : a big trawler blasting eerily with her hooter again and again as the sails were stripped off her, and answered by another, rounding Bourtsi with her engines at full power, high bow-wave falling white from her prow, while the other caiques made way for her as she surged past overtaking them, making straight for the shipyard by the old mill, where the summer will be spent in long preparation for the next autumn season.

It was one morning walking back to *Astarte* along the quay after watching the trawlers being undressed, as it were, to their night-shirts, that I first met La Kaloyerina.

Shapeless of body, hung with a blue-black faded peasant dress, bare-headed she shuffles and lopes along by the water's edge, her face old and lined, snub-nosed with sallow skin stretched taut across high cheekbones that give to her face something of a Mongol look, a distinction that is repeated in the slant of her eyes. It is her eyes that rivet one's attention : eyes that have a peculiar stoniness in their glance, a hardness that does not entirely go even when she smiles – baring the gold-buttressed teeth between the gaps in her gums – as she did at that moment as she came opposite me, stopped, and asked me quite suddenly if I had any clothes that needed washing.

My first instinct was against entrusting even my laundry to a person of such appearance, but then as we began to talk I became interested, and later when I had seen more of her, chatting like this at the quayside or drinking a glass of wine with her in Mitso's taverna opposite, it became clear that La Kaloyerina, 'the nun', had not only a startling appearance but a personality that matched it, and with them both an even stranger history.

A doorway in Skopelos

Looking up from the harbour, Skopelos
Chapel over the sea, Skopelos harbour

On Skiathos everybody knows her, and though this in itself is no particular distinction on so small an island, with La Kaloyerina there is more to it than that. People fear her . . . the women believe she is a kind of witch, generously endowed with that dangerous potentiality, the 'evil eye'. La Kaloyerina made her reputation during the war, when Skiathos and the rest of the Sporades were occupied, first by the Italians, then by the Germans. She was one of the foremost in the island's resistance leadership, working often as not, as she preferred to do, quite alone; her special concern was the safe conduct of escaped allied airmen and soldiers from the mainland, to look after them and hide them, and send them on their way to Skopelos and Alonnisos from where by caique and at night they were shipped on to neutral Turkey.

There are many stories of her activities at this time, most of which she will tell willingly enough herself, if she is in the right mood, and the stories can be corroborated by others of the islanders who worked with her. Once, during a cold winter, she had a band of airmen under her care who were painfully lacking warm clothes. She had them hidden somewhere on the island – La Kaloyerina kept her own counsel always, and the place is secret still – and she decided that unless proper clothing were found for them they might die. So she set out on foot through the snow to a hide-out in the hills where a number of active guerrillas were camping. The men, it is said, were holding some kind of conference when she arrived, and were not too pleased to be so rudely and unceremoniously interrupted, especially by a woman.

'I need warm clothes, boys! Lots of them, and quickly!' The request, though a little peremptory, seemed a reasonable one and she was assured that everything would be done as soon as possible to get her the clothes. But they had misunderstood La Kaloyerina.

'No! I need them now! Or the men will die. . . .' Thus far the historian can vouch for the dialogue. What happened afterwards no one knows exactly, and the possibilities are interesting. At any rate, not many minutes later, La Kaloyerina emerged from the hut carrying four or five pairs of trousers, and an equal number of pullovers and jackets.

She was arrested eventually and taken to Volos to be tried. There she made a rather famous speech in her defence, appealing in her bold straightforward way directly to the judge. 'I would help anyone in trouble, anyone running away, *anyone* hunted.' Pause, and then, fixing her stare once more on the judge: 'And one day even *you* might find yourself running, and I would help *even you*. . . .' One wonders whether the Italian shivered slightly to hear such a prophecy spelled out to him by this fierce dishevelled woman in the dock; but I think he believed her, and it may have been because of this speech that La Kaloyerina was not shot, but shipped off to various detention camps in Italy and later in Germany. Flogged, tortured, starved . . . she says she bears the scars of her beatings still on her back, and I do not doubt it. In Europe she had many adventures, not the least extraordinary was how she nearly became a Lesbian, and was loved by one of the nuns.

And now she's just a poor rather terrifying-looking old woman who took my laundry then, and continues to do so every time I come into Skiathos in spite of rival bids, and makes a great profit on it too, which is only right. She is a familiar figure of the harbour front, her greasy hair stranded and knotted in a bun behind her, loose wisps falling about her shoulders, flicked back impatiently as she moves, her bent legs with drooping thick stockings rolled down to her knees, pushing along before her a pair of broken-down sandals.

And yet – she is La Kaloyerina, a woman with a name, and she knows it. The men treat her in a queer half joking, half respectful way; they treat her as a man when she feels like it, and drink and smoke with her. The women, as I have said, do not like her, and they use her name as a terrible bogey to pacify troublesome children.

There is a mystery, still, about La Kaloyerina. Several hundred allied servicemen passed along the Sporades route to safety, and through her capable hands in Skiathos. The English paid their resistance agents in gold in the Aegean and elsewhere, and La Kaloyerina certainly got paid – though how much, and where it all went to, is a problem that still evokes lively discussion and heated argument in the coffee shops of the village.

Is she rich, with a vast stock of sovereigns cached away somewhere? Or is she really as poor as she seems? There are two factions in Skiathos who hold and canvass these opposing views, the majority preferring the former and more romantic possibility. Myself, I am inclined to the latter: any money that once she had has gone – lost, spent on others perhaps as much as on herself. She has no children but she has a husband, a rather nice nondescript character, and I have seen her go the round of the restaurants collecting scraps of food wrapped up in newspaper, and she hands them to him as he waits outside. But the islanders say that is only a blind, and the question of La Kaloyerina's wealth or poverty must remain unsettled, a mystery, and this too, I feel, is only as it should be.

The hills inland from the harbour provide just the sort of country that guerrillas might thrive in, and La Kaloyerina conceal her wards. A long walk through valleys green with olives, slopes terraced with vines took me up among forests of pine and chestnut to the harsher north shore of the island, a coast of cliffs and fallen storm-beaten boulders, and a small jutting peninsula : Kastro. Here lies the ruined village of Old Skiathos, perched upon steep cliffs, protected on all sides by walls of sheer precipice that dive a hundred feet to the blue-crystal sea below. Rubble of houses, broken pottery, breached stone walls, wild flowers – only a few chapels have been preserved where priests and the hardiest of the faithful still come to worship on special saints'-days.

The islanders moved here in the Middle Ages, driven to this gull's nest high over the open sea by the ravages of pirates and the insecurity of the times, forced to abandon their rich valleys in the south and the sheltered double harbour where their main town had flourished since classical days. Here they survived for many centuries, suffering several sieges, one terrible sack, and countless assaults. They returned to the site of their present village only in 1829, and the fortified ruins of Kastro are left now to crumble in the sun and face alone the last relentless attack of the waves and wind.

3

Skopelos: Vangeli's Island

From the ruins of Kastro, and again from high on the hills of Skiathos as I walked back to the village, the island of Skopelos filled the eastern horizon. There was something almost forbidding about that skyline, so much bolder and higher the contours of those pine forested mountains than the more gentle slopes beneath me. Skopelos means 'rock', in the sense of reef, or barrier in the sea, and looking at it now across the few miles of water I could understand how the name was given. I had already been too long delaying, considering what I had told Vangeli in Panormos, and now I decided it was time to move.

It is some sixteen miles by sea between Skiathos village and Skopelos harbour and that, as a glance at any chart will show, is by the shorter, fine-weather route, round the north-west cape of Skopelos, *Gourouni*, the Hog. The cape has its name not merely from the chance resemblance to a pig's back jutting into the sea; *gourouni* in Greek is a common enough epithet of disgust and profound dislike, and the headland with the tall white lighthouse flashing through the nights its warning to shipping well deserves the islanders' hostility. From Skiathos to Gourouni in a small boat is a long enough haul, and there is still another nine miles along a coast without shelter, sharpened with a continuous line of massive cliffs, until the last headland is rounded and Skopelos itself breaks upon the eye.

Turning the last cape, as I did with *Astarte* one early morning, the sea-traveller finds himself entering a broad open bight surrounded with tall hills edged with rock precipices sheer to the sea. Directly ahead is the village itself, and at first all that can be seen is a dark outline of cliffs descending in jagged steps down to the water, surmounted by a dazzling white wall above which the domes of chapels, the grey slate and dark red tiles of the roof-tops gleam in the sun. Some time later, and only when the long harbour mole is rounded, the whole village comes into view, circling a corner of the bay and rising in white terraces to the green hills.

At the head of Skopelos Bay the hills are less steep, and beginning behind the high wind-breaks of flourishing bamboo edging the sand, rises the broadest and richest valley of the island, olive groves and orchards, stretching away only a distance of about six miles, to the bay of Staphylos and the south coast.

Traces of the castle dominating the harbour and overlooking the sea cliffs can only be seen on entering the harbour itself. Little but a crumbling tower of rock and brown brick remains to tell of the once great medieval citadel that made Skopelos for a time famous.

In 1205, when the 'crusaders' had taken Constantinople and the Greek Empire had fallen, the islands of the Aegean were divided up between the Frankish adventurers who had followed the Doge's standard. The Sporades fell to the lot of two brothers, Andrea and Geremia Ghisi, and the fortification of Skopelos was carried to the limits of the site's natural advantages. For seventy years the Ghisi remained dukes of Skopelos, extracting from their Orthodox subjects the maximum of taxes to afford their building and their pleasures, lording it over them from their rock castle high above the sea. By then a Greek Emperor was once more on the throne of Byzantium and by a bold stroke of judgement summoned a certain Licario, a renegade Frankish knight, turned pirate, whose exploits were re-sounding throughout the Aegean, and gave him command of the imperial navy with the task of regaining the Aegean islands for the Empire.

Licario undertook his mission with enthusiasm, and island after island fell to his ships. In Skopelos Fillipo Ghisi was not afraid. His men-at-arms boasted that even if all Romania fell they would still hold out in their fortress, and the duke himself was so confident that he was fond of rashly quoting a line of Ovid: *Major sum quam ut nihil possit fortuna nocere* – 'I am so big a man that fortune cannot harm me', and contented himself with preparations for the expected attack.

Licario was prepared to take his time. He had learnt that there was one weakness to Skopelos castle: although the island itself had plenty of water, there was no spring in the fortress itself – the defenders relied on water cisterns hewn out of the rock cliffs beneath them. He chose therefore the month of September, after a particularly hot and dry summer, when there had been no rain for over six months and when, because of the constant false alarms, most of the water supply was already consumed. Just when the duke was thinking that he was safe for another year at least, because the conventional campaigning season was almost over, Licario and his fleet sailed into Skopelos Bay, landed soldiers and sat down round the fort. The castle was too strong to force, and Licario did not bother to try. He did not have to wait long. The water gave out and the castle surrendered, Fillipo Ghisi was taken a humble prisoner to Constantinople, and the Sporades returned for nearly two centuries to Byzantine rule.

Skopelos has changed much since the time of Licario and the Ghisi dukes, but still the oldest houses crowd round the castle rock, mounting it seems one on top of the other, separated by narrow cobbled streets and flights of curved steps.

As I wandered about the village and the surrounding hills, I began to realize that coming north from the Cyclades I had crossed a decisive line of latitude, one that marked a new style of island living, affecting not only the climate and the scenery but as one might expect the architecture as well.

The islands have always been rich in timber and one of the basic materials for building is wood. Older buildings in Skopelos are constructed entirely with a timber framework, and many of the houses are braced out at first-floor level on beams of chestnut or cypress, projecting across the street. Because of the comparatively high rainfall – the annual average is nearly forty inches – the flat roofs of the Cyclades are rare and replaced by sloping semicircular 'Byzantine' tiles or blue-grey slate, and often these pitched roofs are curved, their hips and ridges picked out in white. But the most dramatic and attractive use of timber, still most evident in the older cottages about the castle and the big merchant houses spreading with the village round the corner of the bay, are the balconies that hang over the winding narrow streets, balconies with carved wooden columns supporting the roofs over them, crowded with pots of herbs and climbing flowers and vines that fill the close cobbled lanes with the scent of basil and jasmine, honeysuckle and rose.

It was beginning to seem to me that in the Northern Sporades all the conditions for a kind of Aegean paradise were present: the islands were green, and mostly forested; there was water in plenty; winters were mild – snow fell, but seldom lay for more than a few days. The

summer weather I could already feel was considerably more tempe-
rate than that of the islands farther south – not so hot, yet with the
purity of Greek light undimmed. The *meltémi*, that in the Cyclades
roars out of the north sometimes day and night for three weeks on
end, here did not blow, I was told, with such consistent and senseless
violence. It cooled, which was, one felt, its purpose in the divine
scheme of things, but did not carry its duties to extremes; its sensible
habit was to drop when there was no longer any need for it in the
evenings, going down with the sun.

This did not mean to say that there were not frequent exceptions,
and dramatic ones, and although Skopelos harbour, as I was
beginning to see, was not a good one, being exposed to the north,
I made it my base, partly because of its central position, with Skiathos to the west, Alonnisos and the 'outer Sporades' to the east,
partly because I had begun to like the place so much – and perhaps,
even then, the vision of Panormos was stirring in the back of my
mind; but most of all because places are really the people who live in
them, and already in Skopelos I had begun a friendship that was to
grow as time went by.

Vangeli was waiting for me on the quay when I came in, and as
soon as he had helped me moor, took me up to his house a few streets
above the harbour, where Alexandra his wife, the old couple who
were her mother and father, and the two little girls Makhi and Eleni
were there to welcome me. I was invited to lunch, and in the days
that followed, to many other meals, until finally I was informed that
there would be no more invitations: I was simply expected to attend.
From then on, though I had done nothing to deserve such kindness,
it seemed as if I had become one of the family. There was a room upstairs, Vangeli told me, where I could sleep whenever I wanted, if
ever I felt like a change from *Astarte*, or if ever the harbour became
too rough and my berth too uncomfortable. Vangeli had put down
two permanent moorings in the harbour, a light one near the outer
mole and a heavier one farther in; with his usual generosity he
insisted that in bad weather I use the heavier – an anchor, he said, 'so
heavy enough to take *Queen Mary* – no! *Queen Elizabeth!* Notice,
please, that I put them in the sea myself, so –'

'They must be pretty good.'

'Exactly.'

It was at meal times that I particularly enjoyed the company of the Hannas family, each one sitting in his or her own place round the big table in the low raftered kitchen – and perhaps the 'each in his own place' had something to do with the harmony so apparent in the family, and in whose reflected glow I found such warmth. The old man, Vangeli's father-in-law was aged eighty-four, a gentle figure whose physical incapacity made it difficult for him to be much more than a benign though sometimes querulous onlooker, who had passed over in most cases the power of decision to his energetic son-in-law. And yet he retained a dignity – as also had the kindly short-sighted grey-haired old woman his wife – a dignity that needed no artificial prop, nothing of mere lip service. He was the oldest member of the family, and if in conversation Vangeli might show at times a certain impatience with some of his diffidently offered views there was never any doubt as to the respect and love in which he was generally held. Alexandra was a perfect match for Vangeli, unassuming and yet with a quiet sense of humour, as placid as he was temperamental, her nature as calm as her husband's was inclined to be violent. But the head of the family, the person who drew together all the threads of their lives, was Vangeli.

Makhi and Eleni worshipped him, and it was a pleasure to see the three of them together – Vangeli playing with them with a roughness that at first used to make me almost anxious but which obviously they expected and enjoyed. I noticed that the two little girls never called him *patéra* or *babá*, 'father' or 'daddy', but simply 'Vangeli' like his friends, and he told me that one day a couple of years before, both children had solemnly come to him saying that they wanted to ask him something. Makhi, the elder, was the spokesman of the two, and she said: 'Eleni and I have been thinking. We know that if we call you father you will be a father to us; but we want you to be a friend as well, so we want to call you "Vangeli" like your friends do . . . may we?' Vangeli agreed, and so it has been ever since.

The Hannas house in Skopelos, situated on the corner of two sloping streets, has three floors to it, cellars below, and by any standards it is a big one. It seemed that the hall, kitchen and living-room were always full of people. Visitors would call at every hour, women relatives and friends, to sit with the grandmother and Alexandra to gossip and embroider together the beautiful and complicated patterns on cushion covers and shawls and tablecloths;

but the majority were men who called, to talk to Vangeli, either just to chat, sitting with the coffee, the glass of ouzo or of wine that they were always offered, or to ask some favour, his help in matters as various as the best way of writing a letter to some government ministry, or to settle some dispute between neighbours over a land boundary.

'For me,' Vangeli has said in his charming English, 'the best thing is to have *so much* so that I can *give it away* . . .' I began to realize that this was no empty phrase of his. He enjoyed being in a position to help others, though sometimes – as for instance when people knock him up in the middle of the night to ask his help – he is driven to desperation by the constant calls on his time and energy. If his time is limited his energy is not. People came to him not only because he was comparatively educated and had friends in influential positions, but also because they knew that once his interest and sympathy could be enlisted he would put the whole of himself into whatever was required of him. I have sat at a café at one end of Skopelos harbour and seen Vangeli at the other end, coming towards me under the great plane trees : to cross that distance, a mere hundred and fifty yards, usually takes him about twenty minutes, so many times will he be drawn aside confidentially by people with some request or other, all of which it seems he receives with politeness and patience – though normally patience is not one of his most noticeable virtues. Being possessed of a remarkable fluency in his own language, with all those skilled though natural accompaniments of gesture, tone and facial expression notorious among Greeks, his frequent voicing of either dislike or disagreement was always something of a dramatic occasion.

The family is not in the ordinary sense rich, yet they are comfortably off. Their worth lies not in ready cash or in things easily turned into money, but like so many island or country Greeks it consisted of land and trees. The estate at Panormos is about three hundred acres. Most of it is mountain with pines yielding something from the resin regularly collected, but there are also orchards, mainly plums, and some four thousand olive trees scattered over the main Panormos valley and by the shore of the anchorage itself, and it is mostly on the income from the oil that the family live. Another project that Vangeli had set in motion the year before, and which he was now beginning to regret, was the ice factory, situated in a vast barn belonging to the family along the road to Staphylos and Agnonda, on the outskirts of Skopelos village.

The barn is a rambling antique structure, built of whitewashed stone with a tiled and slated roof raftered with giant logs darkened with smoke and age, with space enough inside it to contain a whole two-storeyed house, while around it and adjoining are stables for a dozen horses, mules or donkeys, and storehouses for grain and hay, olives and oil. In fact the stables are used hardly at all now, the only inmates at present being Takis, a middle-aged truculent and sexually frustrated male donkey, and Foola, a pretty Skyrian pony whom I was later to get to know almost too well.

In the barn itself are set, among other machines and remains of machines, two great diesel engines of venerable age which are attached to a complicated network of pumps, pipes and cylinders. Although Vangeli explained to me carefully the stages in detail by which water was here turned into ice, I managed somehow to retain my original ignorance of the process, remembering only that ammonia was one of the principal agents; perhaps because whenever I am there I am overwhelmed with wonder at the extraordinary series of puffs, hisses, grinds and general explosive uproar put out by the engines, and too fascinated by the spinning wheels, the circular pumps, the array of pulleys, maze of pipelines overhead and underfoot, to pay attention to talk of such a precise and scientific kind. It must be added too in my defence that the noise is so great in the ice-factory that it is difficult to hear a word spoken unless it is shouted. I only know that every few hours, by pulling a cunningly devised row of levers Vangeli, his face streaked with sweat and engine oil, clad in filthy trousers and a stained torn tee-shirt, can hoist out a number of gleaming blue-white blocks of ice which are laid down into the gloved hands of porters, loaded on to a trolley and hurriedly rolled down to the harbour.

Ice is important to Skopelos in the summer, not merely to keep drinks cold and food from going bad: its manufacture on the island has revolutionized the fishing trade. Previously, before Vangeli set his engines going, the pumps pumping and the ammonia freezing, ice was brought from Volos, a long expensive sea journey on the *Paskhális* or *Katerina*, melting rapidly below the sun-blazed decks of those big caiques and doled out in jealous fragments to the fish shops, fish packers and fishermen in Skopelos and Alonnisos.

Skiathos also had started an ice factory of its own, but as far as the *eremonisia*, the 'deserted islands' to the north-east, were concerned it was in no position to compete. In any case, Vangeli said, putting his mouth near my ear and shouting above the sniff, clacker and snort of his infernal machines, 'Skiathos ice is no good! It is *terrible*! If you put it in water, and drink —' he made a horrible grimace and passed his hand with a gesture of finality across his stomach, from which I understood that if you were fool enough to drink Skiathos ice and died quickly you were lucky.

But the ice factory was not an undertaking that gave Vangeli much pleasure. Apart from the smallness of profit it brought, after taking into account the running of the engines, breakdowns and repairs, the labour involved in keeping such a plant in constant action took up practically all of his waking hours. He was trying to find someone to train to help look after the engines, but so far he had met with little success.

I used to walk along to the ice factory of an afternoon, to spend an hour or so in Vangeli's company and relieve the monotony of his vigil. The engines needed careful watching and attention but only every half hour or so; the rest of the time he was free, but whenever I I found him he was always doings something. Among many amazing things in the great barn, such as a loft fitted out with cobbler's tools, a furnace, a boat and parts of other boats, a water cistern, an olive crusher, two granite millstones each nearly five feet across, and an oil press, there was a complete carpenter's bench, and it was usually here that I found him busy. 'I make different things, to pass the time —' he would say airily, as I examined with astonishment the various products of his casual but expert craftsmanship. The main work of the moment was an entire new cabin top for *Makhi*, his caique, jointed and with panelled sides. While engaged with this he would also take up and finish other smaller objects, usually designed as presents for his friends. He made several things for me, hanging boards on which to cut bread or vegetables, or a wire loop, shackled and strong, a stern-warp on rocks for *Astarte*. It was impossible for him to be still for a minute, unless it was with complete exhaustion, but even the opportunities of the barn could not satisfy him for long, and there were times when I found him depressed and cursing the fate that had locked him up in this gloomy prison. 'For me this is *worst* thing of all – tied like a donkey, a dog. . . .'

Everything for Vangeli was either 'worst' or 'best': there were no in-betweens.

At midday Alexandra or the two little girls would arrive with a basket of cooked provisions, and often we would eat at the little table all together amid the hum and roar of the machines. Water and wine were always cold at the factory, and sometimes a melon would be triumphantly extracted from the ice-compartments, frozen so solid it was necessary to take a saw to it. The old grandfather often came to the barn, to sit for hours silent and motionless on a chair by the millstones, his tiny shrunken figure bent forward a little, the tweed cap tipped still to a jaunty angle on his white head, with only his gentle rather sad eyes following every movement in the barn.

There were other visitors too; not only more people who came to ask advice or a favour from Vangeli, but his friends to solace him at his work, and notably among these was one who came often in a professional capacity: a man called Yiórgo Frantzésko.

It would be difficult to find two men more different from each other, physically as well as in temperament, as Vangeli and Yiórgo, and the fact that they were close friends and could often be seen side by side rendered this contrast all the more striking. While Vangeli was small and wiry, with movements quick as a bird's and sharp features seldom in repose, Yiórgo was a slow bull of a man, the trunk of his body so immense that it was perhaps just as well that his powerful legs were not quite as long as, among lesser men, the rules of proportion demanded. Upon his vast shoulders sat a head with a bald and shining dome, a face chubby and with a snub nose, glasses through which he blinked shyly and kindly at the world outside, an expression in his round blue eyes chiefly of humour and of constant surprise. As is often the case with big men Yiórgo possessed a nature entirely mild and equable: his great strength was never used against his fellow men but was employed exclusively in wrestling with the iron and steel of engines; for Yiórgo was a mechanic. Yet to say simply that Yiórgo was 'a mechanic' is as misleading, as much an understatement as to point out the prime minister to a complete stranger and describe him as 'a politician'.

Yiórgo's fame as a mechanic is spread far and wide among the islands and his name in moments of engine failure on the high seas is invoked much as once would have been a god's. From all the Sporades and beyond caiques limp into Skopelos harbour, their cylinder heads cracked, their pistons mere shadows of themselves, bearings gone, shafts broken, propellers twisted and gaskets blown . . . all of which for a very moderate fee can be put right in less than no time by the tireless Yiórgo. Although Yiórgo has gathered round him through the years much excellent and modern equipment, among which is a fine electric lathe, perhaps his main talent is improvisation. Whereas another mechanic situated in so remote an island would be frequently sending to the nearest big town for spare parts, Yiórgo prefers whenever possible to make what is needed on the spot, working equally skilfully with iron or steel, copper or brass, welding, soldering and forging, crouched over his lathe, the metal shavings whirling in a gold or silver cloud about his head.

Yiórgo came along to inspect *Astarte's* engine. The engine, he said, when he had looked it over carefully, was fine; or rather, being basically such a fine machine, its present condition appeared all the more shocking. He remarked heavily that in his opinion people who didn't look after their engines didn't deserve to have them. I have seldom seen Yiórgo angry, but in the following months during which he undertook to see the engine right, he did have moments of irritation and despair, and these occurred in connexion with such discoveries as the state of my tools, which had somehow become caked with rust, and similar continuous negligences on my part which he found inexcusable, regarding them not as I did, as unfortunate oversights, but as the most serious of moral lapses.

Nevertheless, in spite of these differences, we became friends, and it wasn't only in relation to mechanical things that I saw a great deal of him. His workshop when I came to Skopelos was already a kind of meeting-place, and being situated conveniently next door to a coffee-house it was possible at a moment's notice to have refreshments brought in by the patient proprietor who deposited his tray wherever he could find a space – on a heap of scrap-iron, a pile of bolts, or on some leaking and up-ended engine with which Yiórgo was then engaged. Coffee, tea, ouzo; orange and lemon drinks, cognac or Yiórgo's own favourite, soda-water; or just plain glasses of water . . . all served at the right temperature – an extreme of either hot or cold – these were the beverages on which Yiórgo's uninvited guests thrived, lounging on broken chairs or empty gas-cylinders, discussing the latest news from the radio, or events on the islands, or with laughter exchanging jokes and stories of the past; or more often than not just sitting or standing about, contemplating infinity, or futility, or the great design of life, with one eye upon Yiórgo's deftly working hands, soothed by the rhythmic purr of the lathe, the tapping of his tools.

In a curious way the atmosphere of the workshop provided a perfect background for reflection, for me as much as for the others: I sat half listening to the talk around me, half absorbed with my own imaginings that flew, hovering, about a certain curved calm-water cove on the far west of the island: Panormos, with its coronet of pines, quiet shores, deserted – waiting, surely, for such imaginings to alight? For us the occasional entry of one of Yiórgo's clients became almost an intrusion.

Those who came were a mixed lot of people, a fair cross-section of the island. First the caique captains, grisled sun-blackened men, unshaven and with lines of worry etched about their eyes, bearing in upon their shoulders the shattered or merely recalcitrant fragments of their engines, who stayed behind to listen to Yiórgo's careful verdict or to watch the miracle of reparation take place. Then there was Vangeli, of course, passing on his bicycle to the ice factory, dropping in for a glass of lemon tea, or bringing a piece of metal he was bent on fashioning to his own purposes, or to borrow a tool. Or there was Louisa, Yiórgo's charming and educated wife who was a school-teacher on the island, looking in to the workshop on her way to do the shopping; and Kosta the tall harbour-master to whom I had taken an instant liking, a handsome fellow who spoke slowly and to the point, and who had already made *Astarte* welcome in Skopelos harbour.

The trouble with Kosta was that he had so little to do; for although Skopelos is the 'capital' of the Sporades, in terms of movements of boats, numbers of fishing craft, trawlers, cruise-ships and foreign yachts, Skiathos was by far the busier harbour. It was a pity that a man so capable should have so little work; but with his family he had bedded himself deeply into the island life, and if he spent much time in the taverna testing the excellent *tsipuros* of Alonnisos and Pelion it was partly because his company was enjoyed and sought after and also because he had to spend his spare time somehow; and if he had developed an admirable resistance to alcohol it certainly did not prevent him from carrying out his duties, such as they were, with firmness and tact.

There was also Lakis Asteriadis, tall and dark, aged thirty, younger brother of one of the two doctors on the island; Lakis spent most of his time at Athens studying at the University to be a pharmacist. One day he would open a chemist shop in Skopelos, he told me, and get married. Then there were the two doctors themselves who dropped in on their rounds or just for a chat, Lakis's elder brother Stammatis, and Zachariadis, both of whom were cousins of Vangeli; and there was Kosta the postman, and Captain Mikhális Tchoukalas the gentle short-sighted master of the *Pródromos*, the biggest caique in the harbour, whose dark blue steep-sided hull seemed a permanent fixture of the port; and Grigor, an open-faced most likeable man who had been for many years making ice-cream in America and who now loved above all things to fish; and many others; and the only thing in common between them was their friendship with Yiórgo and their enjoyment of the informal atmosphere of his workshop, the convenience of the coffee-tray so near at hand and the shade of the plane tree outside the door, and the little tables with comfortable chairs set out under its branches.

From Yiórgo's workshop or just outside it, it is possible to observe almost everything that goes on in Skopelos harbour. Opposite, a dozen yards from the door, the inter-island caiques, *Paskhális* and *Katerina* discharge their anchors and warp themselves alongside the quay, unloading not only passengers but everything that is needed on the island, from baskets of fruit to iron bedsteads, sacks of cement to sides of beef.

In contrast to the *Kyknos*, the only other means of public transport between the Sporades and the mainland, a fast steamer that carries only passengers and has so deep a draft that she must anchor out in the harbour, the *Paskhális* and *Katerina* belong to the Sporades and are part of them. Their captains and crew are Skopelots and Skiathites, they carry messages and greetings between the islands as well as passengers and freight, and if they take twice as long as the *Kyknos* this, in a country where the national philosophy wisely maintains that a few hours here and there will make little difference to anyone, is not held against them. The two caiques are almost an institution in the Sporades: they are the lifelines of communication between one island and another and from them all to Volos, and they look the part – weather-beaten, patched up yet gay with bright worn paint, with all the character and jauntiness about their battered rigging, their deep curved timbers that is the lasting beauty of Aegean craft.

The bigger and older of the two is the *Paskhális*, measuring some sixty feet in length and more than a third of that across; and for the *Paskhális* I have a special affection. Built in Skopelos at the end of the war she is one of the last caiques of any size to be turned out by that island's shipwrights. Her owner is a certain Nikos Paskhális, a Skiathite, who lives in Skiathos. 'Paskhális' means 'Easter Man' and it is typical of Greek unself-consciousness for an owner to call a ship after himself. The caique has a long bowsprit, a magnificent sheer *pérama* bow, and under the proud overhang of her stern there is much splendid scrollwork picked out in gold. On the lower deck around the stern is a carved wood balustrade, a broad taffrail, painted yellow and brilliant green, which lends an added dignity to her impressive lines, giving her something of the look of a medieval galleon.

Captain Eli too is a man who seems to go well with the look and feeling – both pregnant and rakish – of his ship: a big man, and very dark, a boisterous piratical fellow, a man of moods alternatively gloomy and jovial, he wears a black beret aslant over his broad forehead, his trousers somehow hitched up along the under-curve of his massive belly. Captain Eli's belly is in some ways the most significant feature of the man, and strangely corresponds to that apparently excessive beaminess of his ship. On a lesser man and on a lesser ship such over-rotundity might give an impression of softness and sag, might hint of ungainliness and the seedier end of middle age. From the *Paskhális* and her captain one draws a very different conclusion: the great beam of the caique, the belly of her captain – these are the surety of their worth, signs not of their weakness but of their strength.

That the *Paskhális* is a most seaworthy vessel and her captain a fine seaman, no one can doubt; the proof is in the experience of so many successive winters ploughing backwards and forwards through the stormy Sporades. It would be difficult to imagine that the *Paskhális* should ever founder; and yet, once, she did.

Close by Cape Kalamaki and the entrance to Skiathos Bay is a rock, a black speck hardly discernible in the sea, like the dark fin of a submerging shark: this is the Mavromándilo, the 'black handkerchief'. The rock is a dangerous one, and it has a history of its own,

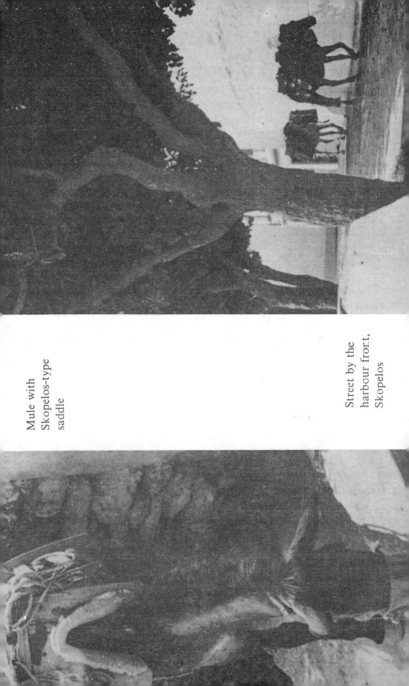

Mule with
Skopelos-type
saddle

Street by the
harbour frort,
Skopelos

Yióyo outside his workshop on the Skopelos waterfront

Skopelos harbour

told too in a story of Papadiamandis, the Skiathos writer of the early part of the century, who wrote exclusively about the people and legends of his island. Two brothers, young fishermen, lost their lives near this place, and their mother crazed with inconsolable grief took herself to the rock where, dressed in the usual black headscarf, she wept in mourning for her sons. She stayed on the rock a very long time, refusing to be taken off, until eventually she lost her strength and drowned.

The Mavromándilo is well known to everyone with a boat in the Sporades, not least to Captain Eli. One winter's night, however, rounding Kalamaki into Skiathos bay, the *Paskhális* was suddenly enveloped in a dense fog – a freak event, rare enough for the islands even in winter – and the helmsman, mistaking one light for another, put his wheel hard to port and ran the caique straight up on the rock. Fortunately it was flat calm, and the damage was slight. She was refloated the next day.

I have had the privilege of travelling on the *Paskhális* many times, and the experience has always been memorable in one way or another. Captain Eli, among his other virtues, has a sense of humour, of sorts. He likes to leave the steering to one of his passengers and wander round the deck ostensibly to collect the fares but really to chat to his friends. At times too he will retire into the little cabin with the single bunk behind the wheel-house and remain there deep in thought or sleep for hours on end, deaf to all demands of either passengers or crew.

One journey, turning north into the Gulf of Volos and approaching Trikeri I was taking a stroll round the deck, stepping carefully round a couple of donkeys and heaps of live trussed chickens, and climbing up to the wheel-house was startled to see that there was no one inside. Yet I noticed that the chains attached by pulleys that run aft along the deck from helm to rudder were moving. I looked in and saw that in a sense I was mistaken, there was someone at the wheel, a small boy: so small that he could only see out of the cracked glass window ahead by standing on his toes; and whether he was operating the wheel, or the wheel him, it was hard to say. We were heading for the Trikeri promontory at about nine knots, and closing fast; in a few minutes the *Paskhális* would be trying to scale the cliffs. I was about to do something dramatic when Captain Eli shouldered his way into the wheel-house, swept the boy, as if he were a fly, from the

D

wheel, and made the necessary adjustment. We stared down at the rocks sweeping by the caique's side. Captain Eli, perhaps because he thought I deserved an explanation, spoke. 'He's going to be a captain,' he said, rather gloomily, and then chuckled throatily, 'If he doesn't wreck us all first.' The boy was his son.

If the *Paskhális* is the queen of Sporadic caiques then the *Katerina* is a no less worthy lady-in-waiting. A little smaller, slower, she is nevertheless a fine and interesting boat with a handsome young captain aboard her and a charming one-eyed mate called Apostolis. The *Katerina*'s engines are old, and need Yiórgo's careful tuning. Sometimes her departure from Skopelos is delayed a few hours, the passengers waiting anxiously, the crew lounging from the rails : from the depths of the engine-room there comes a fearful and continuous clanging, as if some powerful man has been let loose with a sledge-hammer among all that heap of hot metal. Suddenly Yiórgo will emerge, dripping with oil and sweat, but with a triumphant smug expression on his round good-natured face. '*Endáxi!*' He waves his hand and the engine shudders into new life. Apostolis rolls his one good eye and the crew bend to the anchor winch. There are cries of farewell, and the warps splash into the harbour water; and if the wind is right, up will go the staysail, and with a triple blast of her horn the *Katerina* stands out to sea.

Arrivals and departures are not all that can be observed in ease and comfort from Yiórgo's workshop and from under the trees outside. Beautiful crimson caiques from Khalkis glide in occasionally, loaded to their booms with melons. The Skopelots converge at the waterside, and as the grimy captain lounges watchfully by the tiller the boys set up the brass scales and the melons are auctioned on the spot. I have seen two of these melon-caiques in at the same time – a most ill-judged reunion – moored within fifty feet of each other along the quay. The delighted crowd surged from one to the other and the captains, growing desperate, each stubbornly determined to get rid of his own cargo, slashed their prices lower and ever lower, caught in a ruinous cut-throat contest in which only the islanders could have won.

There is a rush, too, for the fishing boats when they come in, and much noisy bargaining with the tired fishermen over the shining heaps of blue and silver in the bottom of their boats; and queues form at the fish packers, and there is usually Vangeli, demanding from the fishermen and also getting – because they are all friends of his – fish for his magnificent black cats that follow at his heels, and Aegean oysters and other shell delicacies for *mézes*, that essential and civilized Greek accompaniment to wine, to be enjoyed later in the evening when the harbour lights are on and we shall repair to the taverna, sitting inside, among the wine barrels, because the nights are still cool.

And so I made Skopelos *Astarte*'s harbour that early summer, sailing out from it eastwards under the tall green bluffs with the white monasteries half hidden high among the pines, and sailed to Alonnisos and beyond to the *eremonisia* where no people live and there are only gulls and eagles, rocks and the sea; but always I came back, sooner or later, to Skopelos, where already I was beginning to feel at home, to Vangeli and Yiórgo and the cafés under the plane trees, and white belfries and church bells, and old caiques gazing sleepily at their own reflections in still water by the quay.

4

Kosta and Paraskevoúla

Skiathos, too, drew me back to it many times, though for different reasons. There is a certain pleasure in simply returning to a place one likes, where one is known. It was good to drop anchor under Bourtsi and tie up beside the fishing boats, to find Gus cheerfully waiting to take my gang-plank and tell me the latest news. I had some painting to do: the deck needed another coat, the mast re-varnishing. Skiathos harbour was convenient, if inclined to be hot, and the tavernas were only a few paces from the quay; and in the evenings, when the sun had mercifully fallen behind the ragged silhouette of hill-top roofs, there was Gerry, the island judge, a most pleasant and civilized Greek who spoke several languages fluently, with whom I played chess. There was time to consider the future.

Up till now, when I had thought about the search for my ideal anchorage, I had always visualized some derelict cottage conveniently situated on the shore which I would rent – perhaps – and use as a boat-house for *Astarte*'s gear. Beyond that my imagination had been blurred. It was enough, at that time, to find the place, to lay a permanent anchor, drop a marker buoy. When the finding of it had seemed so uncertain, how could I dare to think of more?

But now everything was beginning to look different, new. I had sailed back to Panormos several times: sometimes it seemed too perfect to be real; and as I thought about it, and kept returning to it in my mind, I could feel, almost against my will, the hatching of a more ambitious dream. Why not buy some land there – build, well, perhaps more than a boat-house?

The implications of such an idea – even supposing it were possible – seemed to so threaten, overthrow the structure of my present way of life that I needed a second and vital confirmation. I decided to wait in Skiathos for Angelina to arrive; the television series in which she was acting allowed her a few weeks escape from England, and my letters had made her curious and excited to know what I had found. It was necessary now to make some kind of joint decision. Waiting in Skiathos I found myself speaking English again. Relatively the number of foreigners, mostly English, on the islands was large: there were at least four; and in such a small community where foreigners were still rare birds it was difficult not to meet them all.

There was Mrs. Harper, known generally on the island as Rena, a Greek though married to an English businessman, an attractive ebullient woman who occasionally enlivened the harbour scene by riding her horse at a gallop between the café tables on the front. She had bought a few pieces of land on the south coast, on behalf of English friends of hers; she was also building a house of her own and as the idea of Panormos began to take shape, gave me much useful information about the problems of island building.

A new arrival was an elderly gentleman who had spent most of his life ostrich-farming in East Africa, and was now considering Skiathos as a place to retire. Just lately a box of his with money and papers in it had been stolen from the room he was renting in the village; the islanders were horrified at this outrage done to a foreigner presumably by one of themselves, and the village was buzzing with scandalized conjecture. He was away in Volos for a short time, and returned one afternoon on the *Paskhális*. A deputation was waiting for him at the quay, and the box with its contents intact was with much ceremony handed back to him: it had been found deposited by the guilty one, whose torments of conscience had overcome his greed, on the altar of a church.

There were the Crosfields, Paul and Terry, who with Panayioti, an architect, and various other useful and essential people, were busy planning to build a house. Listening to them talk inevitably made my own plans appear more within the bounds of possibility, and I began to look upon their problems, concerning land and building, with a certain vicarious interest.

The Crosfields had already become involved in a quarrel over the boundaries of their land, a quarrel finally settled mostly through Paul's good sense and good humour; but not always were such disputes solved so peacefully. One English family, expecting to find their villa ready when they arrived, were met as they stepped ashore with a summons. They found themselves involved in a lawsuit about a right of way from their land to the road, and were helpless spectators of a noisy legal battle fought out in the stifling heat of the Skiathos courthouse that culminated in the entire court taking to the sea in boats to examine at closer quarters the scene of the dispute.

This sort of friction between foreigner and Greek, while entertaining enough to an observer, clearly did no one any good, and as I returned to my idling in the Skiathos sun, waiting for Angelina to arrive, I hoped fervently that in Skopelos I would have the luck to avoid any unpleasantness of this kind.

I am not quite sure how I met the little boy called Kosta. I can only remember the time when I didn't know him, and then the time when suddenly he was a permanent and accepted fixture of the boat whenever I was in Skiathos.

He was always there, waiting for me on the quay every time I put in. I became so accustomed to his welcome that between getting the anchor ready I would glance up and automatically scan the group that always collects whenever a boat arrives, and see him, standing apart, hands in pockets at the water's edge, too shy to wave at that distance for fear I wouldn't recognize him. As soon as the warps were secured, the engine off and the gang-plank down he'd come scrambling across it to greet me with a voluble and excited explanation of how, day after day he had been expecting me, how he'd given up hope almost that I would ever come back to the island, that maybe I'd got wrecked in that storm a few days ago . . . how only that morning he was up on Bourtsi and had seen the red sail coming between the islands. . . .

By this time he was quite out of breath, and usually underwent a sudden fit of embarrassment, momentarily overawed by his audacity and good fortune at being, as it was clear he was, a part-owner of the boat whenever I was in Skiathos.

There would follow a polite and calmer exchange of news: Where had I been all this time? How I could find so much to do in Skopelos or Alonnisos when Skiathos was so obviously so much more interesting? And then he'd tell me what he had been doing since my last departure, how many times he'd been swimming, that he earned some money sorting boxes on the quay for the *Paskhális*, helped his father in the pine forests . . . And having then run out of conversation he would immediately look round for something to do, tie up the dinghy alongside, or seize a brush and start scrubbing furiously at the deck, or take the ropes apart that I had just carefully coiled and set about recoiling them with infinite patience.

Although I was sure I had never invited Kosta aboard in the first place, I couldn't help liking him now that he was there. He was very shy, aged twelve as he always said, but seemed at least a couple of years younger, and even then was small for his age. His face was perfectly round, with his hair cropped to a bare toothbrush half inch. There was something appealing about him, his large round eyes perhaps, his big mouth so readily stretched in a wide grin. He was very thin, and this thinness was accentuated by his extraordinary assortment of ill-fitting clothes. His ambition, he said, was to become a sailor like his elder brother, but I am afraid he will never be much more of a sailor than I am, which is of a most limited kind, with a profound preference for calm weather and the reliable warmth of summer winds.

Kosta's father was a resin-collector and woodcutter: he was always hard at work in the hinterland of pines, and I never saw him; the family lived in a cottage some way outside the village of Skiathos. But as I got to know Kosta better I occasionally caught a glimpse of his mother, a bent, prematurely aged woman dressed in that loose hanging black-bodiced petticoat, a shawl over her head, that is the everyday attire of peasant women in the Sporades. I used to see her sometimes, standing half hidden, almost effacing herself – doubtless following Kosta's fierce instructions – at the corner of some building on the front, giving her son a lecture about not bothering me too much, or about being properly polite, making sure that he was dressed at least cleanly if not well, while Kosta who was going through that stage of being intensely ashamed of all female, protective influences, especially when demonstrated in public, shrugged and nodded impatiently, and ran off as soon as he got the chance.

I used to give Kosta a few drachmae every now and then, strictly in payment for the odd jobs he was always doing about the boat, and once a pair of shoes and some bathing shorts – these being luxuries as far as his family were concerned. One morning – it must have been when I didn't know him very well, because I can remember how the incident startled me – I was having breakfast of a boiled egg and toast when Kosta put his head through the cabin hatch. I invited him to join me, and after several refusals, which was his way, he accepted. I then asked him if he'd like two eggs rather than one, and when he hesitated I insisted. . . . He ate one egg, and a piece of toast with evident enjoyment; but the other egg he carefully wrapped up and stuffed in his pocket. I couldn't help asking him what he was saving it for, imagining that he wanted to keep it for later on in the morning. He replied, quite simply, that he was going to take it back home to give to his father.

From then on, at midday, if Kosta was still around which he usually was, we'd step across the quay to Mitso's taverna and eat together, though Kosta's stomach seemed seldom able to stretch enough to accommodate even the not very large helpings of beans and potatoes that he ordered, while the sun burned down through the awning over our heads and the quay glared white, too hot to touch with bare feet, and sea and sky beyond the islands melted together like colourless metallic plate.

Little boys in Greece, and especially on the islands, seem to live remarkably happy and healthy lives. Until about fifteen, they are at the beck and call of any adult who cares to make use of them. There is an abrupt, matter-of-fact relationship in these errands which both adult and boy take for granted. For small services the boy does not expect any reward, but for anything that takes up more of his time he will be given a few drachmae. At about fourteen or earlier, when most boys from poor families leave school, they go to work – minor but still hard working jobs, such as waiters' assistants, or builders' helps, and most commonly of all in the islands, work with the nets and on the fishing boats. The partnership of captain and boy is one that can be observed in action on any small caique in every harbour of the Aegean.

Children on the islands can also be strangely proud. I was having supper at an outside taverna with Paul and Terry, and we were eating *keftédes*, a kind of spiced meat-ball and a Greek speciality, when a little boy aged no more than six or seven appeared at our elbows trying to sell us pistachio nuts. 'Pistachios! Buy my pistachios!' None of us wanted to buy any, but Terry thought that the boy looked hungry, so she speared a meat-ball on a fork and offered it to him. The boy tried to ignore the *keftéde* and pushed forward his basket of nuts. 'Pistachios!'

'We don't want any nuts,' said Terry in Greek, 'but take this, it's good!' The little boy would not take his gaze off the meat-ball held out in front of him, but as he looked and looked, he kept his basket firmly between him and the tempting mouthful, repeating, 'No! No!' until eventually the strain became too great and he turned and fled.

Before long *Astarte*'s harbour crew in Skiathos was augmented by a little girl with the improbable name of Paraskevoúla. She was the youngest of that enormous family of which Panayioti was the oldest, he being about thirty, she ten. Probably it was because Paraskevoúla knew I was a friend of her brother and had seen him on board with me that she first began to take an interest in the boat. For a long time I had been aware of her little face peering at me from behind a kiosk every time I came on deck, or sometimes she just stood watching me from the edge of the quay. This constant surveillance gradually began to have an unnerving effect on me, the more so as whenever I caught her eye she would turn her head quickly away and pretend either to examine some other event of interest taking place among the cafés, or to be wrapt in profound and speculative study of the empty sky; and whenever I went ashore when she was at her usual watchful post, she immediately took to her heels.

One of Kosta's privileged occupations which he took very seriously was to guard *Astarte* when I was on land. This was entirely unnecessary : I have never found the need to lock up the boat in any harbour of the Sporades. But at least it gave Kosta a great deal of pleasure, though his presence attracted his friends, and therefore did in fact give him something to do – to keep them off. One morning when I returned from buying some water-melons I found Paraskevoúla on the boat. She had managed to cross the gang-plank – a hazardous enough crossing even for an adult – and was just then with indignant exclamations driving Kosta step by step across the deck.

Kosta might know how to repel invaders of his own kind, but was clearly hopelessly inexperienced in dealing with girls. What Paraskevoúla had been saying to him as she forced him back towards the cabin hatch I shall never know, but poor Kosta had been rendered quite speechless, powerless to make his authority felt.

Of course this was only the beginning. Paraskevoúla was back most days after that – it was the school holidays and the children were free – and as she grew more confident gradually allowed herself the freedom of the boat, on deck and below. Her habit was to burst in during the morning and set about what she imagined was clearing up the boat, washing up, and generally ransacking my possessions, going through every shelf and locker and rearranging everything to such an extent that I could never again find anything I wanted without asking her. She even began to let Kosta order her about.

When Angelina arrived, waving from the upper deck of the *Paskhális* as the caique nosed alongside the Skiathos quay, Kosta and Paraskevoúla were waiting with me. They received her at first with suspicion, soon dispelled. They began imploring us to take them to Skopelos where neither of them had ever been, and one clear morning, having obtained permission from their mothers who came down in their best dresses to see their children off, we left. Kosta was wearing a faded but scrubbed pair of long trousers, his new canvas shoes and his most respectable shirt; Paraskevoúla's short dark hair was carefully brushed, and she wore a bright cotton frock. For the first few minutes at least they were on their best behaviour. Kosta took the tiller. 'I can steer for hours,' he said. 'I think it's going to be rough. Paraskevoúla will get sick, I know.' The sea was a glassy calm. 'Are we going to put the sails up?' he asked anxiously. I said I didn't think so. I could almost hear his sigh of relief, though I think he also wanted to redeem himself. The last time he'd been out with me under full sail along the south coast of Skiathos the effect of the sharply heeled boat, the roar of the *meltémi* in the rigging, had reduced him to tears.

Two nights later we saw them off back to Skiathos on the *Kyknos*, just as we had promised their mothers. The departure of the children left us free for what had been uppermost in my mind for some time: to set sail together for Panormos.

5

Panormos: Saints and Treasure

Whenever I have come into Panormos by sea – until the new road is open it is the only way, except by the mule-track across the hills – I have had an anxious feeling that the place might have changed while I have been away from it: that someone might have cut down the pines and cypresses, burnt the olive trees. I suppose this time it was a fear that the picture of the place kept in my mind and suddenly exposed to someone else might only have been wishful thinking.

Everything was just the same. As we turned in under the island of Daseiá we could see the white walls of Vangeli's house high among the pines far up the valley, the ancient caique derelict upon its beach by the cottages of the outer bay; and then, as we went in farther, the sudden view of Panormos cove itself, opening off at right-angles from the bay, a winding inlet of blue water, with the resin-collector's cottage and the reflection of the old retsina barn welcoming us at its end by the still water's edge.

For the next ten days *Astarte* stayed at anchor at the south head of the cove, warped from the stern to a fir tree spreading over the water. We beached the dinghy or tied it to the ruined jetty, and wandered about the shore.

Not much was said between us about what exactly we were doing; it seemed better not to talk about it too explicitly. We would pause at the headland dividing the outer bay from the inner anchorage: here between some fine olive trees there was a rubble shell of a small cottage that once housed boat-builders who had stopped work fifty years ago.

'This could be a good place.'

'Yes. Beautiful.'

Or we'd stop by the little point covered with young cypresses. 'This is lovely, just here. . . .'

We must have walked past the rock, either under it or above it many times. It was really a kind of small cliff about fifteen feet high, suddenly jutting out from the hill, facing the water. A grove of tall firs and cypresses grew in a depression on one side of it, to the south; to the north the earth sloped down to the edge of the sea, and here there were olive and almond trees, until the black turrets of the biggest cypresses in the bay struck attitudes of grave soliloquy before the gallery of distant pines. We sat at the foot of the cliff, climbed on top of it. The base of the rock was only a few yards from the water. We looked westwards across the anchorage to the dark, wooded peninsula that was the barrier against the open sea; to the north-west, Daseiá, across the bay's entrance; beyond, Skiathos, the northern cliffs, and far beyond Skiathos, a distance of some thirty-five miles, the dim slopes of Pelion.

We came back to the rock the next day, and that evening made a fire and cooked supper. I poured red wine from the wicker flask and held our glasses against the sunset sea.

'Wooden balconies,' I said, 'overhanging the cliff.'

'Big verandas, lots of shade.'

'And a courtyard?'

'The olive tree will stay in the middle of it. . . .'

It was going to be of stone, a house built of solid rock, with walls half a metre thick. . . . Angelina would have a big kitchen, open, in the summer, for coolness, and there were to be wooden columns supporting the wide verandas. . . .

'I ought to have a study,' I said.

'Why not on top, with another veranda?'

We lay back on the rock, the stone still warm from the afternoon sun, and watched the moon sail over the hills.

'Mustn't forget *Astarte*,' I said. 'There's a good place for a jetty, just there by the rocks.'

'After all she found Panormos.' The synthesis of land and sea, boat and house.

'Listen to those pines.' No breath of air touched us. Panormos water lay a pool of black and silver, unruffled, still as a photograph. And yet there must have been wind somewhere for we heard the sigh of it in the trees, on the headland opposite, dying away; taken up at once by the pines behind us, like long waves falling upon sand.

'Could you live here?'

The wind reached us, a breath warm with summer, heavy with the scent of resin and herbs.

'Anyway,' I said, 'it's impossible.'

'Yes, but isn't it enough just to imagine it all?'

And so the whole question rested, outwardly at least, when I saw her off on the *Kyknos* for Athens and England a few days later. But as far as I was concerned my mind was made up: I knew now what I had always wanted to do with my perfect anchorage, once I had found it – build a small house on its shores and live there, with *Astarte* moored at the bottom of the courtyard.

Would Vangeli sell us a piece of Panormos, and that particular piece with the cliff and the olive-trees? Or rather, would he be willing to try and persuade his father-in-law? Slightly discouraging was that only a month or so ago I had heard how a shipowner had been pressing to buy the point that divides the cove from the outer bay, and I remember Vangeli's smile: the family would never sell any of Panormos, the old man was determined, and he was right. He had already refused several offers. After all, he had created Panormos as it was today, in the sense that he and his wife, Alexandra's mother, had started when they were young, started from nothing, planting trees – firs, cypresses, fruit-trees, almonds – grafting the wild olives with cultivated shoots, tapping the pines for resin, ploughing the level spaces with wheat . . . so that there should be one day what there was now, a flourishing estate with natural boundaries, all of one piece, and their own.

There seemed not one chance in a thousand that they would agree to part with a piece of Panormos, even the smallest fragment. But I knew that most things, even the unlikeliest, were possible. Hadn't the idea of *Astarte*, right at the beginning, been itself wildly improbable? Clearly the whole question turned on Vangeli. If Vangeli could like the idea of us living at Panormos, as his neighbours, then it was just possible that he might be able to persuade his father-in-law. The next logical step was to put the question to Vangeli, and this I was not very anxious to do: uncertainty seemed better then than an outright refusal, but though I put it off for as long as I could, the uncertainty in the end grew too much to bear.

Tentatively I opened the subject one day on board *Astarte* in Skopelos harbour. To my delight Vangeli was enthusiastic; it was as if he had been half expecting it. He knew that this was a serious step for us: Panormos was not to be the site of just a holiday 'villa', but a house to live in, for Angelina and myself and, when and if we had any, our children. He would do everything, he said, to help; first he would speak to Alexandra, and then he would try and talk his father-in-law round. It would be difficult, he warned, and it might take time: it was a question of waiting for the right moment.

Nothing could have made me happier, and he could see that. 'I'm leaving this evening,' I told him.

'Where to?' It was hardly necessary to answer. 'Skyros? Alonnisos? Skiathos?' He laughed. '*Me to kaló* – go with good . . .'

I spent many days in Panormos, thinking, planning, walking about the shores of the anchorage and the hills behind. I had forgotten my old fears of complications, getting tied up, involved. I used to sit on the little cliff in the afternoons listening to the goat-bells sounding through the pines, waiting for the herd to pass underneath me, scrambling over the rocks and through the shallows, about eighty fine horned animals, with the herdsman and his dog behind. The goatherd was a dark handsome fellow with a quick smile. He walked with a slow swagger, his bag slung over his shoulder, his long crook in his hands, and though we seldom spoke to each other except to say good morning or good evening, I took a great liking to his presence, mostly invisible, with only the sad notes of his pipe above the trill of the cicadas in the heavy heat of noon to mark his seat under some olive tree on the hillside.

Sometimes I climbed higher and looked out to sea past Daseiá to Skiathos and the double horns of Trikeri, straight down the Evvia Channel in the direction of Thermopylae. I could see Cape Arte-mision clearly in the evenings: the blunt finger of distant cliffs lay darkly on the reddened sea. From Skiathos in 480 B.C. triremes from Themistocles' fleet kept watch against the approach of Xerxes' armada, and there below me in the straits between Skiathos and Skopelos that doomed squadron of the Persian fleet, attempting to outflank the Greeks, must have slipped through, oars muffled in the dusk, only to meet its end in the stormy sea-graves of the Evvian 'Hollows'.

Here it was impossible not to be aware of the past. Yet the Northern Sporades have always been a backwater in the turbulent history of the Aegean. The islands suffered with every invasion that swept Greece; the only difference was that when the Sporades were raided, burnt, their inhabitants carried away into slavery, it was of little significance to the main current of events.

It is believed that the islands were originally peopled by Dolopians and Pelasgians, the primitive first inhabitants of much of the Aegean. Skopelos was colonized by Cretans after the fall of Knossos, Skiathos by Ionians and later Khalkidians.

Both Skopelos and Skiathos joined the Delian Sea League, and in the third century B.C. the Sporades, caught as between two fires in the struggle of Rome with Macedon, were sacked by each opponent in turn. From then on the islands were treated as no more than counters in the often violent game of Greek and Roman politics – passed by Mark Antony over to the Athenians, back to Rome again, until the Emperor Hadrian restored their liberty. In A.D. 267 a horde of barbarian Goths and Heruls, floating through the Bosphorus in five hundred ships, ravaged the islands. . . .

After Licario had ousted the Ghisi dukes in 1276 the plunderings of the Sporades became so frequent that life became hardly worth living : many of the islanders emigrated to Evvia and took up piracy themselves. Skiathos and Skopelos, and especially Panormos, became notorious pirate harbours, and the business became thoroughly organized. Pirates worked on a regular fixed tariff: 'The captain was entitled to three *denarii* of spoil for every two which he had spent on fitting out his vessel; but if he attacked the lair of a fellow-pirate, his gains, in consideration of the extra risk, or perhaps by way of salve to his professional conscience, were assessed at twice the amount of his outlay. . . .'

Insecurity seems to have been the most constant theme of Sporades history, for in 1453 when Constantinople fell to the Turks, the islands were occupied by Venice at the request of the inhabitants. In spite of the occasional misconduct of the Venetian rectors the islands did not fare too badly, and their governors could hardly be blamed for imagining, when Khaireddin Barbarossa made his second devastating cruise of the Aegean in 1538, that the islanders would assist in the defence of their homes against the Moslem invader. In fact the people of Skyros handed over their masters without a blow, and at Skiathos the rector, determined to hold out in the near impregnable Kastro in the north of the island, was murdered by the Skiathites whom he had armed, and ropes were let down the cliffs for the Turks to enter the castle. Not that the islanders gained anything by this act. 'Barbarossa was so indignant at the murder of his brave opponent that he ordered the instant beheadal of the men who

had betrayed their commander, and carried off the rest of the inhabitants into slavery. . . .'

The Sporades remained under Turkish rule for 290 years, a
period shorter by a whole century than many other parts of Greece.
They seem, also, to have had a comparatively easy time under the
Turks and were allowed a wide degree of self-government. Their
main obligations consisted of paying taxes and contributing a certain
number of sailors to the Ottoman Navy. During the Greek Wars of
Independence the Sporades offered a great number of fire-ships to
the raiding Greek squadrons. Perhaps because of this and the sharp
reception the Turks got when they tried to collect the taxes and the
sailors, the Sporades, became known as the *Daemonisia*, or 'Demon
Islands'. In those years the Sporades suffered nearly as much from
the Greek freedom-fighters as from the Turks. A tally of shipping
contributed by the Aegean islands to the insurgent Greeks in 1803
gives some idea of the comparative wealth of the Sporades at that
time. Skopelos offered 35 ships, a total tonnage of 6,300 tons, 525
sailors and 140 cannon. Only Hydra, Spetsai and Crete could afford
a more powerful contribution.

It was not until 1830, when they became part of the new Greek
state, that the Sporades gained their freedom, and at last some sem-
blance of security.

As I looked down upon the bay and the straits beyond, the calm
sea shining in loops of silver, running out like a river from under the
black Panormos pines, I wondered : did 'inanimate' objects not have
the power of memory in some – however vague – sense of the word?
The sea – no. The sea, I thought, was too big, too overwhelming and
too self-absorbed to retain the imprint of life and death, however violent, however dramatic. But trees, earth – could not rocks remember?

Late one afternoon I was joined by a tall white-haired old man
with a broad, pleasant face and blue eyes shaded by a cap. Barba
Yiorgi, he was called, and he was helping collect the resin for Vangeli though he lived, he told me, in a cottage under Mount Dirphis,
the two thousand-foot peak, highest in the island, whose summit was
just visible between the branches of the almond trees. He was leading his mule and donkey-foal back to the resin-collectors' cottage to
tether them for the night, and as I knew he would, he came back for
a talk. I was clambering through the bushes that conceal the heaped

stone ruins of a little chapel of Ayia Sophia, the Holy Wisdom, that lie a few yards inland from the cliff. Barba Yiorgi was waiting for me as I stepped down. He looked at me knowingly. 'You'll never find it,' he said.

'Find what?'

'The treasure, of course.'

Ah, the treasure. Greeks are fond of treasure, and all the best places have some. Still, the Greeks are probably right after all: it's just a question of knowing where to look. It was good to hear of some at Panormos.

'This treasure,' I said, 'how do you know it's here?'

Barba Yiorgi looked at me with kindly scorn. 'Everybody knows about the treasure at Ayia Sophia. But no one's found it yet, that's the trouble. It was hidden just before the Turks burnt the chapel down.'

'When was that?'

There was a pause of four or five minutes, in which I forgot that I I had asked him a question, but during which time he had obviously been painfully calculating. Suddenly he spoke. 'Eight hundred and fifty years ago.'

I felt obliged to point out to him that this figure must be an exaggeration: the Turks only appeared in the Aegean five and a half centuries ago.

'You are an educated man,' said Barba Yiorgi. He gazed at me with admiration. 'I may be a few years out. But the treasure is there all right.' He nodded gloomily. 'But where, exactly? That's the point.'

He described, with accompanying gestures, the box or tin in which the priest managed to hide all the gold and silver of the chapel, besides a great quantity of coin, before the Turks broke in, murdered him and the chapel's defenders and set the place alight. It was said that the priest buried the box under the floor somewhere, though as the old man said, with a sly wink, this was probably a trick. There was nothing under the floor – people had dug there already. It was somewhere though – but where, now? We have entered into a pact: whatever we find we share. There is a further treasure still waiting to be dug up, according to Barba Yiorgi, across the water, somewhere among the rocks and almost impenetrable pines of the peninsula. This lot was hidden, he said, by the klephts, the *andártes* –

fighters in the Greek revolution – who also hid their weapons with the money before they escaped. Panormos, said the old man, was the scene of much bloody fighting between the Turks and the Greek patriots, because of the anchorage. The money, he added, was in gold: English sovereigns. (Most Greek treasure is.) It was as if to whet my appetite.

'But have you really looked for it properly?' I asked him.

'Have I looked for it? Of course I've looked for it. What do you think' (indignantly) 'I've been doing all these years? I'm seventy-four, you know. . . . But if you live here as some people say you might. . . .' he paused, waiting hopefully for some affirmation or denial of this rumour, and went on, rather dejectedly: 'you're bound to find it, sometime. . . .'

'Half and half,' I said quickly. 'Same as the other one, the priest's. You can help me dig it up.'

Cheered slightly, Barba Yiorgi pointed out to me the place where fifty years ago there had been a well. It was filled in now and impossible to recognize. 'And there were steps,' he added, gesturing vaguely about the earth and thistles where we stood, 'big steps made of marble, going down to the sea. We found them when we were digging for Barba Kostis (Vangeli's father-in-law) but we covered them up. That was years, years ago . . . when I was a young man.' He fell to ruminating a while and then, accepting another cigarette and, it seemed, about to move off, he turned suddenly and pointed a finger at me – 'You know about the dragon I suppose?'

'Dragon?' I almost felt like looking over my shoulder. Where? 'No, tell me about it . . .' Another weakness I share with many uneducated Greeks: almost as much as buried treasure, I like dragons. Legendary dragons, as opposed to fairy-tale dragons – there is an important distinction – are quite rare.

Barba Yiorgi sat down on 'our' rock and waited importantly for me to light his cigarette. 'The dragon,' he began, choosing his words carefully, 'lived just here,' he waved his arms around, 'here in Panormos. And if it hadn't been for the blessed Ayios Rhiginos' (the old man crossed himself) 'the dragon would probably still be here today. You know about Ayios Rhiginos, the martyr?'

'Yes,' I replied, 'a little. I've heard of him. But go on . . .'

Later I found out much more, as much as I could, for by far the most popular and most personal saint venerated in Skopelos today is the martyr Rhiginos. He was Bishop of the island in the first half of the fourth century, and when he arrived to take up the governance of his see – landed on the long beach just north of Panormos where the pines tumble down from the mountains to the yellow sands' edge – he seems to have had a presentiment of his violent end. He is said to have fallen on his knees on the beach and called out aloud to God, in a moment of simultaneous fear and dedication, to spare him his fate. The place is called, from this most human cry, *Eleos*, Mercy.

Rhiginos was by all accounts a man of great learning, and something of an ascetic; at the same time he had a reputation for gentleness, and was loved by poor and ordinary people, whose interests he took to heart. That he had courage no one may doubt, for one of his most dramatic acts, for which he is still remembered by the islanders, was the slaying of this dragon that had long been the plague of Skopelos. The dragon, which had its lair at Panormos, presumably in some cave deep in the pine forests, possessed a nature as savage and horrific as its appearance. Its habit was to clamber up the valleys, smashing cottages with a single blow of its tail, seizing sheep and goats, and as often as possible human beings, crunching them like prawns between its jaws. It had so ravaged and terrorized the countryside that it was responsible for the severe depopulation of the island and a large proportion of the inhabitants had either been eaten or had fled.

When Rhiginos mounted the episcopal throne he decided that something ought to be done: the monster must be destroyed; and as others, notably bands of hired soldiers, had failed he resolved to make the attempt himself.

The dragon's reputation was so notorious that it was the custom of the neighbouring islands to avoid the direct responsibility of executing those criminals they had themselves condemned to death, by shipping them to Panormos, and leaving them to be devoured there at the dragon's leisure. The Bishop made use of this barbarous custom by disguising himself as a sailor, and having enrolled in one of these doomed ships coming from Skiathos or perhaps Evvia, disembarked with the condemned criminals on the edge of Panormos Bay. No dragon was in sight. He left his companions trembling on the sand and set off determinedly in search of the beast. He had not far to go. Round the edge of a great boulder Bishop and dragon met face to face.

No one quite knows exactly what happened then. There were no witnesses, and after the event Rhiginos himself preferred to maintain a modest silence. In the opinion of Barba Yiorgi, the Bishop had secreted in his clothes a heavy cross which he drew, as one might a sword, and wielded it to good effect; but then Barba Yiorgi, perhaps visualizing the unequal contest in a more realistic light, abandoned this theory and pointing a horny finger skywards bellowed out in his deep voice: '*Theós!*' 'God!' Which as far as he was concerned successfully disposed of the entire problem.

Some say that the Bishop, making use of that gift of rhetoric for which later he became so justly famed, preached the dragon a dreadful interminable sermon. In any case the beast turned and fled. Relentlessly the Bishop pursued it across the hills towards the south of the island, still preaching his sermon, the fiery words homing like maddening hornets into the dragon's ears, until hunter and hunted reached a point on the coastline between Staphylos and Agnonda. There, faced with the sea before it, the Bishop behind, the dragon was forced to make a desperate choice: a leap to death or another sermon from the Bishop. As the dragon flung itself off, the cliff opened, and the monster was engulfed in the awful fissure. This chasm, a dramatic crack in the cliffs, strewn with boulders and crooked pines, is easily visible from seaward today; they call it *Drakontóskisma*, Dragon Schism.

So may perish all dragons! Modern students of history may smile at such a literal account of so distant an event; although it is a pity not to believe in dragons, if only a little. They would suggest that the dragon merely represented some force of Evil rampant in the island at the time and purged by the energetic new Bishop. The theory is lent some fractional support by the fact that Rhiginos was deeply involved in the contemporary struggle over the Arian heresy, and later with the revival of paganism in the Empire.

It was in A.D. 361 that Rhiginos me this greatest challenge, and the fearful presentiment of the beach at Eleos was fulfilled. Julian, surnamed the Apostate, had come to the imperial throne of Byzantium, and throughout the empire the temples of the ancient cults of Asia, Greece and Rome were restored and re-endowed. As the general failure of the movement became increasingly apparent, a certain desperate fanaticism was allowed in Greece to darken the names of those old and weary Olympian gods who, already half asleep beneath the clouds of their mountain-tops, refused to stir again.

An eparch, armed with soldiers and an imperial writ, descended on the Sporades. Bishop Rhiginos was inevitably singled out for forcible reconversion. Soft words were followed by threats, threats by torture. But the good Bishop stood firm, as the chronicler puts it, 'like a rock on which the furious sea beats in vain'. Finally, on February 25, A.D. 362, the saint was taken to the Old Bridge just outside the town of Skopelos and beheaded.

Rhiginos, canonized, became the special saint-protector (*polyoukhos*) of Skopelos, and the islanders, who had followed the brave example of their Bishop and held firm to the faith, were allowed many centuries of undisputed and peaceful veneration of the martyr's remains. But in 1068 Skopelos received an unwelcome visitor: William, King of Sicily, for some reason known as 'the Good'. One of the first great collectors, William had as his particular hobby the amassing of holy relics. His soldiers landed, marched to the church where the Bishop lay, dug him up, and before the eyes of the outraged but helpless islanders, sailed away with him.

The saint's bones were taken to Cyprus, where they remained intact until 1740. At this time the citizens of Skopelos had grown rich from the trading of their ships throughout the Mediterranean, and with their increasing wealth and responsibilities they had developed a new sensitivity to the reputation of their island. A monk was dispatched to Cyprus to request the skeleton's repatriation, and though this was refused he managed to return to Skopelos in possession of the saint's severed right hand.

The memory of Ayios Rhiginos is still very much alive in Skopelos today, though some sixteen hundred years have passed since his execution. His day is celebrated on the 25th of each February with a solemn procession through the town during which the sainted hand is exposed to the pious view of the populace. There is a memorial shrine on the old bridge where the Bishop was martyred, and peasants with their mules and donkeys riding into town cross themselves as they pass, and so also the passengers in the new bus as it rattles across the bridge on its way to Staphylos and Agnonda. A candle is kept burning day and night behind the little glass door, and there is an inscription in classical Greek on the marble face which few islanders can read.

The bridge is a good place to go, especially of an evening when the full summer heat of the open shore has become unbearable; it is good to wander along the path by the dry river bed, listening to the *meltémi* as it dies away at dusk among the giant bamboos, and, under the broad leaves of the Bishop's great plane, to sit and smoke, dangling one's legs over the parapet edge. Soothed by the cool green light that seems to grow there between the forest of fruit-trees, one may spare a thought perhaps for dragons, and Bishops, and the old gods.

Panormos, too, is a place to contemplate such things, and others also – the sea-fight in the bay in 360 B.C. and the capture of six Athenian triremes, the ruins of the ancient city in the valley, one of the earliest on the island and so strangely abandoned, the chapel of Ayia Sophia itself and the curly-cornered capital I found near it, identified by the photograph I sent to the British Museum as Byzantine work, sixth century: the time of Justinian.

Ayia Sophia must be very old, and I believe that like many of the oldest Greek chapels Ayia Sophia was once a temple. But to what god or goddess? Athene, is my guess: because the early Christians took care always to render the transposition from the old religion to the new as painless as possible. Was the chapel a mark for the eparch and soldiers of the Emperor Julian when they came so confidently to Skopelos and thought to shake the faith of old Rhiginos? Was the cross, so lately installed in the temple, thrown out again, and the image of the goddess reinstated? And anyway, the islanders who came down to worship there, did they notice much difference?

It was Barba Yiorgi who later led me to a rough terraced wall overgrown with bushes, a few paces from the rock and a place I must have passed a hundred times, and drawing aside the branches pointed out to me an ancient marble column, seven foot long, embedded in the stones. After that I did a little careful searching myself, and in the same loose stone wall found two more capitals – Byzantine, probably, but at present I can only guess. What a place for a chapel, and indeed a temple.

And what a place to live. . . . Vangeli was taking a long time finding the 'right moment' to approach his father-in-law; but it was well that he did, for when he came riding over from Skopelos on Foola his Skyrian pony, he brought – grinning all over his face – good news, the best news. Alexandra had approved, the old man had agreed. 'You are an islander now, a *Skopelitis*,' said Vangeli, delighted to see me so overcome, 'and you will be my neighbour, and this makes me very happy. . . .'

It was October, and too late to discuss details, to measure land, sign papers. Besides it would have been impolite, I felt, to push ahead so fast. Things as serious and important as these, in Greece especially, deserve not to be hurried. I was more than content. The next stage could wait until the spring.

The weather had been bad, but now the first gales of autumn had blown themselves away and perhaps the most beautiful time of year in the Sporades was to come. I planned to make a short visit to Skyros again, before finding a place to lay-up the boat and return for the winter to Angelina and England. But Vangeli invited me to a *panayiri*, the festival of a certain saint, Ayios Artemios, and by way too of celebrating my own great good fortune, I gladly accepted.

The night of the feast was still and full of stars glittering with the first chill of autumn. My footsteps rang on the cobbles of the crooked streets as I made my way out of Skopelos, past the silent ice factory, between the high walls of gardens that cut off the trunks of orange trees and pistachios, and I walked with the dust soft underfoot across the Old Bridge where the ghost of Rhiginos sleeps among the leaves, out along the road through the olive groves towards Staphylos. I had thought I would join others making their way to the chapel, but I saw no one and knew I was already late. In a few moments lights came into view between the trees, and there came the sound of voices and chanting, and the bitter-sweet faint smell of incense.

I had only seen Panayióti Galatzánou behind the crowded counter of his narrow little shop, the walls of which were hung with that peculiar assortment of goods – packets of detergent, clothes-pegs, dried fish, barrels of split peas – that is the usual ware of the general grocer in the islands. Galatzánou seldom seemed to shave, and his clothes like most of the islanders' were old, worn and undistinguished; yet here he was, throwing open the doors of his family chapel to more than a hundred people, half of whom were invited to dine with him and his family in the rooms adjoining when the service was over. I saw him now, as I pressed with the others into the little church bright with candles and shining with light reflected from brass and silver, ikons and polished wood: he was standing by the lectern on one side of the ikon-screen, face uplifted, his deep voice leading the congregation in a chant that everyone joined.

Outside the doors of the chapel people dressed in their Sunday best stood about in groups, talked and greeted each other. The chapel seemed to be built on to the rest of the house, and I wandered freely through the simple, whitewashed rooms, out into the courtyard behind where women watched over huge cauldrons of steaming garlic-flavoured beans, where young goats roasted upon spits and towers of new bread leaned against the walls.

I was tasting the *mézes* of fried liver, kidneys and entrails that an old woman had thrust with a glass of *tsipuro* into my hands, when I heard the chanting suddenly change note. The voices seemed to be coming from the front courtyard. I hurried back in time to join a procession led by the priest, with an ikon held reverently by two men before him, winding its way in cheerful voice round the chapel three times. When the last circuit had been completed the priest and a few of the more faithful disappeared once more into the church, but the rest of the congregation seemed to think that their religious obliga-tions had now been fulfilled, and the crowd dispersed about the house and courtyard. I found myself next to Vangeli as we were borne into the dining-room. There was the usual argument over places and in the end I sat with Vangeli at the head of a long table with Kosta the harbour-master on one side and Alexandra opposite.

After the *mézes* came the dinner itself, heaped plates of hot meat, bowls of green salad scattered on the tables, and wine. The wine was served in two-gallon wicker demi-johns, and it was Galatzánou's own; it was a deep red-black, with a pleasant musty flavour, and it was strong. Already it seemed generally known that soon I was to live at Panormos, and I was frequently congratulated with warm smiles and raised glasses as if, curiously, it was I who was doing them the honour of wanting to live on their island.

I remember looking at my watch when we first sat down, and saw it was nine o'clock. I did not glance at it again until three hours later, but to account for that period in detail would be difficult. I remember most of all that there were an extraordinary number of toasts, most of which were initiated by Vangeli who as usual on these occasions was in excellent and contagiously high spirits. We drank first, and soberly enough, to our host, and to his family, to the priest, to St. Artemios – long may he protect us. (Though who was he?)

There followed a pause in which Galatzánou held the floor and made a long speech, frequently interrupted, his flask raised in benediction as he proposed a toast to his guests, neighbours, fellow-islanders—the sweep of his gesture deliberately including me within it, so that I was made to know that I could never be anything else but an islander, and of this island, and that evening felt strangely that I had been one all my life.

Vangeli stood up and replied. I recall him drinking his own health, a suggestion loudly acclaimed, and I remember my own growing and frustrated obsession with the desire to uncover the identity of the saint in whose honour we had ostensibly gathered.

My neighbours whom I asked replied evasively, and usually began to recount the deeds and virtues of those better known men, St. George, or St. Demetrias, until I began to suspect that nobody knew, or cared much anyway, and that St. Artemios must have been invented simply in order that the people of Skopelos could meet and enjoy themselves once a year.

I remember too that there was much singing, in which Vangeli took a dramatic part, a guitar being produced from nowhere – the old folk-songs of the islands, sentimental love-ballads with occasional tunes of such a lively rhythm that the women were shouted into action, and a space cleared, and the *syrtó* danced between the tables.

At about midnight people started to go home, and only a hard core of drinkers, dancers and singers remained to raise the roof of Galatzánou's hospitable home. It was nearly three o'clock when the party finally broke up, stumbling in happy procession between the silent olive groves back to the village, and the last echoes died away from the white walls of the chapel with another whole year to pass before so many assembled again in praise of St. Artemios, whoever he was, with singing and laughter to gladden his ancient bones.

The frequency of saints' days and holidays in the Sporades has been remarked upon by foreigners, often with despair, a long time ago. The Venetian 'rector' or governor of Skyros in the sixteenth century complained to his government that 'his island would be most productive, if only the Greeks could be persuaded to cultivate it assiduously. But there were only two working days in the week; day after day the people were keeping some festival . . .' 'So passes our life,' the rector, evidently a serious man, wrote.

Things are not much different today. Hardly anyone is so hard-worked that he has no time to take advantage of the holidays provided by so crowded a calendar, and few have not enough money – so little is needed – to celebrate these occasions in simple yet adequate island style. As I became a more familiar figure on the island I found myself often invited to these festivals, *panayiria* as they are called, and came to realize what an important part they played in island life.

Panayiri, from which our word 'panegyric' is directly derived, means a 'celebration, in praise of', and with it to me at least there is a strong feeling of 'gyration' in the sense that usually an ikon is taken in procession round and round the chapel, and afterwards there is the country dancing of the circular Greek kind, in which all (*pan*) take part.

Most mountain chapels in the Sporades seem to be devoted to the Panayia, the 'all-holy' Virgin Mary, in one or other of her many aspects. Not far from the mule-track between Skopelos village and Panormos are two chapels to the Panayia, *Hypermakho* and *Polemistria*, the Mother of God discovered in a somewhat unusual guise, that of war : the all-holy Battle-Virgins. Near the latter there is a stream called *vromonéri*, 'foul-water' and it is here that a band of Turkish raiders who had landed at Panormos and were making their way, as they thought secretly, towards Skopelos were ambushed and massacred by the islanders, who no doubt chose the place because it was close under the eye of the warrior-goddess on the hillside. They called it 'foul-water' because the stream was stained with Turkish blood.

The Panayia's great day is August 15, exactly superceding the ancient pagan festival of the goddess Diana, but most of the chapels have their own special days, each one different, scattered throughout the summer. The hills of the Sporades are studded with chapels ; take any path inland and after an hour's walk in any direction you will have passed two or three, their white walls, blue or pink washed domes gleaming between the trees. In the *molos* area of Skopelos village, the ancient quarter built round the castle rock there are no less than thirty.

At a good *panayiri* the pilgrim arrives the evening before, carrying – depending on the remoteness of the chapel – a bag stuffed with wine and provisions on the back of his mule or donkey, and also perhaps his wife, his grandmother and most of his children. The women sit about and chatter, gossiping with their friends and relatives, the children play together, romp over the hills around; the men, however, prefer to take things, in principle at least, more seriously.

The service in the chapel that night might well last until the following dawn, or after. Perhaps by eleven o'clock in the morning the final chanting, swinging of incense is done, and the dark shawled older women emerge from the warm candle-gloom to blink their eyes in the sunlight. Meanwhile others have been busy. Long tables have been set out under the cypresses or planes, piled now with dishes of food, flasks of wine. Some ouzo will revive the priest and his marathon night-worshippers, and then the feasting begins. Later the musicians – there are always three or four – with accordion, guitar, *bouzouki*, and the haunting deep-toned clarinet of the mountains, will set up their instruments and themselves at some point of vantage. The quick island rhythms will sound forth with all their inevitable sad gaiety, and, as the sun sinks and fires and lamps are lit, beat to time the stamping feet of the dancers, now swinging in a great circle under the trees.

Such was the *panayiri* that I attended in the hills above Panormos valley, a chapel belonging to the scattered group of cottages known as Mourtiró. Vangeli had told me I ought to go, though he wasn't going himself – he had some trees to cut down. He called to me across the water, from the window of the retsina-barn, in English: 'You must go to the *panayiri*!'

'How far is it?' I called back.

Vangeli waved his arm vaguely. 'Not far,' he said, and as I seemed doubtful he added, 'Take Foola! My very good pony! Lakis is at the *kalivi*, he will show the way. . . .'

'All right,' I said. 'Thanks.'

I could see Foola tethered to a carob tree, browsing in its shade. She was a fine little pony, a chestnut, one of that breed famous on Skyros for surefootedness and strength. I had never ridden her before. An hour later I went ashore. No one was about, except the goatherd invisible somewhere on the hillside; I could hear one or two sleepy goat bells, but the piping had ceased. Other people rode Foola without any difficulty, so why shouldn't I? I approached her with confidence. 'Good little Foola,' I told her gently. '*Fooláki mou . . . ela 'do koritsi mou . . .*' much as I had heard Vangeli, who knew her best, address her.

Greek ponies, horses, mules and donkeys wear roughly the same sort of saddle, constructed of wood with leather or felt nearest the animal's back. The saddle is pommelled, in front and behind; the rider is normally carried side-saddle and so has something to hold on to with each hand. Looking back on it I can think of no good reason for doing what I then did: I led Foola to a rock, adjusted the loops of rope that pass for stirrups and mounted her astride. Before I had time to put my other leg in the stirrup-rope Foola was off, her dark mane streaming in the wind of her own momentum.

She headed straight for the white wall of the woodcutter's cottage, only at the last moment jinking nimbly aside. If by this preliminary feint she intended to dash me head first against the wall, she very nearly succeeded: I remained with her largely through good luck. As Foola dived under the low branches of almond trees and careered down the winding path, following the twists of track between rock and bush without slackening her gallop, I suppose I should have admired the surefooted skill with which in the best traditions of her breed she overcame the obstacles in her way; instead there was only one thought in my mind – to get off. I chose a clump of bushes approaching on my left, trusting that the leaves did not conceal as so often horns of jagged rock, made a quick judgement of speed and distance and as we hurtled by threw myself into it.

'It's better riding side-saddle,' the quiet voice of the goatherd suggested from under an olive tree above the path, as I rose from my resting place. 'Thank you,' I replied with dignity. 'I'll try that.'

Foola was chewing at some thin grass a few paces away. She seemed quite unmoved. '*Koritsáki mou,*' I murmured insincerely as I took her head rope again. To jump up backwards on to a pony's saddle is a feat easily accomplished by Greek islanders. After several attempts I managed it, swaying dangerously on the saddle-ridge, and once again before I was properly settled Foola was away, this time at a fast trot. I tried all the English words and sounds I could think of, all of which only served to redouble her energies. Every time I tugged savagely at her head-rope she turned headlong down the hillside. I came off, more or less intentionally, twice more, but not so painlessly as the first time; the last part I walked, with Foola in docile step behind me.

Lakis stuck his head out of the window of Vangeli's cottage as we came up through the olive trees. 'Why don't you ride?' he asked, and then noting my dishevelled appearance, laughed. The grandmother explained to me kindly where I had gone wrong. There is only one way you can stop or slow down a pony or a donkey on Skopelos: you make a prolonged blowing noise between loose lips, a sound similar to that made by a child blowing bubbles in the bath. This I obediently practised for some time until according to my instructors, by now including Alexandra and the two little girls, I had got it as near as possible word perfect. I only hoped I would never have to use this addition to my vocabulary, at any rate not on Foola, for whom I had developed a secret dislike.

I persuaded Lakis to come to the *panayiri* with me, and offered him Foola to ride. He agreed to come but gave some vague reason about preferring to walk, though he claimed he knew all about the vital bubbling noise. We left Foola behind.

Lakis said he knew the way well. By the fifth or sixth path intersection we were lost. In the end we climbed up the wrong side of the valley, caught a tantalizing glimpse of the chapel far away among the cypress tops, got lost again in the wooded valley bottom and arrived at last hot and thirsty, just as the service was finishing and the panegyrists were settling down to eat and drink.

I was shown to a place next to a grocer whom I recognized from Skopelos. 'What about your shop?' I inquired politely.

He raised his arms in despair. 'Yes! My shop! Closed! *Tina kánoume?* No business today – or tomorrow. . . .' He seemed glad of my sympathy. Nothing had changed since the rector of Skyros made his sad complaint. In the Sporades one had to be ready to make these constant sacrifices.

Lakis and I had to leave not long after, but apparently the assembled company kept their uproarious vigil throughout the following night. It was in Skiathos that I was able to attend a night-long *panayiri*, an affair again of the Virgin, but altogether a much bigger and more important festival.

Panayioti had primed me with much ouzo before I left the village so that my memories of the whole occasion are pleasantly blurred, but I recall the heavy shadows of great trees, the pattern of leaves printed upon the moonlit chapel walls, around which it seemed several hundred people were moving. Far below across the sea the moon path pointed to the misty mountains of Evvia.

As this was the second night a great number of people were stretched out on blankets and rugs asleep or resting under the trees.

They were mostly women and children, and did not seem to mind when people walked, danced or drank over them.

Oil-lamps smoked from the branches, hung outside the chapel. There were two groups of musicians and several portable wine-shops dispensing retsina to the crowd. The musicians were conducting themselves in typical Greek fashion: the spirit of uncompromising, unco-operative individuality carried to a self-destructive extreme. Being two groups they should – one would have thought – have played alternately; at least if they were determined not to do that, they could have separated. Instead they had taken up positions within spitting distance of each other, both by the chapel door. As soon as one group struck up, the others seized their instruments and selecting some song with a rhythm and mood entirely at variance with that already being played, launched into it with enthusiasm. The resultant discord can be imagined, though I must admit that the local panegyrists did not seem to care, and if a man dancing his lonely *rebétiko* got mixed up in the larger circle swinging to the *kalamatianó*, this only appeared to make it from the onlookers' point of view more lively and more interesting.

The *panayiri* had exploded all over the countryside. Young men with guitars and their own chosen companions sat together under the twisted olive trees. From the shadows as I passed they called out to me, glasses raised. A girl was dancing alone amid a silent half-circle. I stood and watched her for a moment until a young man stood up and joined her, and she moved about him with hips a-swing, arms curved, outstretched. The oldest dance in the world.

But it was time for me to leave. I also had a pilgrimage, of a sort, of my own to accomplish. Tomorrow, or rather as it was two in the morning, today, I would leave for Skopelos again, meet an old friend of mine, David Gaunt, companion of an earlier Asiatic journey, and set sail for Skyros and the grave of Rupert Brooke.

6

Skyros: A Poet's Grave

The sea-road from Skopelos to Skyros passes by a small, low island midway between the two, a kind of staging post for those who prefer short voyages, a shelter if necessary from any sudden or contrary winds, and a place too of its own peculiar interest and charm. Skantzura is practically a desert island, or at least so it appears as one approaches, scanning its low rocky shores thinly covered with *koúmara* bushes, thyme, myrtle and wild olives that no one bothers to cultivate.

Fishermen come to Skantzura. The island's coasts are a rich hunting ground for the *rofós*, the Aegean grouper, and there is also a kind of grey-green stone, similar in its cut form to thick slate, that is occasionally quarried there. Two men were sitting in their fishing boat as we dropped anchor in the cove on the south-west of the island, and told us they had been fishing there for two days. They were waiting for dusk to go out again.

David Gaunt at that time was a keen fisherman. He had a theory, which I used to share, that if one lived on a boat one should fish, and live on the fish one caught. But whenever I had tried to put this theory into practice – dangling tempting bait into the blue depths, trolling lines astern, casting hooks cunningly concealed in shell-fish (laboriously collected off the rocks) from the dinghy, and even armed with spear-gun, mask and flippers sinking through the green-glass paradise of offshore shallows – I had drawn a constant and depressing blank. Such failure had produced its own apology, a theory concocted in self-defence. Each man to his own trade, I said: I would write and fishermen would fish. They would read my books and I would eat their fish; and it would not be my fault if in this exchange the fishermen would consider they'd come off badly.

David, being more optimistic and more practical, favoured rather the all-rounder theory: that a man should be able to do everything as well as possible, write and fish, though not necessarily at the same time; and it was in pursuance of this ideal, on that still morning in the cove at Skantzura that he sat attending his lines at the stern (while I wrote below in the cabin) occasionally uttering with suppressed excitement: 'Heavens, a fish!' or 'Got him!' or more rarely and more tensely, 'A big one, I think —' hoisting up every twenty minutes or so a rather small sliver of wriggling black and silver, red and gold, adding it to the little pile growing on the deck, out of which we were to make *kakaviá*, the famous fish soup, *bouillabaisse* of the Aegean.

The other boat lay over a hundred yards away, on the other side of the cove. The two fishermen sat quietly, motionless, not mending their nets, not even smoking, just waiting for the sun to climb and fall.

A shout from David brought me on deck. It sounded like a big one. His usual practice, after shortening the line, was to jerk the fish high over the rail and catch it as it came over. The fish flew up from the sea, David reached out his hand and just as he did so a cry from the fishing boat rang out over the water. '*Don't touch it!*' The fish landed with a thump on the deck.

It was a *skorpio*, one of the few dangerous denizens of the Aegean marine world, a pinkish savage looking fish with two poisonous spines on its back which if embedded in human flesh can inflict a nasty swelling wound that usually requires the attentions of a doctor.

We shouted our thanks to the fisherman; but how, at that long range in the second the fish was visible in the air the Greek could recognize it and shout his warning, remains to me a mystery.

That afternoon we visited Father Petros. Skantzura belongs to the great Lavra Monastery on Mount Athos, and Father Petros is the last incumbent of the tiny and decaying monastery on the island. He and two other families that seem comprised of old women and chickens, make up the entire population of the island. The old monk welcomed us and led us up a crumbling staircase along the balcony and into what served as both the guest-room and his study, where he offered us ouzo, water, and little squares of *loukoumi*. I had met him before at Skopelos, a kindly looking man with a white beard and gentle blue eyes. Afterwards I saw him more often, whenever he came to Skopelos, as he was a friend of Vangeli's. Between the two there was always a kind of stock repartee that was repeated with slight variations whenever they met.

'We're coming to Skantzura with a boat-load of girls for you, Father.'

'How many did you say?'

(Waving a hand airily) 'Oh, four or five.'

'You'll never manage them, you're too old!'

'But they're for *you*, Father —' at which the old monk would bend his beard to me and say with a twinkle in his eyes, 'What a thoroughly evil fellow this Vangeli is, don't you think?' And when I agreed he would chuckle silently into his whiskers.

There was bad news months later of Father Petros. He was being recalled to Mount Athos. At first I thought this must be a step up, knowing the horror with which most Greeks would regard a place as lonely as Skantzura, but Vangeli told me this was not so, that most monks would prefer the island, however remote, simply because of the independence such a post gave them. There had been some violent but unspecified quarrel between the old man and the two families on the island, and looking back at our visit when we sat at the broad table in the barely furnished upper room, the sunlight streaming through the dusty windows, I can remember the ugly expression of the old woman who brought us our glasses of water, and my sympathies are all with the monk. We talked of Cyprus that afternoon and as usual I was amazed at the forbearance with which Greeks still manage to discuss this painful subject with Englishmen. We told him that our destination was Skyros, and it was pleasant to hear him say, somewhat cryptically as we left, 'Ah yes, *to Brooke.* . . .'

The following day, anchored in Linaria, the harbour of Skyros, the mystery of this '*to Brooke*' was cleared up. In Greek *to* is the definite article, but neuter; the answer was that Rupert Brooke having grown into a legend, even in Skyros, had also become a kind of institution. 'The Brooke' referred originally to the place of his burial. At Linaria we were told to go up to the main village on the other side of the island, to see *to Brooke*, and we went.

The village is on the east coast, built high above the sea round the ancient fortified hill where now stands a fine Frankish castle. It was here, at the palace of King Lycomedes that Thetis hid her young son Achilles, disguised as a girl, when she heard that the Greeks wanted him as a leader of the expedition against Troy; and it was here too, from these high cliffs, that Theseus met his death.

Not far below the castle there is a small square, like a bastion, overlooking the sea, where there is a statue of a naked youth, 'the Muse of Poetry' set up in honour of Rupert Brooke; though in my view the sculpture does no one any honour, least of all the sculptor. Brooke was not buried here, but in Tresboukes Bay, a large and sheltered anchorage several miles in circumference at the barren south end of the island; after stocking up the lockers with provisions we sailed round there from Linaria.

The hills around Tresboukes Bay are uninhabited and bare: brown rock, stunted trees. A few ravines opening from the shore are filled with olive trees; it was in one of these narrow valleys that we hoped to find the poet's grave.

We spent two days in the search, clambering ·up and down the stony slopes, cutting our shoes to pieces on the rocks and stumbling over the many tortoises that thrive in this deserted corner of the island. At last, anchored close to a beach on the eastern shore of the bay we started up a valley that we were sure must be the one. Nearly a mile from the sea, where the sides of the ravine closed in and the light was a pale green filtered through olive leaves, we found it: an incongruously Victorian marble tomb, wrought-iron trespass rails round the Pentelic slab. A fine olive tree grew at the head of the grave, spreading its branches over the marble. It is unusual in rough country like this to hear birds, but in this olive grove the air was full of them; in Greece I have never heard so many sing together. We rested for a long time by the grave, listening to the birds, and cicadas, and the distant jangle of a goat-bell. It was afternoon and the sky had become suddenly overcast. Experimental gusts of warm, sage-scented wind sighed down the valley, shaking down black olives over the tomb.

Brooke had been in this olive grove on the 20th of April, 1915. There had been a battalion exercise round the shores of the bay, and he and some of his fellow officers had rested here in the afternoon in the shade of the trees. He had remarked on the strange peace and beauty of the place. Three days later, at the age of twenty-seven, he was dead of a septicaemia contracted probably in Egypt a month before.

The Brooke legend has grown its own Skyriot trappings. We were told in Linaria how it had all happened, how before the war the poet was visiting Greece and came to Skyros; how he found the olive grove in this little valley and spent the whole night there in the company of his closest friends, drinking much wine, talking and making merry. He loved the place so much, he said, he wanted to be buried here. Many years later, say the Skyriots, the British fleet with Brooke on board, was steaming north to free Constantinople from the Turks. The poet was dangerously ill, and when his ship came abreast of Skyros – strange destiny! – he died. His friends who were with him remembered his wish, and buried him with honour in the place he had loved and chosen so many years before.

I have said that our visit to the grave was a kind of pilgrimage, but perhaps this is too strong a word. But we were both involved, indirectly and from a distance, with the ghost and legend of Rupert Brooke. David was educated at Rugby and King's College, Cambridge, as had been the poet. As a schoolboy and adolescent I used to have two heroes; Byron, who made my first years at Harrow more tolerable, and who later influenced my choice of publisher, and Brooke, because of whom I chose to go to King's. I had been given a book of his poems when I was fourteen. I suppose hero-worship is endemic with boys, whether it be for poets or racing-drivers. Certainly mine meant a lot to me, and I am glad that when they ceased to be heroes it was not by means of some violent palace revolution, a rolling of heads, with still-warm thrones immediately offered to others. . . . My heroes did not topple, they merely receded – as I learnt more about them and they became more real. Grave-visits have had a certain significance: Byron at Missolonghi, Brooke at Skyros, they commemorate feelings and emotions that were buried long ago.

Now there are no heroes, and the horizons are strangely bare; probably this is just as well. When I think of Rupert Brooke I feel an affection for him, a respect, but mostly sympathy. I have a perhaps unusual picture of him in my mind : an amazingly lonely figure in spite of all his friends; and sad, with some terrible lack, heart-void; and sometimes I have seen him, a lyric runner through endless woods, with a world of only himself and the flying leaves, with the hungry infant furies closing in the shadows behind.

As we walked down from the grave, left quiet and peaceful among the olive trees, and stood on the pebble beach looking out across that sheet of inland water, it was difficult to imagine the scene on that April night fifty years before: Tresboukes Bay crowded with ships – the overflow from Lemnos, stepping-stone for the Gallipoli assault.

No less than four British and French battleships were at anchor, besides cruisers, transports and smaller vessels, and the French hospital-ship to which Brooke was transferred the day before he died.

Brooke died on the afternoon of the 23rd, and the orders for the Allied fleet were to sail for Gallipoli the next morning. There was not much time. His friends decided to bury him on Skyros that same night.

A procession of boats approaching across the water, lights dancing under the clouded moon; military commands in lowered voices, men with lamps posted every twenty yards. . . . It took the coffin bearers nearly two hours to negotiate the ravine. Three volleys, then the Last Post; a cairn of marble rocks heaped over the grave and a pencilled epitaph in Greek:

> Here lies the servant of God,
> Sub-Lieutenant in the English Navy,
> who died for the deliverance of Constantinople from the Turks

That night, anchored off the beach at the entrance of Brooke's valley, an exceptionally dramatic storm burst on the island. We should really have moved to a more protected place, a cove we knew in the north-west of the bay, but we stayed where we were, partly paralysed by the sight and sound of this prolonged and apparently cosmic detonation. It lasted all night, and it was impossible to sleep. We smoked, shivered and drank coffee; deafened with thunder, we kept our faces pressed to the closed portholes. Gusts of wind tore across the sea, buffeting *Astarte* and heeling her over with the violence of their impact, and blue lightning slashed down at the mountains around. We had the doubtful privilege of observing, less than a hundred yards away on the beach, a stunted tree struck by lightning burn and smoke in the rain. *Astarte*'s mast, thirty-five feet above the water, was twice as high as that poor trunk of scorched wood.

Almost as disturbing as the lightning, was the wind; if it had set in hard from any one direction we would almost certainly have dragged anchor. But through the night the wind burst on us from every quarter of the compass. We seemed to be in the dead centre of the storm.

Next morning when the storm had exhausted itself we left Tresboukes, and passing by Linaria anchored in a small bay to the north, a natural deep-water harbour overhung with steep forested hills. Instead of staying one night as we had planned we waited five days, in almost continual rain and gales while the food ran out and the gas-cylinder emptied.

We were in the bay of the marble quarries, from which for centuries the famous multicoloured Skyrian marble had been shipped to the west, especially to Rome. A quay built of these enormous blocks, a derelict crane rusting beside it, was all that remained. Marble red-veined, green-grained, streaked with chocolate and yellow lay half cut in titanic cubes beside the abandoned machinery, as if the last ship – said to have called some thirty years ago – had left in a hurry, suddenly and inexplicably, fearful, half filled, never to return. In modern times an Italian and then an English company had worked the mines, and high in the hills – steep climbing on goat-tracks through the mist and pines – ruins of modern buildings, the houses of clerks and officials, crumble beside fluted drums of Doric columns, the ancient platform of some temple that once looked out from this great height across the windy sea to the west; and stooping among the rubble one may pick up among the older, dateless fragments of pottery, the bright blue and white of Worcester and Spode, the patterns gleaming strangely in the rain.

Somewhere up here could well have been the place where Theseus was buried. When the Athenians captured the island in 470 B.C., a she-eagle, 'tearing up the soil with her talons', revealed the spot. The Athenians dug there and found a gigantic skeleton, fully armed, with a bronze lance and sword beside it. The bones were carried back in triumph to Athens.

The mines themselves are eery places, especially in rain and cloud : acres of quarry, gashed mountain, heaps of fragmented rock, twisted rails and a broken British steam-engine turned on its side at the bottom of a pit. A family live in a cottage down by the bay. Polite but somehow un-Greek in their watchful reserve, they added to the strangely depressing atmosphere of the place that was not altogether caused by the weather. They talked with gloomy nostalgia of times that even they could hardly remember, of steamers at the quay, a hundred workers, mule-trains and rollers, foreigners and money – times that could never come again, because the Skyrian quarries are forgotten; after two thousand years they are almost exhausted, and by modern economic standards no longer worth the working.

The family kept bees, however, and this interested me not only because we had run out of sugar and were glad to buy some honey, but I had come across a quotation referring to bee-keeping in ancient times, and mentioning Skyros. According to Columella, 'Celsus says . . . that after the fading of spring flowers bees should be trans-ferred if necessary to places that can offer a more liberal diet of the late flowering blossoms of thyme, marjory and savory – Skyros being a favourite place to transfer bees from the Cyclades.' It seemed to me a long journey for bees, and perhaps a dangerous one for the ships' crews, presenting startling possibilities should escape from a mad-dened swarm become necessary in mid-passage. Did bees become seasick, I wondered? And had the custom of carrying Cycladic bees to Skyros fallen into disuse?

To these questions I could receive no satisfactory answer, and it was with relief that when the wind dropped one night we put out to sea again. It was time to lay up *Astarte* for the winter. Vangeli had assured me that this could be done at Vassiliko, on an island opposite Alonnisos, but it would need careful preparation. I was slightly sceptical as to whether it could be done at all, *Astarte*'s hull with her comparatively deep keel being very different from an ordinary caique's. There was another reason for hurry: the storms of the last ten days had given clear warning of the changing season; the blue smile of Aegean summer had long gone from the sea.

7

Granddaughters of Lycúrgos:
A Berth for Astarte

The choice of a place to lay up *Astarte* had been worrying me for some time. If we were to make a home in the Sporades it was essential that I find somewhere convenient where the boat could be easily slipped at least once a year.

At Panormos, close by the rock where we planned to build the house, was a perfect beach which in the old days was used as a slip for boats and caiques – and who knows? even galleys, triremes – but there was no winch or chains, or any of the specially fashioned giant logs needed for the job. It was an omission that sometime in the far future I was determined to rectify. Meanwhile Skopelos had no proper equipment for the task except in a cove on the north coast where no one lives and where I was not keen to leave *Astarte* for the winter months, while at Skiathos the operation would have been expensive, and there were various problems concerning the shallow ness of the lagoon.

Vangeli had given the matter much thought and decided that the best place was an island called Xeró, where a great friend of his lived, a fisherman Kosta Malamiténiou and his family, who would gladly keep an eye on the boat. *Astarte*, he said, could be pulled up in front of his cottage.

'Kosta has three fine girls,' Vangeli said. 'One is Elsie, my goddaughter. They are all *naftiki*, they know about the sea, boats – they will take good care for *Astarte*. You must go to Xeró. . . .'

The island lies eastward from Skopelos, clinging to the south coast of Alonnisos as if split from it aeons ago in some terrible upheaval of the mountain tops that now lift their rock summits above the sea. Xeró means 'Dry', and it is the first of the *eremonisia*, the deserted islands, though in fact there are still fourteen or fifteen people existing on its barren shore, half of them at Vassiliko, 'Royal', a cove hidden as is almost every one of the natural harbours of the Sporades, concealed within folds of hills grey-green with wild olive, brown and grey with rock and sunburnt earth. Three or four cottages, rust-red tiled and whitewashed, cluster at the head of the bay, surrounded by fenced in plots dedicated hopefully to the cultivation of vegetables and even corn in a field fitted in behind, before the rocks and wild · olives take over again and the hills are given up to thin herds of goats. At anchor in the bay one forgets again the existence of the outer sea. Here it may blow round the compass and yet in the shelter of these hills no swell may ever penetrate, and only the wind as it shrieks down the valley may tell of the storm that has burst upon the Aegean beyond.

Because the cove is so sheltered, and also because the slope of the beach is just right, neither too steep nor too gradual, the place has always been a favourite one for careening and slipping the fishing boats of Alonnisos and Skopelos. At any time of the year there can be seen drawn up at the head of the cove at least three or four caiques, and in winter there is a line of a dozen or more, their broad hulls propped like stranded whales upon logs of pine, rough beams sloping to the sand to support their bellies, where four months' barnacles and weed encrust the planks.

Down by the shore at Vassiliko lives Vangeli's friend Kosta, his wife Kalliope, and their three daughters – Athanasia, Elisavet and Elsie. These are the three granddaughters of Lycúrgos. And who is Lycúrgos?

Follow the steep path up the little valley and you will find yourself on a high narrow ridge, a knife-edge between north and south, an altar to the wind and sun where stunted trees cower and there is a small patched-up cottage where two very old people live alone but together, Theódoros Lycúrgos and his wife. There is a story told about these two, a remarkable one considering the close-binding conventions of island society, that when they were young, at about the turn of the century, they lived together and were married without benefit – or rather, without hindrance – of clergy. Kosta the fisherman was one of their sons ; there were others, some of whom were killed in the war, others were shot as hostages before their parents' eyes. Lycúrgos is a magnificent old man whose age remains uncertain. His children and grandchildren put him at ninety, but that was some years ago ; rather than invite catastrophe they have kept him at that respectable age ever since.

He walks bent nearly double now, hobbling on a stick, but once he must have been very tall. He wears the old-fashioned baggy trousers, sometimes leggings, and a tattered brown woollen waistcoat; on his feet thick stockings tied up with strips of leather. His face is deeply lined, with a powerful straight nose, drooping white moustache; from under shaggy brows he looks out at the world with still-clear grey eyes, steady and penetrating. When he comes down to the shore to lie against a rock in the sun and watch the men working at their boats, people greet him respectfully, ask after his health and listen carefully to what he says; and if he is feeling especially friendly he will accept a cigarette that someone has the courage to offer him.

Vangeli has a great admiration for the old man; he calls him 'philosopher'. He knows Vassiliko, and Lycúrgos and the family there particularly well. During the war the cove was the last staging post of the northern trans-Aegean escape route across to Turkey. Vangeli's elder brother was the chief resistance agent on Skopelos, organizing the caique night-tunnel between the islands and across the sea. The Italians got wind of his activities and he managed to escape to Turkey; somewhere in the Dodecanese he died. Vangeli, his brother, was 'questioned'. The questioning lasted most of the day and night and at the end of it he was carried home unconscious by his family. He came to Vassiliko and beyond to Iura to lie low for a while. He took over his brother's work and the stream of escaped prisoners continued to flow eastward from Vassiliko. When the invaders raided the island the families at Vassiliko fled into the caves on the high wind-blown back of the island, and Lycúrgos, an old man even then, used to wait on the shore to meet them. . . .

The old man and his wife live up on the ridge, Kosta and Kalliope with their daughters in a three-roomed cottage below at the head of the cove, and it seems that the strength of character and kindliness of the older pair, with their grace and extraordinary good looks have been inherited by their children, and grandchildren. Elsie is eighteen, and Vangeli's goddaughter. She is the tomboy of the family, with brown hair cut shorter than her sisters', an expert with the *kalamáki*, trident of night fishermen used to spear octopus and fish in the rock shallows, and yet with her sisters skilled in the arts of sewing, weaving and embroidery. Elisavet comes next, a year older, with long honey-coloured hair plaited in double strands down to her waist; straight-nosed and grey-eyed she is the living image of some sculptured Athenian *kóre*. Athanasia is the oldest and also the tallest, aged twenty-one. She has large liquid dark eyes and a gentle expression. Her slow smile had become even dreamier these last few months because she had become engaged to be married.

Kalliope, the mother of the girls, kept to the old style of dress, white embroidered bodice, her oval face framed always in her shawl, broad dark peasant's skirts pleated about her thin body – a style abandoned by the girls who managed to give the appearance of being modern, with their simple dresses of printed cotton, without seeming in any way out of place. Kosta was entirely the man of the family, tall, blue-eyed with greying hair, and yet shy and reserved; unlike the usual image of himself the Greek male often tries so hard to project, he was both unassuming and gentle. He supported his family by fishing, and owned a fine though small caique built twelve years ago in Syra, painted twice yearly by his daughters with red and green lines round the hull, the wheel and eye designs in different colours on each side of the prow, and the caique's name, *Theodoráki*, after their grandfather, Theódoros Lycúrgos, carefully figured in black and white upon the bows.

At first I was worried that because Kosta was away so often much of the responsibility for looking after *Astarte* – should they agree to do it – would fall upon the girls. But as Vangeli had said, they were certainly *ναυτικοί* – 'nautical' – and I could see now that with the girls in charge of her *Astarte* would be safe.

Kosta's fishing grounds were to the north-east: out of the straits between Alonnisos and Xeró to Kyra Panayia, Iura, the shallows of Psathura – an island where hemlock still grows wild – where gleam among the weed and rock the walls of an ancient long-drowned city, and the steep depths about Piperi. He was away days on end, sometimes as long as a week; alone usually but sometimes he took one of the girls with him to help with the lines and the crayfish bait, the nets and the multitude of hooks of the *paragádi*.

Often when I was at Vassiliko Kosta was away on one of his fishing expeditions. Once when a gale had started up and he had not returned, I could feel the tension in the family, the anxiety that only showed itself in the occasional off-hand calculations of his probable anchorage. 'It's north-west, the wind,' said Elsie, 'If he was at Psathura he'll be in Planidhi by now. . . .' 'Or Ayios Petros,' said Elisavet. And Kalliope their mother, crouching on the low stool by the hearth set in Sporades fashion in the corner of the little room, stared into the flames, adjusted the black bubbling cooking pot, murmuring to herself, 'The wind, what a wind . . .' while the whole house shuddered and jarred, and the old tiled roof seemed about to be torn off at any moment, and outside where I went for a reassuring glance at *Astarte* the branches of the fig and the mulberry tree clashed and clattered in the gale.

And then, a day later, long before I could even hear an engine, I'd see Athanasia in the middle of a sentence hold up her hand for silence, and the girls would stare at each other. 'Father.' The girls could recognize the beat of *Theódoraki*'s engine long before she rounded the point; and the whole tempo of the cottage's life changed rhythm – wood thrown on the fire, the tiny coffee-pot rinsed out and filled with water, set on the fire-iron to heat, the bed cleared ready for him to sleep . . . and the girls would be waiting on the beach as the caique came in, Kosta with four days' beard upon his face, stooped at the tiller as he let go the anchor, and as the prow nosed in towards the sand Elisavet's gold hair flying as she jumps to take the rope. . . .

Nothing much was ever said when he stepped ashore. In answer to the girls' silent inquiry Kosta, who never spoke much anyway, might utter, 'good', or 'quite good', or simply 'nothing', but it was a pleasure to watch them cross the sand, the father with his tall daughters in a group together, and to see Kalliope's warm face at the cottage door, her slow, inward smile.

I felt I could now ask them if they would look after *Astarte* for the winter. Since I had come to Vassiliko I had become a familiar guest at the cottage – originally on the strength of Vangeli's friendship and later, as I would like to think, because I began to know the family myself. Their response was more enthusiastic than I could have hoped. 'Of course, gladly,' said Kosta, 'we can pull her up here in front of the cottage, Anagnostou and Niko will come and set up the winch and chains and *vasa*. . . . And in the winter, you needn't worry, the girls or I will be here. There is always someone at Vassiliko. . . .'

Living winter and summer at Vassiliko meant a life more primitive even than that led by Greeks in the most remote of mountain villages. The family had to be almost completely self-supporting, growing all their own vegetables in the little plot fenced off from the

goats outside the cottage door: potatoes, tomatoes, aubergine, onions
and the rest, which are eaten with the staple of their diet – fish,
caught by Kosta, or by the girls themselves on the moonless night
expeditions that they make, all three together, round the edges of
the bay.

In summer life is not so difficult: fishing is comparatively easy
and the fine warm weather makes everything more pleasant, so that
living space, instead of being confined to the tiny rooms of the
cottage, can flow out into the open air – under the old mulberry
tree where in hot weather we used to eat, or the long bench by the
brick and stone oven against the wall of the house, where everyone
gather to sit and talk and watch the cove and the sun setting behind
it. Looking after the sheep and goats is simpler, too – Kalliope and
the girls take it in turn each day, disappearing at dawn up the
thorny hillsides and returning only at dusk. It is from wool sheared
from the sheep that the family takes its main activity: weaving –
though this is an occupation kept mostly for the winter.

The family's two most valued possessions are a sewing-machine
and an old wooden loom. Blankets, soft wool-and-cotton sheets,
cushion covers, tablecloths, bright patterned material out of which
they made their winter dresses – all are woven at this loom, and the
regular thump and shuttle of wood on cloth must be a familiar accompaniment to the winter gales howling round the cottage. All the
girls can weave, but Athanasia is generally allowed to be the expert,
and she is also the artist of embroidery. In the same way each of the
girls has a special kind of work at which she is considered to be best.
Elisavet knits, calmly and quickly, her serious grey eyes locked in
daydream so that suddenly to speak to her means waking her from
some deep contemplation, of Australia perhaps where she would like
to go, or of the shadowy face of the man whom one day she will
marry. Elsie is the mistress of the sewing-machine, and is skilled at
dressmaking, while Kalliope confines herself mostly to the spinning
of the wool and to the complicated lace work that ends off the
materials completed at the loom.

I did not know the Greek for 'weaving' and it became a joke
whenever I saw Athanasia at the loom – they'd say, 'Penelope,
Penelope —'

I used to wonder at first what they did with all these useful and
beautiful things they make – each girl had a wooden box full of their

own work – and they told me: all this was their trousseau, the lace-work, embroidery, woven materials, all for the new life that each one expected when she had a house and family of her own, the fruit of careful, painstaking labour, begun from the age when first she could hold a needle, each piece lovingly laid by. . . . When Athanasia brought out her work, proudly showing them to me, piece by piece, and folding them away again with care into the wooden chest, I could sense a new feeling about them: these were no longer the furnishings of a distant dream, they were real. Because of Athanasia's engagement these things had taken on a new significance, for her sisters as well as for herself.

It was clear that Athanasia would not be sorry to leave Vassiliko for Patatiri, and this apart from the obvious advantages and attractions of married life. 'There's always something happening in Patatiri,' Elsie said, wistfully. 'There are people to talk to. Here there's nothing, and nobody.'

Vassiliko is a lonely place, but in summer at least there is some movement in the cove, boats dropping in from Alonnisos, fishermen anchoring for the night – not often, once a week perhaps, and then in spring and autumn the captains and crews of the big caiques come to slip their boats on the beach by the cottage, all the men well known to the family, and most of them in some way related.

In autumn too there were the sponge fishers, from Lemnos mostly, with their rock-scarred, battered and paint-scraped caiques, their ancient rusty diving equipment, air pumps, safety lines and patched rubber suits hanging over the rails . . . strange, piratical looking men these, drifting about the sea for six months on end, locked up together in the cramped, airless and oily holds of their boats, men who practise a dangerous profession in which fatal casualties are not particularly remarkable, who live this peculiar half-life for half the year partly for money, partly for the alleged excitement of it all, breathing the slightest arrogant hostility for the landsmen and the homesmen on the shore.

Arrangements for the slipping of *Astarte* were nearly completed – Vangeli had told Anagnostou (who owned the necessary equipment and lived in Alonnisos) to be ready on a certain day and he, Vangeli, would come on his caique *Makhi* to help in the operation – when a north-easterly gale blew up and for five days all communications between the islands of the Sporades were cut, the gates of the wind shut fast, and every vessel afloat ran for shelter. I was not too disturbed by the delay as I still had much to do in the way of preparing *Astarte* for the winter, packing up the gear and seeing to the engine, and made use of the torrential rain for washing the sails free of salt.

Several other boats came to shelter with *Astarte* in Vassiliko : a great grain-caique from Volos bound for Samos, a splendid scarlet painted ship of the *pérama* type with clipper bow and long bowsprit ; a small iron steamer also from Volos bound for Khios heavily loaded with cement, her funnel black with soot, her sides streaked with rust and red lead bright as blood in the rain, as if she had just escaped from a clawing fight with some vindictive sea monster ; and the *Ayios Dimitrios*, a caique once blue and white, not much bigger than *Astarte*, a sponge-boat from Lemnos with eight men aboard.

The captains of these three assorted vessels, with an escort of at least one of their crew, used to row ashore in the short spells when the rain left off and only the wind howled down the valley, clouds pouring grey and red-black across the sky, and gathering by the wood hut in the corner of the beach, taking cover under the overhanging tiles, met for company and talk, the exchange of hopeful weather forecasts, and unlikely sea-tales.

I enjoyed listening to these men, to the captain of the cement-steamer especially (a most unfriendly fellow), bull-necked and black whiskered, in gumboots, blue trousers, serge jacket and a black beret stuck on the side of his head. He spoke very little, but when he did it was usually to the point ; as when he gruffly advised the captain of the grain-caique to put out another anchor to the east, advice which the latter scorned to take and which resulted that night, when the wind veered a few points, in the caique crashing against the iron sides of the steamer – causing an uproar of cursing and shouting that lasted two hours from midnight, and which prevented anyone in the cove including myself from getting much sleep. The Khiot grain captain, a thin grey-haired man of lugubrious expression who wore a rather unsuitable cloth cap so big that it came down over his ears, had maintained that the fault was the steamer's, but the next morning the necessary adjustments of warps and anchors had been made, and everyone met as usual on the beach prepared to forgive and forget.

There was nothing in the way of sea-stories that I could contribute at this daily gathering of shipmasters on the beach. Yet I found my-

self, ironically enough, closely questioned as to the future behaviour
of the weather. This was because, of the fleet at anchor at Vassiliko,
Astarte was the only vessel that possessed a barometer. To those not
familiar with such an instrument a barometer seems to take on
magical and oracular properties. 'What does the barometer say?'
was the first question that greeted me from one of the captains when
I came ashore. To which I would make a carefully noncommittal
reply. 'Steady,' I'd say, or 'up a bit . . .'

'And what does this mean?'

Again a dodging of the issue, based upon ample experience of
British weather forecasts, those masterpieces of linguistic evasion.
'More wind,' I would say, as a gust sent me staggering, raindrops of
a new squall lashing at the side of my head. 'Rain, too.'

It was no good taking my barometer too seriously, though to those
captains I would never have betrayed its failings. *Astarte*'s glass is a
fine, sensitive instrument, yet one of that over-zealous kind that
suffers, I suppose, from a superabundance of energy, not properly
directed or controlled. It will, for instance, during long periods of
absolute calm register the approach of a most violent storm, cancel
this warning at the last moment – just as, one imagines, the first blast
is about to hurl itself over the horizon – immediately substituting a
more optimistic forecast which again is rescinded in favour of what
appears to be the onrush of the final cataclysm. All this, besides its
routine diurnal rise and fall.

Against the breaking of a summer *meltémi* barometers should
never offer an opinion : there is no change of atmospheric pressure ;
yet *Astarte*'s barometer never fails to become active, climbs steeply,
dives, hesitates, drops further, and finally soars to frantic heights, all
of which might drive a lesser man into a state of nervous and physical
exhaustion, forcing him to spend his time taking in anchors, putting
them out again, battening down this and that, changing course,
postponing passage after passage until at last he gives up, contenting
himself with a permanent mooring in some impregnable harbour.
. . . To such a condition I have long ago refused to be driven, and to
live at peace with my barometer it has been necessary to cultivate
nerves of steel. The captain of the sponge-boat used to row across to
Astarte to inspect the magic instrument himself, and from him I
learnt that the sponge-fishing industry was in slow but sure decline.
Each year from Lemnos fewer boats put out, returning with, on

the whole, an ever smaller supply of sponges. Most depressing of all
was the rise of the synthetic sponge, easy to manufacture and so
much cheaper, appealing to a public rapidly losing any discrimination it ever had. The outlook was not promising, and the islanders
themselves were becoming less enthusiastic about this way of earning
a living. The rise of living standards in Greece during the last few
years did not attract them to a kind of work and working conditions
that savoured more of the eighteenth rather than the twentieth
century.

I was able to confirm this myself when I went on board the sponge-
boat at the invitation of the captain: one of the divers had a bad
boil, and as usual in the remoter parts of Greece it is generally
believed that all foreigners are doctors in disguise, or at any rate
carry around with them medicine chests stocked with the latest
panacean drugs.

A ladder led down into the hold. An oil lamp hanging from a
beam shed its yellow glare upon a scene exactly like, I imagined, the
fo'c'sle of some Nelsonian frigate. There was no standing head-room
and I had to crouch, making my way forward over coils of rope and
pieces of diving equipment, past the big oily fly-wheel of the air-
pump to where in the bows eight primitive bunks were ranged, four
on each side of the hull. The deck overhead was leaking, and buckets
had been placed between the bunks to collect the water as it dripped
through.

Three or four of the crew were already down there, one asleep or
trying to sleep, laid out on his blanket. Another man was sitting on
his bunk, sewing. The yellow light threw his half-bearded face into
relief, dark eyes and white teeth gleaming as he smiled. There was a
strong damp smell of diesel oil, sweat, and sour air.

The diver with the boil lay propped up against the mast. Friendly
jeers greeted him as unwillingly he pulled up his trouser leg, and one
of the men jocularly handed me a long knife. The boil was as big as a
fried egg, and must have been extremely painful; there was little I
could do for him except recommend a hot poultice. Incredible
though it might seem there was not even any antiseptic on board,
much less such luxuries as bandages and lint, and these had to be
supplied from *Astarte*. The diver had wrapped his swollen leg
in a dirty piece of cotton, torn from an old shirt.

It was obvious to me that he should not dive again until the boil

Skopelos
main street

Astarte at anchor at Vassiliko

Theodoraki on the *vasa* at Vassiliko

cleared up, but neither the boat as a whole, nor the diver himself could afford such sick-leave. They gave me as a present a small amphora they had fetched up, attractively shaped and encrusted with molluscs. That afternoon there was a lull in the weather and the sponge-caique left. Next day the gale died down for good, and by afternoon sea and air glittered in still sunlight. The hills about Vassiliko were green with new grass and bright with flowers; the *koúmara* bushes were in scarlet bud.

I walked up to the ridge where old Lycúrgos and his wife sat on the bench against the cottage wall, warming themselves in the sunshine. Together we looked down, hundreds of feet, to the startling blue waters of the cove. Sounds of the grain-caique's winch noisily at work echoed up through the calm air; faint sounds too of angry voices. The steamer and the caique had got their anchors mixed.

The sun sank amid the debris of the departing storm. Above me the sky glowed a pale, luminous green, and a new moon set its thin white sail. The year was going out fast, and there was still work to be done.

Vangeli arrived on *Makhi*, as I hoped he would, early the next morning. Anagnostou also came with his son Niko and another helper on their own big trading caique.

Makhi's deck was piled high with pine logs that Vangeli at great trouble to himself, let alone expense, had cut down from the forests at Panormos, and which were to be used in the slipping of *Astarte*. I was glad to see him. His only regret, he said, was that it had stopped raining. 'Ah, the autumn I love the best – especially the rain! In Skopelos the rain is very beautiful, and very beautiful for the trees. . . .' It was one enthusiasm I found difficult to share with him; for the work that lay ahead I preferred to be dry.

The method of hauling boats ashore in the Aegean is primitive, but in principle it is simple, and it needs to be. As there are no tides it is impossible to leave a boat on a mudbank, wait until the tide is out and then set to with scraper and brush. In the Aegean it is necessary to take the whole boat out on to land, and because the quality of Greek anti-fouling paint is poor the average caique must be slipped three or four times a year. If this is neglected, a growth of weed and barnacles will so encrust the hull that the boat's speed and efficiency will be seriously reduced, and besides this there is the ever present danger of worm, the notorious teredo, whose workmanlike and rapid depredations into a wooden hull are a caique owner's constant fear.

At Vassiliko that morning the same sort of equipment in use in every *karenáio* or boatyard in the Aegean was being got ready on the shore; I was already familiar with the system having had *Astarte* slipped two winters running on the island of Aigina. As we arrived and dropped anchor close to the beach Anagnostou and his son were busy levering the *vasa* down the slope of sand.

The *vasa* is the wooden base upon which the hull is to rest, and consists of two long and large logs of wood laid side by side and yoked together at each end with iron bars and chain. A gap of about three feet is left between the logs, and it is into this space that the keel will eventually fit, so that the weight of the boat is taken along its whole length – the curves of the hull being accounted for by a series of different sized wedges added along the length of each log.

With a normal Greek caique, which is practically flat-bottomed with a keel only nominal and often less than a foot in depth, the *vasa* seldom need any alteration: set closer together for a smaller boat, farther apart for a larger. For *Astarte*, however, allowance must be made for the extra depth of keel, and some of the wood Vangeli had brought from Panormos was now carried ashore to reinforce the *vasa*, to be built up on each side to make enough room for the keel to fit in between.

Astarte was now anchored from the stern, her bow pointing to the beach, and held in position by a rope ashore. Fortunately there was no wind. A tall wooden capstan-winch was being set up at the head of the beach, and rusty steel cables with double blocks or pulleys were being unrolled along the sand.

The girls were there, ready as they had promised to push round and round on the capstan when the time came, and with Anagnostou and his son there was also Agallos, joint owner of the *karenáio* and tackle, a cheerful captain of a caique that in summer took Greek tourists from Skopelos to Alonnisos, and who was now wading into the shallows barefooted, with trouser legs rolled up, cap on the back of his head, pushing out into place sections of what looked like enormous wooden ladders.

These were the *skara*, and they form the runway down which first of all the *vasa* will be dragged, until the logs float in deeper water, and then also the road back up which the *vasa* and *Astarte* would be hauled.

As soon as the *skara* were properly tied and well in line the *vasa* were levered down, slipping easily on the wet wooden rungs, until they floated out to *Astarte*'s bows. There now remained the problem of getting the *vasa* underneath *Astarte*, evenly in position, a log on each side of the keel, and Vangeli and I took our places with a boat-hook on either side of the bowsprit. As Anagnostou and Niko hauled on ropes from the stern, trying to pull the twin logs back under the boat, Vangeli and I pressed down with all our weight with the boat-hooks on the *vasa* below us. The buoyancy of the logs, with the extra wood we had put on them, was considerable. There was a great deal of shouting and from the beach cries of encouragement. After several attempts we did it, the *vasa* were pushed down and back, fitting firmly under the hull.

I pulled on the shore-rope while Niko paid out on the stern anchor: boat and *vasa* together moved slowly towards the beach. The *skara* were of course floating on the surface of the water, and again with boat-hooks, but more easily, we pushed them down until the *vasa* ran up over the first rungs and we grounded. The first part of the operation was completed; it was now simply a matter for the capstan-winch, and a slow hauling up the beach.

A long wooden pole was fitted through the top of the capstan, and with much laughter the three girls galloped round taking up the cable's slack.

'You were going to tell Mikháli about the engagement,' breathlessly said Elsie to Athanasia as they swung round on the winch.

'Yes,' I said, 'I want to hear all of it.' The cable tightened and the pace slowed. As the pressure increased Niko sat under the winch keeping a hold of the loose cable as it came free. The weight of both boat and *vasa* – the latter weighed at least half a ton, and together they must have been well over six tons – was taken on iron stakes and chains buried deep in the sand under the fig trees; but I needn't have worried: a caique of at least eight times that weight was already propped up farther along the beach.

'It was in Patatiri,' Athanasia said. 'Father told me to sit on the stool at his feet. It was in the evening —'

Elsie interrupted excitedly, 'Father had spoken to me just before, so I knew what was coming!'

'He didn't say anything for a long time – then he began. "I have arranged for you to become engaged," he said. "Do you know Yiórgo the son of —?" I nodded. "Do you like him?"'

'And what did you say to that?'

'*Yes*,' said Athanasia, blushing at the memory of it and giving an extra hard push on the capstan so that her sisters, laughing and momentarily off balance, nearly tripped over the cable.

Kalliope looked up from her spinning at the cottage door. 'If you talk so much, Mikhális will never get his caique up!'

It was a long haul. We took turns at the capstan, two at each end of the pole, moving round like horses at a well – or 'like donkeys,' Elisavet laughed, dancing in front of us with a carrot dangling from her hand. It was not particularly hard work, but slow. Each full circle brought up the boat a few inches.

I asked Athanasia how well she knew Yiórgo at that time, and though I suppose I should have been ready for it, her reply startled me. She had not known him at all. Of course, she 'knew' him in one sense : she knew how he looked and what his voice sounded like, who were his family, his brothers and sisters, what each of them had done and said from their earliest days, and she knew of his friends . . . but she had not even spoken to him.

'You must have said *good morning*. . . .'

She laughed. 'No, not even that.' They had passed each other often, she said, but always she had turned her head away. . . .

The engagement had taken place a few months ago. All Yiórgo's family had gathered – about twenty people – and were waiting in their own house. The previous week Athanasia, helped by her mother and sisters, had been making *glyká*, sweets, literally – cakes made from various ingredients: spices, sugar and finely-ground nuts; hundreds of them. When all was ready and the day came, Athanasia was dressed most carefully and in the company of her parents and sisters went down to the house. She carried an enormous tray of the *glyká*, and also numerous presents for everyone – shirts, ties, socks for the men, stockings and dresses for the women. The ceremony that took place was a formal introduction of the bride to the bridegroom's family. Athanasia (she said her knees were knocking together and she wanted to run away) had to make a kind of obeisance, *metánia*, by which she crouched down, touched the floor with her two fists and kissed the hands first of Yiórgo's father and of the rest of the family, in order of precedence. In return she was presented with token pieces of money, ranging from 100 drachmae notes to gold sovereigns.

Followed several visits exchanged between the two families, each time with more presents, *glyká*, pieces of money. Yiórgo himself went through the same obeisance to Kosta and the rest of his fiancée's family. Athanasia went to stay with Yiórgo's family in Patatiri for a fortnight, later Yiórgo came to stay at Vassiliko. And now Yiórgo is away on a ship; the engagement, as usual, is a long one: a year.

As *Astarte* climbed out of the sea and came to the shore-end of the *skara*, Anagnostou put down log rollers greased with goat's fat, and as he carefully watched the boat's advance drove a wedge under the end of this or that roller to keep the direction straight. By midday *Astarte* was at last in position, well clear of the water. We broke off for half an hour to eat, and to be ready for the last stage.

Before I had met Athanasia and known of her engagement I had been inclined to condemn arranged marriages out of hand, without having thought much about them. 'You see,' said Athanasia, 'I now have two fathers, two mothers, two different sets of brothers and sisters. . . .' I was beginning to see in how sensible a pattern the arranged marriage was formed. A normal girl of Athanasia's age waiting, longing to fall in love. She is just waiting for the word, the finger of her father to point to a certain young man. The very fact that the boy will be known to her so slightly is here an advantage. The door to her suppressed affections is suddenly thrown open.

The length of the engagement is part of the well-planned pattern. One year – to fall in love, to grow the necessary emotional and physical attraction. And as in Athanasia's case, after the first few visits, in which the young couple, on their best behaviour, learn to know each other a little, there is often a long parting – Yiórgo goes away on a ship. Romantic letters are exchanged. Yiórgo is teased mercilessly by his shipmates. Athanasia dreams alone of her lover far away on the high seas.

When the marriage itself finally takes place society does not for a moment relinquish its guiding hand. The wedding is celebrated in the fullest glare of village publicity. The bride and groom can never forget that their own personal union is only a part of it : two families have publicly united.

Next, the pattern of married life is very different from its counterpart in England or America. Here there is none of the sudden isolation of the young couple. The nights they have alone, but little more. In the day the man is out of the house, working, or with his own men friends in the coffee-house or taverna. The woman is at home, helped by a delighted company of her girl friends and relatives, all going about the long and hard business of house-keeping, in a country where standards of cleanliness are high and everything is done by hand. In this way, by the participation and attention of others, at least the edges of so dramatic a change of life are softened. The transition is a gradual one. Everyone is helping to make it all easier, more interesting, more exciting, and even the bad parts can be comforted into gentler acceptance.

Basically the marriage is kept as formal as possible. A man does not expect to share all his interests with his wife, nor she hers with him. There is little privacy, and as a result little opportunity for any behaviour other than that expected of them. Only within this framework, and gradually, may tenderness and understanding between husband and wife begin to grow.

Of course, for those accustomed to a more modern, individualistic approach to marriage, the system would seem intolerable – as intolerable as theirs would seem empty and depressing to a girl like Athanasia. But at least the Greek arranged marriage, I had discovered, had more to it than at first I had thought : there was a great deal of serious social planning concealed within its formal stages, and much humanity ; also, it worked.

The dowry side of it, however, seems to be of more doubtful value. Elsie had told me of the two little white houses high on the hill above the village of Patatiri – Kosta's and Kalliope's savings : two houses for two daughters. The eldest (there were four, originally) was already in Australia and married ; Elisavet would follow probably next year. One of the houses was for Athanasia when she got married in six months' time ; the other . . .

'The other must be for you, then, Elsie,' I said.

She shrugged her shoulders with exaggerated unconcern. 'I don't want to get married, ever.'

But for girls of really poor families dowries, or rather the lack of them, can frequently be tragic.

Lunch over, we returned to finish the work.

The *vasa* had to be removed from under the boat, not only because they would be used again to haul up some other caique next week or in a month's time, but also because their position on either side of the keel prevented me from doing any of the scraping, washing, and finally painting, that I had to do in the spring when she was re-floated.

How were they going to take away the *vasa*? In a Greek *karenáio* practically everything is done by leverage. In Aigina I have seen *Astarte* moved bodily, *vasa* and all, twelve feet sideways across the beach, to make room for another caique. This was done, in a few hours, by two men, shifting seven tons of wood and metal, each with a fir pole used as a lever in their hands. At Vassiliko there was no need to shift the boat to one side, but it was necessary to build up two blocks, one at each end under the keel, to raise the boat so that the *vasa* could be dragged away. The blocks, short columns of wood, were built up of wedges, laboriously hammered into place, and the boat was finally lifted a fraction by a jack.

Astarte now rested on these two columns, bow and stern, under her keel. The pine trees Vangeli had cut down at Panormos were propped up on each side of the hull, and the wedges on top of the *vasa* knocked away. The *vasa* were then unyoked and slid down singly into the water, later to be pulled up and put together again for the next caique. A few more columns of wood were built up under the keel to take the weight more evenly, and the work was done.

A wind was getting up, sighing through the fig trees. If we wanted to be back in Skopelos harbour that night and before another autumnal gale, we must leave at once.

We said good-bye, and Vangeli went to start up *Makhi*'s engine with a gas blow-lamp. 'Where is Barba Lycúrgos?' I asked. It wasn't only that I wanted to say good-bye to the old man, but I felt I ought to see him, for another reason. A week before, when I was here at Vassiliko, he had come down to the beach and called out to me across the water. I rowed ashore and asked him what he wanted. 'I'm constipated!' he said, his long lined face and drooping white moustache a picture of indignation and woe. 'And what's more, it's been eleven days! Give me something to take – you must have lots of things on that boat of yours. . . .'

The Khiot captain and two of the divers were sitting near-by, and they grinned broadly. 'Take some figs, Uncle!'

'Figs, my child?' He fixed them a look of scornful impatience. 'I've eaten kilos of figs this last week. And have they done any good?' Muttering, he crouched down on a rock.

The Khiot was sympathetic. 'Yes, that's bad,' he said. 'Now, when I was in Rhodes once . . .' An animated discussion followed to which everyone contributed details of experiences, their own or of others whom they knew well, in which such symptoms had been successfully dealt with. Most Greeks do not suffer from the constraints and inhibitions affected by Europeans about the natural functions of the body ; these and allied topics are generally discussed with complete freedom. Various sovereign remedies were proposed to solve the old man's problem – paraffin, camomile tea, even Shell engine oil (high viscosity), and the captain from Khios stuck by his own cure-all, ouzo, in large quantities, which he maintained was the answer to every ailment, physical or mental' All of these helpful suggestions grandfather Lycúrgos stubbornly rejected : either he had already tried them, or he refused to believe they would help. 'No, I want the Englishman to give me something!' He turned to me again. 'If you can give me something to clear me out, *tha sou kamo Theó*!' I'll make you a god!

I rowed back to the boat and dug among the lockers. Eventually I found a bottle filled with a black and potent looking mixture labelled 'Cascara Evacuant' and *take with caution*. I returned with it to the beach. 'This,' I said confidently, 'will do it.'

A glass, spoon and water were brought out by his granddaughters. I gave him a quadruple dose. He got to his feet slowly, bones creaking, and shook me by the hand. '*Tha sou kamo Theó!*' He hobbled off, grumbling into his moustache . . . 'constipation, a terrible thing . . . *eleven days* . . .'

Now, another four had passed. I was anxious to know my patient's condition. I hoped the dose had not been too strong. When I saw the bent figure of the old man, bowed over his shepherd's crook, slowly making his way towards me along the beach I went to meet him. 'What news?' I said.

He stopped, and looked at me sorrowfully. '*Teepote!*' Nothing!

I'd given him a dose, I'd thought, strong enough to move an ox. 'You must see a doctor,' I said, sternly. 'It could be dangerous, fifteen days, especially at your age.'

The old man shook his head. 'No, no – give me some more medicine!' It was no good trying to make a man like Lycúrgos go to a doctor if he didn't want to. I handed over half the bottle.

He sat down under *Astarte*'s hull on the sand and waved to us as we took up the anchor. He and *Astarte*, and the three girls in bright dresses waving from in front of the cottage, looked strangely forlorn. But *Astarte* was in good hands. We were the last visitors at Vassiliko, probably for a long time.

A few days later, in Skopelos before I left the island, I had a message from Vassiliko. All was well. I too was much relieved ; also delighted – presumably my deification had gone through.

8

Landowner at Last

I returned to Greece in the spring, and from Kymi on Evvia took the
Kyknos to the Sporades. It was the day before Easter, and Easter in
Greece is what Christmas is to the rest of Europe, the most important
of the year's religious festivals. Buses and boats were crowded: everyone was going back to their families for the holidays, back to their
own islands.

It is always good when a foreigner returns to a Greek island, there
is always a warm welcome, an illusion of belonging, and I enjoyed
my return to Skopelos, the multitude of greetings, innumerable
handshakes, '*Kalōs ōrises*!' 'Welcome!' and the formula of reply,
'*Kalōs se vríka*!' literally, 'well that I have found you'. Vangeli was
expecting me and was waiting on the quay, and Yiórgo had seen me
in the boat coming off the *Kyknos* and was there to haul me up on to
dry land, his mighty fingers encompassing my hand.

Perhaps this time it was no illusion: I did belong. Hadn't Vangeli
said to me, *You are an islander, now*? Skopelos was already, it seemed
to me, 'my' island.

Nothing as yet was settled, and though I had Vangeli's word on it
I was still in a state of suspense. But to open the subject of the land at
Panormos straight away, as soon as I stepped ashore, would clearly
be bad manners, especially to a Greek. I would have to be patient.

A drink at a *kafeneion* on the harbour front celebrated my arrival.
'What news?' 'Everything quiet.' It felt an age since I had left, and
then only a day. Everyone was wearing a suit, a collar and tie,
because of Easter, and Vangeli, to match the smartness of his
appearance was at his most charming and urbane. I noticed a large
green and black object parked beside Yiórgo's workshop. It bore a
striking resemblance to a bus. 'What is that?' I asked, with astonish-
ment.

'Our bus,' said Yiórgo shyly. 'The road as far as Agnonda is open,
and it goes there, sometimes.'

The bus had arrived on the back of a large caique a few weeks before, and had been driven on to the quay without the catastrophe that apparently the assembled crowd of Skopelots had expected. I asked Yiórgo if it was a good bus. 'Very old,' he said, 'but the engine's not too bad.'

The problem at that time and in the succeeding months was not the engine. The Athenian company that had bought the monopoly of public transport in Skopelos and Skiathos had landed a bus on Skiathos also, and after promising immediate and frequent services, had supplied the two islands with only one driver. This man, a pleasant enough fellow, though with a somewhat inflated idea of his own importance – he described himself more accurately than he knew as 'conductor of the Sporadic buses' – would jump into his seat at Skopelos, blow his horn and tear off for Agnonda, ditch the bus under the plane trees and take a caique for Skiathos. There he would make a few runs with the Skiathos bus, until, some days later furious telephone messages would recall him to Skopelos where again he would make a few frantic journeys until a stern and indignant summons from Skiathos sent him scurrying back across the eight miles of intervening sea once more.

Oddly enough the main reason for the Skopelots' dislike of this unfortunate man was not because he couldn't run his bus properly. After all it was almost enough just to have a bus on the island, parked on the harbour front, a monument in which to take a justifiable pride; that it seldom ran was of secondary importance. No, the real grouse was that the driver was not a native of the island, a true Skopelot. Did they not have Stammatis, a man born and bred on Skopelos, and with much experience of steering buses on the mainland? I could see that the present conductor of Sporadic transport would not hold his unenviable post for long.

The Easter excitement was mounting. Ianni's restaurant was closed with the others, but the tables outside the coffee shops were full. Most of the men seemed to be down by the harbour, but they sat around seldom drinking, just smoking and talking, and clicking through their fingers their *komboloi*, strings of amber beads inherited from Turkish days, that many Greeks play with for hours on end to help pass the time. We took up my suitcases to Vangeli's house, where I was welcomed by Alexandra and the family. My room was ready for me, and though no one was eating at all that day, being Easter

Saturday, Alexandra offered me anything I might want. I decided to wait with the others, until after midnight.

Foreigners tend to believe that the Greek Church has a powerful hold on its people, comparable to that power and influence exercised by the Catholic clergy in countries like Spain, Italy and Ireland. This is not so. The Greek Church does have a certain power, and it possesses considerable wealth, locked up in monasteries and land. The ordinary village priest, however, is as poor if not poorer than the next man, and nowadays is often less well educated; his influence is limited.

For one thing Orthodox Christianity does not lay so much emphasis on sin and confession – the backbone, I have always imagined, of priestly power in Catholic countries. Greeks may very well become oppressed with the sense of other people's sins, but seldom it seems to me do they worry very much about their own.

In the cities there is a strong and growing hostility towards the Church, based mainly on popular disapproval of ecclesiastical wealth and privilege, but in the villages and in the islands the most notice-able feeling towards the clergy is one of indifference. On Skopelos, for example, one feels that the priests are regarded with friendly tolerance, and little more. Of course there is still the mass of older, and very old people, mostly women, for whom the Church does have a profound significance, and over whom the priests may have some real influence; but the younger generations have turned their faces the other way.

I have the impression that Orthodox ritual is much more impor-tant to the Greeks than the practical teachings of Christianity, and it is for this reason that the Church continues to play a great part in everyday Greek life. The village priest leads the ritual in the big religious festivals, and at the *panayiria* throughout the year; he pre-sides at baptisms, weddings and funerals. Convention and social conformity are enormously powerful in Greece, and with a rapidly growing middle class, are gaining strength.

A foreigner is often confused when he tries to evaluate the influence and importance of Orthodox Christianity to the Greeks because he forgets or underrates the power of the Church as a symbol of Greek nationalism. It is only a hundred and forty years since the Revolu-tion. The leaders of each little Greek community under the Turkish empire were the village priests, and it was they who kept alive the spirit of Greek-Christian consciousness during the three and a half centuries of Turkish domination. They led their people religiously, educationally and politically, and when it came to fighting they were usually in the front line.

In the rest of Europe nationalism and religion were never so closely allied, indeed generally speaking nationalism was quite disassociated from and in opposition to the Church. Foreigners are shocked that in Greece an Archbishop should be a political leader, as in Cyprus – a criticism that to Greeks makes no sense at all. Englishmen and Americans appear to be even more appalled that a 'Man of God' should give his support and leadership to violence and war; but here it might be well to remember that in the last two world wars the soldiers went out to kill each other with the full moral backing, the pious exhortations of their own 'Men of God'. A pacifist, non-violent movement does exist in the world today, but it is not from all the great Christian Churches that it can look for leadership.

Easter in Greece is a religious-national festival. In Athens, with the marching soldiers, crosses, flags, and drums, one hardly needs to be reminded of it. In Skopelos that evening when Alexandra gave me my long unlit candle and I set off for the church, I passed under many bare flagpoles set up over shops and balconies. Tomorrow the blue and white Greek flag would be fluttering bravely from every one of these, and from thousands of others in every village and city of Greece; and it would mean much more than mere decoration.

The courtyard outside the church was crowded, and it was difficult to make my way through the doors. Skopelos town is divided into four neighbourhoods, or parishes, each with its own church. A heavy atmosphere of incense and candlewax and warm breath filled the spaces of the domes. It was about eleven o'clock: another hour to midnight and the climax of the ancient religious drama. I edged carefully through the densely packed mass of women at the back of the church, inching my way to the front where the men stood shoulder to shoulder before the ikon screen.

There were two lecterns, one on either side by the richly carved wooden stalls, and a man stood before each chanting from a great book whose pages he turned slowly as he sang. The chanting was done alternately, verse by verse sung across from each side, the congregation intoning the chorus. Grigor, a friend of Vangeli's whom I knew well, sang from one lectern; his voice was deep and sad. I could recognize most of the faces now, lit by the candle-flames, the fishermen and boatmen, butchers and shopkeepers, but most of those I knew best were on one side of the church, standing beside Grigor – Vangeli, Yiórgo, Lakis, his brother Stammatis the doctor, and others, and they made a place for me to stand with them.

The priest had been behind the ikon screen for a long time. I caught sight of him briefly through the grill of carved wood: he was putting on an additional brocaded robe, and was combing his long grey hair. It was nearly midnight now, and people were glancing surreptitiously at their watches. They began to put out the candles at the back of the church, and the last verses of the chant died away on the incense-heavy air.

There was a stirring in the congregation, an edging forward, and a rustling of clothes, a whispering, and each of us gripped the warm wax of our unlit candles. The priest appeared for a moment in the doorway of the screen, put his hand to his head. In the excitement of the moment he had forgotten his hat, and went back to get it. This time everything was ready.

In the stillness and gloom of the church, he came forward, magnificently robed, his face uplifted, arms outstretched, a lighted candle blazing in each hand. For a moment he stood there, and then he stepped forward holding out the candles before him, and those in the front dipped their candles to the priest's, and turned to their neighbours to light theirs, until the little flames spread back into the darkness and the whole church was brilliant with light, and already we were jostling out with the priest into the courtyard, trying to avoid sizzling each others' hair, dropping hot wax on clothes. Outside in the cool spring air it seemed that the whole night was alive with dancing flames. Silence, and a bell from the clock tower chimed the first stroke of midnight, and suddenly the priest's voice, triumphant: '*Christos anésti*!' Christ is risen! and his face was transformed into an expression of such genuine and sublime happiness. Everyone was embracing and shaking hands, and I found myself turning to my neighbours, 'Christ is risen!' or replying '*Alithós anésti*!' 'Truly he is risen!' while explosions of fireworks rocked the village and from across the bay, at the radio beacon, came the distant rattle of rifle fire.

Later, the priest led a procession round the steep village streets, and afterwards we went back to the house, candles held aloft to light our way over the dark, uneven cobbles. Hot soup was waiting for us, a special favourite soup made from the entrails of young goats, to break our fast a little; but tomorrow, or rather later today, was the real time of feasting.

Vangeli's sister owns a fine house on the outskirts of the village, not far from the ice factory, a rambling whitewashed building with verandas and a courtyard and a walled orchard of lemon, orange and almond trees. Alexandra – she has the same name as Vangeli's wife – is umarried, but though she lives alone there are always children playing about the great garden, and an amazing variety of animals. Besides a pony and a donkey, there are geese, chickens, turkeys, dogs and cats. It is hard enough to count the cats, even more difficult to count the kittens – the sofas of every room are teeming with them. I had only to rearrange a cushion to sit down, when some furry object the size of my fist would step out with tiny hairs on end, hissing fiercely, to challenge the intrusion.

One room of the house is given over to the government as a weather station, a room filled with various instruments to read the wind force and count the sunlight hours, and outside in the orchard is a little tower which measures rainfall. The meteorological officer is a giant swarthy Cretan, called Myron, over six foot and with breadth to match, whose duties are to take the readings, and radio them to the mainland. Myron was a great favourite of mine, kindly and good-humoured, always ready with a joke and a roar of laughter. He took his meals with Alexandra and admitted to me, that Easter Sunday morning when we gathered in the courtyard, that he was very lucky – he had better food, he said, than anyone else on the island, Alexandra was such a good cook.

'But of course she's a good cook,' Vangeli said, sticking his thumbs into his waistcoat as we drank ouzo in the sun, and yellow ducklings darted between our feet and we sniffed the appetising odour of kid roasting in the outside brick oven: 'Isn't she my sister? It's only natural. Am I not the best cook in the Balkans?'

Myron stretched out his great body on a very small chair, rocking backwards on two legs. 'Ah, Vangeli, how is it that you're so good at everything? How unfair the world is that one person should be so talented, while the rest of us . . .'

Vangeli smiled pityingly at his friend's irony. He leant forward:

'Afterwards we shall play *tavli*, and then cards, and we shall see who is really talented and who not. . . .'

Greeks when they play table games like these, cards, chess, *tavli* (backgammon), play with a violence and passion that to the Anglo-Saxon is quite astonishing. There are two gentle looking old men who I see every day hobbling on sticks by the waterside, or sitting quietly reading their newspapers in the warm spring sunshine; I have also seen them inside a coffee shop playing chess with each other, and I would hardly have recognized them.

'If he moves that knight,' one would say, with a ferocious sneer, 'by the Panayia I shall crush him to a pulp!' There are always a few people standing by, watching the game, and it is to these that the players address their remarks.

His opponent moves the knight. 'Right! I warned him! Take *that*, then!' and a castle will appear in his hand, not gently, diffidently sliding out as in more equable climates to remove the knight, but from on high, crash, down on the knight, knocking it and other pieces across the board. 'Got it! I'll eat him up now!' (This 'eating' is part of the jargon of most games as played in Greece: you don't take a piece, you *eat* it. . . .)

I would have thought that one of these games of chess was enough to make the two players enemies for life, but this is not so. The next day I would see them at it again. It is the same with cards, each card hurled down with a great crack of the fist to shake the table; everyone, spectators included, feels it is his business to criticize the play with complete frankness. Yet although Greeks are by no means good losers such terrible, public defeats do not seem to rankle for long. There is always another game to play, and this time the cards may be different, the tables turned.

It was in the ruins of that Easter Sunday feast, the huge dishes of roast kid, potatoes, and salad, cleared away, the dogs and cats happily at peace chewing at the bones, that Vangeli brought out the board and we sat down to play.

Myron tried to distract our attention – he didn't play backgammon – by getting out his gramophone and putting on a series of Cretan dances. In spite of his great bulk he dances the rhythms of his own island with amazing agility, his feet flashing through the intricate steps. As I watched him spin and bend lightfoot under the olive tree, I remembered that a week ago Myron had witnessed a fight –

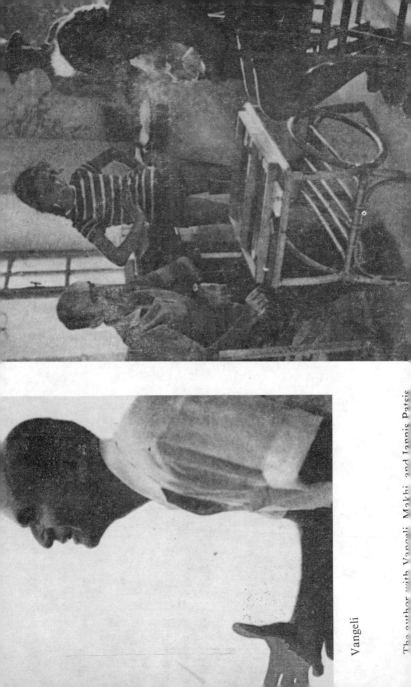

Vangeli

The author with Vangeli, Makhi, and Iannis Patsis

Kosta Mavrikis and
his taverna,
Steniválla

rare event in Skopelos – in Sari's taverna. He had become impatient with the antagonists and in classic style had got up and cracked their heads together. When the policeman arrived, everything was quiet.

After a few games, most of which Vangeli won, he leant forward and addressed me sadly, 'Ah, Michael, what a pity you are so bad at *tavli*, after all I've taught you!'

Some games later, he sat back, in crowing mood once more. Vangeli is one of those who dare to voice, and loudly, what most people really feel: when he loses he complains bitterly of his unbelievable bad luck, when he wins he congratulates himself on his fantastic skill.

'*Och, Mikhaláki mou*! Haven't I told you that I am the best player in the Balkans? A teacher of teachers? A master?'

Once, much later, when Vangeli knew I was writing a book, he asked me what I was going to say about *tavli*. 'I'm going to tell the truth,' I said, sternly.

'Will they believe you?'

'What do you mean?' I replied unguardedly.

'When you say I'm such a brilliant player —'

'I'm not going to say that. Far from it. I'm going to say that you're very, very lucky. . . .'

At last the moment was a good one, I felt, with Vangeli in such euphoric mood, to broach the subject once more of the land at Panormos. I hadn't been able to stop thinking about it all the winter in England, and I couldn't help believing that something, somehow, at the last moment, would go wrong. The old man, Vangeli's father-in-law, might change his mind – why shouldn't he? They might all, as a family, have had second thoughts: a foreigner landing plumb in the middle of their beautiful Panormos. Could I really be so fortunate —?

'Anytime you want,' said Vangeli. 'It is necessary first to make a plan of the piece of land, and then go to the *symvouleiográphos* . . . in English?'

'Notary.'

'Yes. Whenever you are ready.'

I was ready. Except, first, I must re-launch *Astarte*. I left the Easter week celebrations at Skopelos, having eaten too much and drunk too much continuously for several days, and took the passenger caique up the coast of Alonnisos, past Patatiri and Votsi to Stenivalla, the last inhabited cove of the Northern Sporades, where the Mavrikis family welcomed me at their lonely rockside taverna, cracked the red-dyed Easter eggs with me, and sent me on across the straits with their son Mitso in his small fishing boat to Vassiliko.

I received a present of dried figs, appropriate offering, from old Lycúrgos, as befitted my lately immortalized state, and for three days his three granddaughters fed and helped me while I scrubbed and scraped away at *Astarte*'s dry hull and painted the top-sides a dazzling new white. On the last day, with the arrival of Anagnostou and his strong-arm sons and helpers there also came – a pleasant surprise – Vangeli on *Makhi*, and with him to help with the last coat of anti-fouling and the inevitable pumping that would follow when the boat first floated, Grigor the fishing enthusiast and liturgy-chanter of the Easter night service, and Iannis Betsannis who with his father operates a grocer-taverna in Skopelos. With them too came careful instructions from Yiórgo as to how I should proceed with the engine after its four months' hibernation, and with so much help and so many good wishes, and after suitable libations to Poseidon, to Apollo god of embarkation and landfall, to Aphrodite and to Pan, *Astarte* was levered down the *skara* over the sand, with much shouting and 'one, two – all together, *now*!' gathered speed and with a thunder of rolling wood, a cheer, slid the last slope to the sea. Keel under with a flurry of spray, smack and hiss of blue water as she dived, rode out, the goddess born again in the foam, quiet now, afloat on the water like a bird alighted, the green-eyed shining figurehead at the bows smiling down at her own reflection. . . . Beginning again of another Aegean summer.

Grigor sat at the tiller all the way back to Skopelos. Iannis and I took turns at the pump while Vangeli on *Makhi* hovered anxiously around. 'Are you sinking?' – above the noise of the engine – 'Not yet.'

Two days later, with the timbers sealed up again, Vangeli and I were at Panormos, metre-rules and a long piece of knotted string in our hands. I had feared that after all he would not wish to part with just the strip of land we had set our hearts on – the rock over the sea, the olive and almond trees. I need not have worried. 'It's only a little,' Vangeli said apologetically. 'You know my father-in-law . . .' It was just less than a *strémma*, a thousand square metres (which is about a quarter of an acre); but it was enough, and just what I wanted; what I had wanted, it seemed to me, all my life. 'And all this around,' Vangeli waved his arms, 'you know that it is ours, you can do what you like. It doesn't matter. . . .'

Back in Skopelos the next day, we called on the notary in his office, a little upstairs room in the back streets. He looked at us politely over his spectacles and began burrowing into heaps of old papers which gave out, as though they resented disturbance, a musty smell. Once more, I was anxious: usually when a foreigner tries to buy land in Greece all sorts of difficulties arise. All too often the land is found to belong to several people at once, at least one of whom is in America or Australia; alternatively it may be claimed by people quite other than those offering it for sale, in which case the prospective buyer is liable to find himself in the middle of an interminable Greek lawsuit. I had no fears about the ownership, but I'd heard that there was some government rule about not being allowed to break up estates larger, or smaller than, a certain amount. Also there was the question of the forest – private houses built too near a big area of forest (such as the hills round Panormos) were discouraged because of the very real risk of fire. In either of these cases I would require one, or probably several permits, and to get permits, any kind of permit, in Greece is likely to take months. . . . Fortunately none of these obstacles proved insurmountable: the first did not seem to arise, probably because my *strémma* was too small to worry about, and as for the second, the proximity to the forest, Vangeli pointed out, eloquently enough, that the true forest did not begin until above the new road; the distance between my plot of land and the road above was several hundred metres, and though there were many pines in this area, they were small, and interspersed with olive trees, so no one (in their right mind) could call this forest.

There was nothing else that the notary could do but start drawing up the deeds of sale. We were to come back in two days, when all the papers would be ready.

It was raining when we gathered once more in the notary's office, Vangeli, his father-in-law and myself, a butcher and a grocer called up to act as witnesses, and an elderly gentleman who had been in the United States who was to translate to me any of the passages of the somewhat archaic Greek used in legal matters that I did not understand. The ceremony did not take long. The papers were read out. We nodded gravely in agreement. We all signed many times in various places, and the deed was done. '*Kalo riziko!*' Good roots! Everyone shook me by the hand. The old man, Alexandra's father, held my hand in his frail fingers and wished me health and happiness. 'We're neighbours now, you and I! And now you need children. . . .' I was very happy.

We escorted him under an umbrella back through the rain to the house on the corner. Vangeli poured the ouzo and we drank solemnly to my good-rootedness. I sent a telegram. I actually owned a piece of a Greek island, some good red earth, and five olive trees, by the sea.

The first of May. All the caiques in Skopelos harbour had under-gone some mystical regeneration overnight, and when I stepped up on the dew-soaked deck to admire the morning and the pale scarf of mist dissolving in the sunrise I saw that every mast had blossomed into flower. Little Makhi and her younger sister Eleni came down to the harbour carrying bunches of flowers for *Astarte*. Makhi can walk my gang-plank fairly confidently, if she takes it at a run; Eleni pre-fers to cross on her hands and knees. I thanked them for the flowers and climbed with them up the ratlines and tied them high in the rigging. The other bunch, roses, hyacinth and crocus, they arranged for me in a big glass on the cabin table.

It was a public holiday, and the official start of summer. I took the family round to Agnonda that morning, where many other people had come on mule or on foot, on the two or three motor cycles that had arrived on the island lately, and in the bus that decided to run that day. The two tavernas had spread out their tables under the plane trees and by the hull of a great derelict caique that was pulled up on the beach, her prow resting under the biggest plane. The tables were crowded, and all the young men of Skopelos seemed to be there, one with an accordion, another with a guitar, and over by the fruit-trees two *bouzouki* players. After lunch, for which everyone had brought his own and shared it with his friends, there was singing, and later the young men sang to the popular modern Greek rhythms of Piraeus and Athens radio, and the dancers joined hands, old women in peasant skirts and shawls, as well as the younger wives, and middle-aged men with bellies tight under their splitting waistcoats, lean grey-haired woodsmen and the young bloods in dark narrow trousers and white shirts, strung out hand in hand in a long curving line, bobbing to the music – halt, swing, step back, forward again – serpentine among the trees.

The news that I had been given a piece of Panormos had spread quickly, and I was being constantly shaken warmly by the hand, often by complete strangers, and wished *Kalo riziko*! It reminded me throughout that day that much as I enjoyed the junketing at Agnonda I dearly wished to be somewhere else. It was not until evening that I left with *Astarte* and sailed up past Cape Trahili along the coast northward to the island of Daseiá that conceals the entrance to Panormos Bay. I dropped anchor opposite my plot of land and rowed ashore at dusk, and sat for a time on the rock cliff where we had planned to build the house.

I had never owned land before, and the sensation was a strange one. Yet I couldn't help feeling, besides the new pride of ownership, power of possession all signed and sealed, that the truth of it all was somehow very different. I could not 'possess' this earth and rock that I lay upon, these trees whose smooth bark I touched, their leaves above me patterned darkly against the fading sky. If anything, the reverse was true: the land possessed me, and I began to sense that in time as the roots of olive and almond, flowers, grass and *koúmara* bush spread deeper into the soil, so would the branches in the air, new shoots, green tendrils wind themselves even more closely about my life.

I had wanted to start building right away, but this turned out to be impossible: the building unions had not yet come to Skopelos, and although this meant that labour and expenses generally would be cheaper, it also meant that builders were scarce – most of the islanders in the trade had gone to Athens to work at the much higher wages. I had engaged a builder, one Pandelis Kefalonitis, who promised to start work as soon as he was free, at the beginning of September. I had been impatient at the delay, but now I began to see that there were advantages: I needed time to get used to the place, and in a strange way I felt that Panormos must have time to get used to me.

There is a curious harmony of landscape and people in Greece. This is why places have so much character and personality of their own, as if by a miracle of nature man and earth are made of an equal standing, one matched to the other, and if the sky and mountain share in fashioning the man, so the man leaves the legacy of his own complex spirit upon valley, tree and rock.

Against a Greek landscape the human figure is never lost, is never seen so small that there is felt the need for abasement, nor by way of compensation the need to over-inflate his own importance. He is neither the solitary speck, the fly toiling over the terrible mountain face, nor is he the ant indistinguishable from his fellow ants teeming on the limitless plain.

In Greece you are always looking up, or down, but never too far in either direction; and then there are the distances, blue haze over the sea, but always a dim shape of some island or mountain-top, something for the eye to hold on to, and the mind, to keep a sense of proportion. People look the right size, and usually feel it; and in the brilliant light of a sun that is never an enemy recognize each other, each man with his own strong shadow walking before him.

I realized that I had not begun to know Panormos, and to start straight in and build a house before I knew the place or felt I belonged there, would be like a kind of breaking and entering: if I was to live in Panormos I wanted to belong there, to build from the inside, from an understanding of the place, not to superimpose myself ruthlessly, and so lose so much. All this needed time.

In those days I had several visitors, and I began to get to know some of my future neighbours. In an upland valley a mile or so to the south-east of the cove there lived a charming man called Iannis Patsis, white haired and white moustached, who looked about seventy but was really only fifty. His wife had died long ago and his two sons had gone off to work in Athens and on the ships. He had no particular trade, but he was good with a pick-axe, Vangeli said. He was lame in one foot and walked with a limp, and he had an old white donkey that was blind in one eye. Living by himself, he got lonely, he told me, especially in the winter. He had some vines and fruit trees, from which he lived.

Near him lived Andrikos, 'little Andreas,' so called because he was a particularly big and broad man, even on an island where the average height was noticeably above that on the mainland, and his speciality was the iron crowbar, or the great long-hafted twenty-pound hammer used for pulverizing rock. And there was Spyro, tall and very thin, who always looked rather ill, who had two fine mules and lived with his wife and daughter in a cottage in the hills. They all promised to help build the house when the time came.

Spyro used to come down, sometimes with Iannis Patsis and his donkey, to see what I was doing and advise me what to plant in the way of orange and lemon trees, and to make general suggestions about the house and the garden. 'You must have a fig tree,' said Spyro.

'And vines,' said Iannis.

'We'll bring you cuttings from ours. They're strong and grow quickly, and have sweet grapes.'

'They'll grow up over poles,' added Iannis, leaning on his good leg, 'and in summer you'll have shade.'

'And where is the house going to be exactly?'

'Here, on the rock,' I would answer, 'and then out this way, like this —'

'It will be a fine house,' says Spyro.

'And very big,' adds Iannis, and then they nod gravely together and Spyro would call up his mules and ride away, and Iannis would carefully untie his old blind donkey and walk off beside it up away into the trees.

Barba Yiórgi found me once, and told me sadly that he was off back to his cottage on Mount Dirphis, and he wouldn't be down at Panormos very often, at least not this year. I think he really believed I would find the treasure, especially when the workmen started digging the foundations. But most of the time there was no one there at all.

I used to row ashore at night and wander about or just stand quite still while the wind moved the leaves overhead and shadows started from the ground, and the bay was a sea of stars. The most beautiful times of day in Greece are early mornings when the light is brilliant and sharp, and colours and shapes stand out with a clarity that is almost unreal, and in the evenings when a gentler golden light replaces the glare of midday, and trees and hills and sea grow warm, as if soft to touch. But the time to sense the magic of a Greek country-side is at noon. High summer noon, when the whole earth has gone dead or asleep with heat and glare: to walk up a hillside through an olive grove, limbs drugged, head ringing with the cicadas' ceaseless trill; rocks shimmer, sky and sea are veiled in colourless heat haze, the silence is deeper than any other, stillness of leaves, dry thistles, parched earth: an extraordinary tension, a breathlessness, a waiting for something. . . . Walking slowly, steps grate over crumbling earth, stones, sounds magnified like the rasp of breath, crack of twigs, louder than life but without echo. Shade of a plane tree : lie down, sweat cooling, stretch out – wait, listen.

Inevitably I would go to sleep. Sometimes I wondered whether I would dream, and if so, what about; but I never did. But when I woke up and the sun had moved down the sky again and colour and life were flooding back into earth and sea, I felt with strange certainty that there had been some secretive, sly movements about me – branch of a tree changed direction, leaves of a bush moved aside, as if someone had been watching me, the ghosts of the past perhaps, spirits of the place had been looking me over while I slept; and I could almost see their footprints where they had silently gone by, paused, and moved on; and I liked to think, and hoped, that they could see no serious objection to me, and might grow to accept my intrusion.

There is a feeling about Panormos of friendliness. The feeling is in the place. And though this friendliness does not come from the people living there – there is no one in Panormos, not in the inner bay – it comes I believe from the people who lived there once.

Places where no man has ever lived seem neither hostile nor friendly : they are neutral, natural, and in that sense to me sterile. Where there can be neither seen nor sensed the traces of men's work, their living, there can be no character, no recognizable spirit of the place. It is for this reason that the coral beaches, palm lagoons of uninhabited Pacific islands could never appeal to me. Their beauty would tire as surely as the pyrotechnics of a firework display, as the constant view of brilliant, snow-capped mountains, as the featureless though changing vision of the wide open sea. For me a place must have been lived in, and loved, no matter how long ago. Panormos is a place like that. 'For it is possible, at a pinch, to do without gods, but one misses the dead.'*

Panormos is the only good harbour on Skopelos, and here was one of the three earliest settlements, together with Staphylos on the south coast and Glossa, the ancient Selinos, on the north west. According to legend Skopelos, in ancient times called Peparethos, was colonized by Cretans, after the fall of Knossos. The invaders were led by Staphylos, the son of Dionysos and Ariadne, and the original inhabitants, Dolopians and Pelasgians, were easily overcome. Staphylos was one of the Argonauts who sailed with the other heroes under

* Rupert Brooke, writing from Lake Winnipeg in 1913.

Jason's command. Skopelos was an island sacred above all to Dionysos, and when the islanders first began to mint their own coins, silver
and bronze, as early as 500 B.C. they took as their emblem the bunch
of grapes. The legend of Cretan colonization has been curiously confirmed by the discovery by archaeologists on the neck of the little
peninsula at Staphylos of a gold sword-hilt and cup, indisputably of
Minoan style and design.

In the valley that leads inland from the outer bay of Panormos,
the 'all-harbour', is a hill now covered with olive trees that is the site
of the ancient town. The hill is called 'Kastro', the usual Greek name
for ruins upon a high place. Poplars grow near the sea, and behind
them orchards of plum and cherry, almond, apple and pear; and
beyond them the olive groves, trees knotted and twisted with respectable and still potent age, march farther into the hills, climbing the
steeper slopes that rim the valley, halting only at the abrupt forested
escarpments that jut out over the green cultivated land.

It occurred to me as I walked up from the long sweep of pebbled
beach, through the poplars and plum trees towards the base of the
hill, that probably in ancient times the sea came in much farther.
Even now it is clear that a strip of land a few hundred yards from the
shore-line was once covered by water: here they have tried to grow
vegetables, mostly tomatoes, though with only moderate success;
but gradually the salt is being washed away.

I came upon the first visible traces of ancient remains some distance from the base of the hill: broad slabs of hewn stone submerged
in the earth, running out under the fruit-trees. Upon these solid
foundations the cottagers have erected their light walls of heaped
rock dividing the orchards. If once this part of the valley were
covered by sea, then it is possible that these low outworks were
harbour walls, a long jetty perhaps, a quay.

At different places on the slope of the hill as I climbed I could see
the shoulders of great walls still thrusting between the flowers and
the roots of olive trees; a tall embanking wall, about ten feet high,
still enclosed and held part of the hillside. The blocks of stone were
well cut, large, and still fitted perfectly. At the very top of the hill
other remains of ancient buildings, of the acropolis itself, convinced
me that at one time the place must have been a citadel and a town of
quite sizeable proportions. Two large cisterns, or perhaps store-
rooms, lined with brick, are built deep down into the hill near its

highest point. From the top, where I stood, I could see across into the inner cove, to where *Astarte* rode at anchor, and where, if the harbour below were full or out of action, ships could shelter in safety. It seemed a good place to live, if not quite such a good place to defend. The Acropolis commanded a view of the open sea, westwards beyond Daseiá to Skiathos and Evvia, Cape Artemision and Trikeri; but there was an obvious danger of surprise attack: ships keeping close to the coast of Skopelos, coming from either direction, north or south, would remain invisible until they actually turned into the bay.

My guess is that Panormos was abandoned, in company with most sea-shore island towns, at some time between the third and seventh centuries A.D. At that period, such was the instability of the Aegean – ravages of pirates, invasions of barbarian Goths, Huns and Herules from the north and east – that most island capitals were shifted either inland, or better still to some easily defensible hill-top which also possessed a long view of every possible approach by sea. Alonnisos is a good example, where today the main village is still perched upon its mountain crest, high above the harbour and the surrounding seas. A look-out on watch up there could give several hours warning of the approach of any hostile fleet of ships, (it would have been safe to assume that all approaching ships were hostile), time for the men to gather and arm, families to be brought in from the outlying cottages or from the harbour below, time for the animals to be herded up into the shelter of the hill-top walls.

At Skiathos roughly the same thing happened: the islanders moved across the island to their 'kastro' on the wild north coast. At Glossa, the ancient Selinos, the villagers moved uphill, a considerable height, enough to discourage any but the most determined attacker. Now, of course, the Skiathites were returned to their fine original position. At Glossa and Alonnisos, they have started to go back, but as neither of the two landing places below them are particularly good, there is nothing except the tourists to draw them down again.

But Panormos was never reoccupied. Why not? Various explanations are put forward. Two German archaeologists who made a brief survey of the island about forty years ago suggest it was because the place was so cut off from the rest of the island. Communications are difficult as I know well, having many times come over the rough mule-track from Skopelos. Also, Panormos itself is very enclosed –

the valley is narrow, and not very long: not enough space I would guess for a capital village. One of the most cogent reasons, however, for its abandonment must have been its vulnerability to surprise attack.

Sitting now as I write, on the low cliff, with a view of the bay's entrance, the pine-tufted point – called significantly enough *Arapi*, the 'Arab' or 'Moor', I can imagine such an assault. Iannis Patsis is at this moment rowing his boat laden with firewood from the cove to the outer bay. He is the first to see them, the high prows of the galleys nosing silently round the point. We who are on land cannot understand his sudden hoarse shouts of fear, we are even inclined to smile at the way his hat has fallen off with his sudden violent effort at the oars. And then we see them too, the galleys, half a dozen of them perhaps, now that they are discovered throwing aside all attempt at silence, the timekeepers calling out the ever quickening stroke, oars flashing in the sun as they speed towards us. Beside me Spyro, who is planting a lemon tree, has dropped his spade and is waving his hands, crying out incoherently. Pandelis the builder, taking measurements for the foundations, is giving his assistants at the top of his voice a number of contradictory orders. Among these men there is, I regret to say, an element of panic. Most of them are throwing themselves on to their mules and donkeys – those fortunate enough to have brought them – and are making, literally, for the hills.

The attackers, as I suspected they might, have detached a segment of their fleet, two galleys, which are heading fast for the inner harbour. Iannis Patsis has jumped into the water only a few seconds before the foam-pushing prow of the first galley was on him, and as I now recall that Iannis cannot swim, I am beginning to understand how seriously he must regard the situation.

From the outer bay, over in the ancient town, I can hear a confused babble of voices, frantic screams of women, shouts of men. A murderous cry of triumph has burst from the racing ships. They make I must confess, a splendid if terrifying sight – white water swirling from fast-dipping oars, the armed men gathering already at the bows, brandishing swords, spears, ready to leap ashore as the keels ground on the beaches.

At the head of the cove Vangeli is repairing his jetty, and as usual for such watery work is dressed only in a vest and his pale green under-shorts. With him are Andrikos, Yiórgo and other stalwarts.

Here I know there will be a fight, though against such odds it will be hopeless. Vangeli is at a disadvantage without either trousers or shoes but has rushed to the retsina barn where the weapons are stored. An angry shout carries across to me: he has forgotten where he put the keys. Just as well. Now, they too have fled among the pines. Only I am left, having sacrificed myself in the interests of cheap journalism. My only hope is to wrap myself in my largest Red Ensign, and pray that the attackers are not ancestors of future beneficiaries of British colonialism. . . .

We cannot know how many times the ancient city was sacked: plunderings, burnings and massacres were too commonplace to be remarkable. One naval battle that took place in Panormos, however, has been recorded, by the historian Diodorus Siculus.

The date is 360 B.C. . . . 'Alexander, tyrant of Pherae, sent pirate ships against the Cyclades, stormed some and took many captives, then disembarking mercenaries on Peparethos' – as Skopelos was called at that time – 'put the city under siege. And when the Athenians came to the assistance of the Peparethians and left Leosthenes in command of the mission, Alexander attacked the Athenians. Actually the Athenians were blockading such of Alexander's soldiers as were stationed in Panormos. And since the tyrant's men attacked *unexpectedly* Alexander won an astonishing success. For he not only rescued the detachment at Panormos from the greatest danger but he also captured five Attic triremes and one Peparethian, and took six hundred prisoners. The Athenians, enraged', adds the historian, 'condemned Leosthenes to death as a traitor, and confiscated his property. . . .'

Yet perhaps the most important reason for abandonment of Panormos, and for it never being reoccupied, was the rival popularity of the town of Skopelos itself, in the place where it stands today.

Besides the strength of its castle there was also the rich and indeed the largest valley of the island sloping gently back from the shores of Skopelos Bay. This valley has no peer in the Sporades, even in Skiathos, for its constant supply of good water, the fertility of its earth. It was tempting, almost inevitable, to live so close to such natural wealth. The lack of a sheltered harbour remained its only and still potent drawback. But Skopelos Bay, and the bay of Ayios Konstantinos north-west of the castle were better than no harbour at all. In those early days when beaching of boats as opposed to anchoring them was the more common practice the disadvantages could not have been so telling. Later, with the building of sailing ships rather than rowing galleys, with the necessary deeper keels below, it was still possible to anchor in comparative shelter in the curve of Ayios Konstantinos Bay, as indeed during summer at least did the fleet of Skopelot merchant brigs that in the nineteenth century traversed the Black Sea and the length of the Mediterranean, carrying corn for others and the produce of oil and fruit, resin and wine from their own island.

What began as a necessity became in time a convenience. The islanders stayed where they were, and from the siting of their capital village it could be said that some of their special island characteristics have derived. Skopelots face the sea, and facing it northward they cannot conceal from themselves its real hostility; they work upon it, but they do not depend on it. They have their rich valley at their backs, and rely more upon the earth to live than upon the water.

And so Panormos remains, as Yiórgo in his Skopelos workshop once described it, τὸ λιμάνι τῆς σιωπῆς, 'the harbour of silence'. Not that the place was abandoned all at once. People must have continued to live there until well into the Middle Ages, and when the last law-abiding citizen left the crumbling ruins of Kastro in the valley, others of a different kind took their place around the shores of the inner cove. Panormos became a pirate lair, as notorious as once it must have been flourishing. After the pirates, in the heyday of Skopelot mercantile prosperity, Panormos was the winter harbour for the island's merchant marine. The old man, Vangeli's father-in-law, can remember when he was a boy seeing more than twenty Skopelot-owned brigs and schooners at their winter moorings in the cove; and it was to Panormos each January that the islanders came to take part in the ancient ceremony of 'blessing the sea', in which the priest throws a gold cross, or sometimes a ring, into the water, invoking the sea's protection of the ships that would sail upon her in the coming season.

The cottage by the retsina barn, now used to shelter Vangeli's resin workers during the summer, was once a custom's house; a boat-yard that turned out fair-sized caiques in the cove closed down fifty years ago. Only in the last century or so has Panormos become quite so desolate, so deserted. There is the ruin of Ayia Sophia, the Holy

Wisdom, burnt down by the Turks as Barba Yiorgi says, though perhaps destroyed many centuries earlier. All round the edges of the inner harbour are traces of ruins, the shells of cottages, heaps of old stone, and in some places the rubble continues into the water; and when those that are ruins today stood upright and were lived in there must have been others, all signs of them gone now, but ruins then, circling the bay. People have always lived in Panormos, and I believe that those who have done so cannot have helped but love the place. There is that feeling about it. We who planned to build in Panormos again, and live there, would be the first for a long time, and yet after all those who had gone before, the last. Because of this the past was important to me, and I had come to think that the old ghosts, the spirits of the place, if they were really looking on as I believed they were, would not disapprove.

9

Earth Tremors and Island Rivalry

The first shock came when I was buying rope in the little paint shop half-way up the steps. It came as a sensation of slight unsteadiness, lasted for only a couple of seconds and was immediately followed by the sound of falling masonry from next door. '*Seismós!*' I stepped briskly out into the July sunshine, in company with the shopkeeper and his brother, the coil of rope over my arm, still not really thinking in terms of earthquakes but assuming that a pile of bricks had collapsed in the next house where builders were at work.

Everything looked just as it always did, a hot windless morning of early summer, Skiathos harbour gleaming in its customary sultry lethargy. I walked down to where *Astarte* was moored, noticing that there were rather more people about on the front, and that the taverna cooks and waiters had come outside and were lounging about under the awnings. There were more people but there seemed to be less movement: they seemed to be standing about waiting, or listening for something. I bought some cigarettes at the kiosk, and as he handed me my packet the man said: 'Did you feel it? That's only the first – there'll be others . . .' and a grisled boatman at my side nudged me and grinned. '*Seismo!* But only a little one,' he patted me reassuringly on the arm, 'don't you worry about it. . . .'

The second tremor must have come while I was on the quay adjusting the gang-plank which had moved out of position. I didn't feel anything. I suppose I was still sceptical, because it wasn't until twenty minutes later, down in the cabin, that I heard the grind and grate of the anchor chain, a sinister sound that usually means that either the boat is dragging anchor or that the chain of some other craft has been dropped across mine. I came on deck quickly. It was evident now that more people were crowding the open-air café tables; there was a sense of expectancy about them, or at least a calculated calm. I saw little Iannis-from-Constantinople walking out between his tables, a tray of ouzos in his hands, walking delicately as if he expected someone to trip him. Panayioti hurried by me, grinning broadly. '*Seismo!* But it's nothing, absolutely nothing!' He seemed to be enjoying himself.

A small figure jumped aboard and sat down by me at the tiller. Kosta gave a long sigh. 'If you're on the sea,' he said by way of explanation of his sudden arrival, 'you're quite safe. So don't worry.'

Disregarding this advice I stepped ashore, faintly aware of that quickening of inner tension that I supposed must be a natural reflex in human beings when the very earth they stand on shows signs of no longer being quite as solid as they have always expected. I knew that tremors of this kind were fairly common on most Greek islands and in most parts of Greece. Every few summers in the Northern Sporades the islands shuddered gently in their sleep, as if remembering in their dreams some unspeakable horror of long ago. But the horror, after all, is never too far away, the nightmare always ready to be translated into reality. Santorin, in the south of the Aegean, is volcanic, an island that no one can convince himself is asleep for ever; the disasters in the Ionian Islands only a few years ago, and even more relevant to the Sporades, the great Volos earthquake of 1956 (Volos is less than thirty miles from Skiathos) in which hundreds of people perished, does not allow the subject to leave the minds of the islanders for long.

Perhaps also this archetypal, primitive fear gains secret strength from some atavistic memory of a darker age, before even the Olympian wielded his thunderbolt, before Poseidon the earth-shaker ground his teeth in the caverns of the sea: that dim time when man bowed in sacrifice of propitiation at the mouths of caves, at the entrances to the holes of snakes; and when the ground moved under them they knew it was the terrible Earth Mother turning in her dream, claiming her children.

Animals, and certain people, are said often to have a presentiment at the approach of an earthquake, and this occurred to me as I watched the mules on the quay waiting to unload the bricks from a big caique alongside, how they shied and backed into each other and would not be held steady by the muleteers. There were no less than seven tremors that day, none of them serious. It was not until much later that I realized that these were only the echoes of that gigantic upheaval that levelled the city of Skopje some two hundred and twenty miles to the north-west.

An old fisherman was sorting his nets on the quay a few yards from *Astarte*, and as I paused beside him he looked up at me and scowled. '*Theós!*' he said, God! 'Yes!' He nodded vehemently. 'God is angry, angry! Look at the world today, just look around you!'

I did as he suggested, and besides noting that Kosta was successfully beating off an assault of one of his friends who was trying to board the boat, saw nothing that was particularly at fault. The old man was very small and had a great tousle of short black hair; there was two weeks' growth of beard on his burnt, lined face, and his gnarled fingers worked with a sort of frenzy at the threads. He kept muttering to himself, then suddenly addressed me again. 'Look over there, just behind you —' Tourists, some of them Greek, were boarding a tripper caique bound for the beach at Koukounaries. 'Women, women half *naked!*' It was true that some of the women were wearing shorts.

The fisherman dropped his net and automatically accepted the cigarette I offered him. He looked me long and searchingly in the eyes. '*Bah*. Rotten, that's the world today. And there aren't enough men to help me with the nets, either! All the young men go off, to work on the big ships, indeed! Rotten, I said' – he shook his head with rich satisfaction – 'Oh, yes,' hurling my cigarette, unlit, into the sea, 'God will destroy us all. . . .'

I had to buy paraffin, and went to Jimmy Delhiyannis's shop where a group of men were holding forth on the present seismic crisis. The main question under discussion was the whereabouts of the earthquake's centre. Someone suggested Khalkis, and was at once shouted down: no, dreadful though it was, all the evidence pointed to Skopelos; Skopelos, was the centre all right. 'Weren't you leaving for Skopelos today?' someone asked me. I admitted that such had been my intention, and a thoughtful silence fell on the company. Jimmy leaned across his desk and addressed me earnestly. 'You know that the wires to Skopelos are broken?' He sat back. A big farmer who had directed me on my way to Kastro not long ago clapped me on the shoulder. 'I shouldn't go if I were you,' he warned grimly. 'A lot of damage there, that's what they say. . . .'

By the time I left Jimmy's shop with my can of paraffin I was almost persuaded that it would be an act of madness to venture into earthquake country just across the straits, that Skopelos by now was probably a heap of smoking rubble, and that no one would be wanting to go to Skopelos for a long, long time.

I cast off about noon, and as there was no wind, headed under motor to round the north cape of Skopelos, *Gourouni*, the Hog, where a blue-black swell sucked with a sinister rhythm at the base of the great cliffs. At least, I saw, the lighthouse was standing – or was it perhaps at a slight, a very slight angle? I didn't believe what I had been told in Skiathos, at least not all of it. My experience of quakes in Greece was limited to a tremor once in Khalkis, and once I had met and talked with a fisherman on Anaphe, an island near Santorin, who told me how at the time of the eruption he had been at sea between the two islands, and how he had known nothing until suddenly he had seen this huge sixty-foot high wall of green water bearing down at him. . . . He kept his nerve, turned his boat into it and rode safely over. He had been lucky: the other fishing boats drawn up on the beach of the little creek that passes for a harbour on Anaphe had been smashed out of recognition and swept hundreds of yards up the ravine. As little Kosta had said, it was probably safer at sea. . . .

The horizon to the north was empty, sea and sky melted in summer haze. There was no sign of any tidal wave. Yet as I progressed down the green wooded coast, approaching the last cape round which I would have that first and lovely view of Skopelos town, I couldn't help feeling anxious. What if there had been damage, serious damage? I thought of the people I knew in Skopelos, Vangeli and his family, Yiórgo, Grigor, Pandelis and others. . . . It hardly bore thinking of. And hadn't there been a serious earthquake once in Skopelos, long ago? According to Thucydides, in 427 B.C. the island suffered severe damage. It was the same earthquake that sent a tidal wave down the Evvian channel, wrecking the two Athenian triremes on watch at the island of Atalante. 'Also there happened at Peparethos (Skopelos) a certain rising of the water, but it broke not in; and a part of the wall, the town houses, and some few houses besides were overthrown by the earthquakes . . .' Two and a half thousand years ago, but what was that to these ancient seas, these scarred mountain tops?

It was only when I was moored safely in the harbour that I could be certain that nothing much could have happened. I sat at the café next door to Yiórgo's workshop and drank the coffee to which

Yiórgo always treated me every time I got back to the island. Yiórgo sat beside me, grinning hugely at my fears. Yes, they had felt the *seismo* all right, but only slightly. There had been no damage to houses or anything else. In fact the only untoward incident had involved Yiórgo himself. A rock about the size of his head, which meant it was quite a big rock, had fallen through the gap in the corner of his cracked and sagging ceiling. It had crashed on to a mirror, shattering it, and then bounced off harmlessly on to the floor.

All this was quite remarkably at variance with the gloomy forebodings with which I had been fed in Skiathos. It became all the more so when some time later the full effects of the tremors had been calculated and were made known. Skopelos had suffered no harm at all – with the exception of Yiórgo's rock. In Skiathos however fifteen houses had been damaged, though only four with any degree of seriousness. No one had been hurt.

Afterwards I realized I should have expected the sort of loaded comment I had heard in Skiathos. I had always been aware that there was no love lost between the two islands. On this occasion it had been a simple case of wishful thinking.

Once, at a time when I knew the islands only very slightly, I was having a drink with some Skiathite friends and asked them what they thought of their sister island Skopelos. 'Skopelos? A fine island, really. The only trouble is the lack of water there . . . you know, a bit barren. . . .'

I had repeated this remark in all innocence to friends in Skopelos. The reaction had been immediate and explosive. 'What! No water? Here in Skopelos? Good God, we have enough water to drown everyone in Skiathos!'

On another, later occasion I asked some Skopelots, though not so innocently this time, what they thought of Skiathos. 'Skiathos? Well, a beautiful island; certainly. Or rather, it would be, if it weren't for the *people* there . . .'

'The people?'

'Yes. You must have noticed it yourself. They're so *mean*, inhospitable. . . .' And a Greek can hardly say worse than that, especially of a fellow-countryman.

Skopelos prides itself on the generosity and hospitality of its inhabitants: they are proud to call themselves '*philókseni*', which means 'friendly to strangers', 'guest-lovers' – the Greek word '*ksénos*' significantly enough being the same for stranger and for guest. No one can vouch for Skopelot hospitality more wholeheartedly than I ; yet I cannot doubt that I would have received the same kindly treatment in Skiathos. What amused me always was the immense seriousness with which such utterly destructive remarks were handed out. 'Skiathos?' people would say, as if with an effort bringing to mind a place which they are surprised I should want to know about; and then that impressive pause, as if summoning unwillingly their powers of intellect to bear upon so trivial and unlikely a subject, to be considered for the first time . . . and finally the judgement itself, delivered with an air of such total and convincing impartiality that the deliberately hostile content of the words takes a moment or two to sink home.

I have noticed it several times, and admit that I have obtained much secret enjoyment from it, that whenever on an island in the Sporades one falls to discussing some neighbouring island, a sort of lugubrious atmosphere is created ; there is a tendency to use the past tense, as in a funeral oration and there are long, reflective silences ; it feels as if one is talking about some poor, departed, worthless, and probably criminal relative, whose considerable failings are not really to be blamed on himself, and which call forth not anger or bitterness but rather patience and sympathy.

The island that gets the worst of this, and is roundly condemned by both Skiathites and Skopelots, is that odd man out, Skyros, separated from the others by forty miles of sea. As Vangeli put it : 'You see, Skyros is roughly two hundred years behind everyone else. They're *várvari* down there, barbarians, that's all . . .' The compliment is returned by the Skyriots, in a different though no less effective way. Mention of Skiathos or Skopelos there brings no reaction whatsoever. They have never heard of them.

What is interesting, and surprising, is the extraordinary lack of contact between the islands of the Sporades. Skyros of course is a special case, being so far to the south, entirely on its own, and with its own caique communications not with her sister isles but with Kymi on Evvia to the west. Skopelos and Skiathos however are separated by only seven miles of sea ; they share the same caiques, the *Paskhális* and *Katerina* that twice or three times a week pass from one to the other and back again, yet the two islands seem to ignore each other's existence. With Alonnisos there is a slight difference: that island seems willingly enough to fall under the wing of Skopelos. A small caique runs daily between the two, and in summer many Alonnisiots come to work – as at Panormos – in the pine forests of the larger island. Geographically, and also emotionally, it seems that the Sporades are divided into three remarkably separate groups: Skyros in the south; Skiathos in the west, close to the mainland; and Skopelos, Alonnisos and the outer Sporades in a group together in the centre and north-east.

Skopelos has always been the 'capital' of the Sporades. All the modern harbour works in Skiathos have been built by Skopelot builders – most of it done by Pandelis, whom I had engaged for Panormos – and through some technicality and because of her junior status Skiathos does not have complete control over her own harbour. I was at Skiathos when a new 'cleaning up' policy was about to be enforced, mainly for the alleged benefit of tourists. Various shacks and rather picturesque market stalls had been set up on the quay under the hill, and efforts by the Town Council to remove them were being firmly blocked by the Town Council of Skopelos. The anomaly of Skopelot control is particularly irritating to Skiathites because their harbour is so much busier than Skopelos. 'We have a harbour-master,' I was told indignantly in Skiathos, 'a *real* harbour-master, dressed in proper white uniform, and sailors guarding the water-front. In Skopelos what do they have?'

Rhetorical pause, which I fill, defensively: 'Well, they have Kosta . . .'

'Yes, but what is Kosta? Does he wear uniform? Are there any sailors under him? No. He's really just a custom's officer, and that's all Skopelos needs. They have no *right*. . . .' And so on, while an affectionate picture of Kosta passes through my mind, walking with slow dignity along by the quiet waterfront to the taverna at the corner where he will down a few little glasses of *tsipuro* to pass the time. 'Δεν έχει κόίνουση,' as he had said to me rather sadly, 'There's no movement, no coming and going. . . .'

Another ever continuing source of friction between the two islands is tourism. The gentler scenery of Skiathos gives an impression of comfortable ease: across the straits the island of Skopelos with her high mountainous skyline, purple and blue, is inclined to forbid rather than attract. Most of the tourists in July and August are

Greeks, holidaying from their city jobs in Volos, Salonika and Athens. Whole familes come out and spend a month or more in the private houses and small hotels, and their husbands join them for a couple of weeks or as long as they can. Skopelos has fewer tourists, and those that come have usually been there before : they come every year, the regulars. Skiathos has geared itself more successfully to greater numbers, and to the modern requirements of holiday makers, especially the young : already there are two 'night-clubs', at least one juke-box, with the threat of others on the way.

One thing that Skiathos needs badly, from the tourist point of view, and which Skopelos is about to get, is a good modern-style hotel. Rolf Mühleisen, a young German, arrived some time ago with a friend of his, Armin, and they were later joined by Rolf's younger sister Barbara. The plan was to buy some land on the edge of Skopelos Bay and build a small hotel. From the start they ran into difficulties, but finally Rolf managed to buy a strip a few minutes' walk from the village at the head of the bay. An architect was acquired and attractive plans drawn up, a team of builders came from Volos and began to dig the foundations.

The land they had bought was near the site of an ancient temple, identified by a stele discovered there some years before as a shrine of Asklepios ; at that place, on the beach, where the sea year by year advances, washing away the low cliff of sand and earth, blocks of white marble have already been uncovered by the waves, and there are other remains farther in the water, with a scattered multitude of sherds. It was reasonable to assume that on an island the size of Skopelos a temple of Asklepios could not have been very extensive : Rolf's land should have been clear.

Everything went well, until the first pick hit upon marble, and as the diggers worked deeper the outline of walls began to appear, marble blocks and traces of mosaic floor. By chance the director of the Magnisian archaelogical office was in Skopelos at the time. Word reached him of the discovery, he hurried over and in a matter of hours an official order had arrived stopping all further work. The government took over the site. Rolf has spent some weeks arguing with ministers and their staff in Athens – ministers who were usually 'away' or 'out' – and has eventually extracted a promise of partial compensation, though when this money will be paid is anybody's guess. Having lost a year, with a large hole already knocked in his slim budget, one would have thought that he would have given up. But he is negotiating for another piece of land, not far from the first place, which in fact promises to be a more suitable and even more attractive site for a hotel; and he will go back to Germany, work, earn some more money and return to start all over again. Rolf is wondering, rather gloomily, how much more groundwork he is likely to do for archaeologists before he's finished, and is trying not to guess the name of the next god or goddess whose shrine he might uncover.

Foreign tourists are still comparatively rare in the Sporades, but their numbers are increasing every year. Skiathos is already in danger of becoming that sad creature of illusion, a tourist island, and one wonders whether Skopelos though sheltered by her ramparts of mountain and her encircling sea can hold out much longer.

Of course the islanders do not look at it this way. Skiathos wants more and more people, and Skopelos looks enviously across the narrow seas. In Skopelos they say that glib and shady Skiathites board the *Kyknos* in Skiathos harbour and persuade the tourists to get off there and not waste their time travelling on to Skopelos; and the sinister accusation is returned by Skiathites, who imagine the same treacherous blandishments offered to tourists in Skopelos, when the *Kyknos* arrives there first on her way from Kymi.

There has been rivalry between the two islands for as long as any-one can remember, and probably ever since they were first inhabited. At least the Skiathites cannot pin on their sister-isle the attempted theft of the 'Swinging Panayia', though at first they tried to do so.

This near-disaster, Gus told me, took place at the beginning of the century, when he was a boy. The ikon was so called because it had been miraculously discovered, many years before, hanging on the branch of a pine tree in the hills near Koukounaries. The woodcutter who found it brought it back to the village where it was placed in a church and because of its miraculous arrival was long venerated by the islanders. (The woodcutter, incidentally, later cut down the pine tree by mistake, and was immediately struck dead.)

Some priests were visiting Skiathos many years later and paid their respects to the holy relics on the island, among which was this ikon, the 'Swinging Panayia'. Early the next morning, before dawn, when the caique that had brought them was about to depart, somebody saw one of the priests leaving the church with a bulky parcel wrapped up in his robes. Suspicious, he ran into the church, and found the ikon gone from its place.

News of the theft spread through the village in a few minutes. The church bells were rung, and the islanders, woken from their night's sleep, poured out into the streets and rushed down to the harbour. Gus was among them. He remembers the occasion well because he was woken by the tolling bells and neighbours hammering on the door of his father's house, and in the hurry and confusion he pulled on his trousers back to front. The caique with the priests and the stolen ikon was already some distance from the shore but there was no wind and the vessel lay becalmed in the bay. The Skiathites put out in a fleet of rowing boats, and in face of their indignant anger the ikon was hurriedly handed over to them, and was later replaced with much ceremony and thanksgiving in its original position. There had been grave suspicion that the thieving priest was a Skopelot, but fortunately it was discovered that he came from Evvia.

There is another story, though this must be assigned to the realm of distant legend, how once, long ago, the islanders of Skopelos being jealous of that ring of islands that protects Skiathos harbour from the south, set off in an armada of boats, attached strong chains to the islands and began trying to tow them away. Only after a prolonged and terrible fight, say the Skiathites, were the chains dislodged and the Skopelots beaten off and forced to retire. The Skopelots never tried it again, and the islands still remain to shelter Skiathos Bay from southerly storms.

Goat-Hunt to Iura

A telephone-call from Vangeli found me in Skiathos: an expedition to one of the remotest islands of the Sporades, which I had been invited to join, was ready to set off from Skopelos: I must leave Skiathos at once. I had planned to go with Gus to his farm in the hills the next morning, and see the Monastery of the Evangelist, but goat-shooting in Iura only took place once a year, and I had been looking forward to the event for some time. Skyros may have been famous in the olden times for the quality of its goats, but it never had anything like *capra aegragus gmelin*. . . .

The goats of Iura are a special breed, unique almost, akin to the Caucasian ibex, peculiarly robust, tall and with magnificent curved horns; and with expressions on their bearded faces which make the usual contemptuous leer of the domestic animal seem almost respectful by comparison. Once, some time before, I had arrived in Skopelos to be told by Yiórgo and others that an 'animal psychologist', a young Englishman, had specially come up from Athens, had hired a boat and gone to Iura for a few days to study in closer perspective the habits of this isolated species. I met him when he came back. He told me he had bruised his feet over countless jagged rock paths and lain in wait and watched from behind impenetrable thickets the thrashing of ram against ram, long horns interlocked, butting each other into insensibility or flight, while the ring of she-goats chewed thoughtfully at the occasional thistles within their reach and appeared not unduly perturbed at the result of the impassioned conflict. One ram, they seemed to be thinking, was much like another.

The Greek government takes a keen and proprietary interest in the goats of Iura. The only man who lives on the island is the official goat-keeper, who crouches with his wife in a little cottage on one of the few relatively level pieces of rock, high up in the south of the island. His job is not so much to administer to the needs of the goats – they look after themselves, and don't care for interference at any range – but to protect them from poachers, hungry fishermen who might keep a rusty shotgun under their decks, or more organized expeditions from the mainland or the neighbouring islands; though the nature of the terrain in itself acts as a powerful deterrent to most, and is the goats' best defence – indeed the reason why they have managed to survive for so long at all. Nearby is a small chapel and another single room for visiting officials and others who feel tempted, and obtain the necessary permission, to observe this valiant breed subsisting in their natural habitat. Not many people seem to take this unusual opportunity.

As far as the islanders of Alonnisos and Skopelos are concerned the goats of Iura are interesting from one rather crude point of view: meat. Although it would seem surprising that even goats could survive on such impossibly barren and stupendous crags, the truth is that they not only survive but multiply; so fast indeed that it is necessary every now and then to thin them out, shoot a number, and so prevent that dread phantom of the modern world: overpopulation, with all its attendant ills. Yet most people, while deploring the use of shot-guns on the island, would hesitate to carry the comparison between goats and human beings too far. For Iura there is no altern-ative to occasional bloodshed. Even the harassed welfare-workers in the Far East, struggling to instruct the rings of squatting peasants with the techniques of birth control might think themselves well off in their torpid rice fields: the problems involved in setting up a dis-tribution centre of contraceptives for goats on a cliff top in Iura do not bear thinking about.

In any case there is another factor to be considered. Occasionally during the past centuries goats of the domesticated variety have been brought across to browse on the sparse vegetation of the island, and the rare and noble strain of *capra aegragus gmelin* has gradually become, in parts, diluted; and if animals must be killed it is these particular descendants of a lesser breed that the authorities prefer to have destroyed. On Skopelos people had been talking about our expedition for some time – it was just a question of waiting for the permission to arrive from Volos.

I had seen only a little of Iura myself, sailing at a respectful dis-tance under its tall forbidding cliffs, where eagles glide and the goats when they move seem like ants crawling upon the faces of a preci-pice, and I was interested to see more of it; so I answered my summons to Skopelos the next morning, early. I might have known that Vangeli's voice of almost desperate urgency over the crackling line between the two islands was not much more than ingrained mannerism. When finally I moored at the quayside, ready to leave as planned at midday, I was met by a scene of total inactivity. I found Vangeli playing *tavli* under the plane trees.

'Well. . . ?' I began, expecting I wasn't quite sure what – whatever people need for a goat-shoot: a heap of rifles, food, ammunition, blankets, wine. . . . Vangeli waved a cheerful hand at me, shook his dice violently, and hurled them with a curse across the board, his eyes alight with the battle of the game.

'Did you have a good journey?'

'Fine, thanks. When do we start – what's the plan exactly?'

'Start?' He looked at me blankly.

'These goats, Iura. We were going. . .'

'Yes, of course!' His tone was reproachful, as if it was I who had forgotten what it was all about. 'Notice please that we start at six o'clock. Tomorrow morning.'

'Good,' I found myself saying, and ordered some coffee. After all, what did it matter if we started the next day – probably better to start in the early morning, anyway. And as for the monastery on Skiathos, another day when I went there next would do just as well. Besides, it was certainly pleasant sitting here in the shade, the green hills ringing the bay, and I was glad to be back in Skopelos even though I had left it for only a week.

The forestry official on Skopelos, whose district included all the Sporades, was a man called Tomás. It was under his protective jurisdiction that the goats of Iura enjoyed their largely untroubled existence. A goat-shoot such as the one now being organized could only take place under his direct supervision, and it had been to him that the news of the government permission had been sent. I knew Tomás quite well, serious, likeable, young, who was remarkable in Skopelos for never being seen in anything but the most stylish and sober of dark suits. He was always carefully shaved, clean-shirted, with tie and stiff collar. His shoes were always beautifully polished. On Skopelos where suits and ties only appeared on Sundays, the rest of the week being happily lived in the oldest and most varied combinations of easy clothes, his consistent elegance invested him with an unusual distinction. Tomás was well liked on the island, a friend of Vangeli's and a favourite of Makhi and Eleni. He was to lead the expedition, to see fair play between man and goat, to count the carcasses and as far as possible to ensure that the right kind of goat got shot.

Preparations, such as they were, were completed that night. We sat in Sari's taverna eating *mézes* of liver fried in garlic and oil and drinking wine. A stream of men came in to report to Tomás their readiness for departure and their legal ownership of a firearm in a condition safe enough not to endanger too much the lives of others. I had the courage to point out that I had no wish to shoot any goats myself, and this went down better than I expected. At first it was thought that this was because I had no gun of my own, and I had some difficulty in politely rejecting numerous generous offers of weapons that I could use. In this as usual I was helped out by Vangeli. He himself took no pleasure in shooting, preferring to re-serve his energies for catching fish. It was agreed then that *Astarte* and those on board her should be present as observers, rather than take any active participation. Grigor and Vangeli would go with me and do some fishing; another caique filled with the real hunters would meet us at Iura the following evening – providing of course that the weather remained suitable.

We were to leave at six o'clock: such had been Vangeli's strict instructions to Grigor and myself; but it was not until after eight that we finally cast off and headed out towards Ayios Yiorgios in a slightly troubled May sea. We had to put in at Patatiri to collect a half-gallon flask of wine, a matter of a few minutes but as always, when Vangeli is concerned, extended itself over more than an hour. At the quay a dozen people drew Vangeli into conversation on various highly important subjects, it was then inevitable that a certain amount of coffee should be drunk, so that by the time we were sail-ing north-east in the straits between Alonnisos and Xeró it was after midday, and there would be no time for any fishing at Kyra Panayia that afternoon to which Grigor especially had been looking forward.

Grigor, a keen angler with much fishing experience in the United States – of little use to him in the Sporades – was a proud possessor of a magnificent plastic and steel American-made fishing-box. This splendid object which always accompanied us on such expeditions was originally filled with many gorgeous and multi-coloured flies, spinners, silver and gilt 'spoons', all carefully and symmetrically arranged in trays that slid in and out with fascinating facility, artificial bait of colour and material cunningly designed to whet the appetite, stimulate the greed and satisfy even the most perverted tastes of every and any fish in sea or river worthy of its fins. Unfortunately, as Grigor had been forced sadly to conclude, Aegean fish in their attitude to food lack the least refinement, the smallest sophistication; their eating habits are uncommonly brutal and utterly unimaginative. Not for them the rainbow glitter of swivelling steel, the exotic glow of shaded plastic, while the lifelike and terrified grimace of juicy siblings struck in simulated flight leave them quite unmoved. Instead they are more than content with freshly cut chunks of their friends or relatives, dangled with suitable consideration for depth and locality, in front of their noses.

The crude eating habits of Greek fish was a subject to Grigor for constant and rueful reflection. He had abandoned his fine fishing-rods long ago, though not without much painful teasing from Vangeli, and now was equipped like any other Sporadic fisherman with that unromantic minimum of gear, all that is necessary to catch a fish from the smallest of quarter-pound *barboúni* to the biggest of forty-pound *rofós*: a roll of nylon thread wound round a piece of wood, a few hooks of different sizes, some lead weights, and a sharp knife. These now were the lonely occupants of Grigor's shining fishing-box; except in the bottom tray where still were kept for sentimental reasons a few brilliant flies, a spinner or two, and a much thumbed photograph of himself at the lower end of an enormous curved fishing-rod, playing some truly sophisticated but insufficiently intelligent American fish from the banks of a wooded stream in the Middle West.

That morning as we travelled with Vangeli at the helm, Grigor had spent a couple of hours with his fishing-box carefully baiting every hook on his line. Now that it was clear there would be no fishing that day he was sitting on a canvas stool on deck patiently unbaiting the hooks one by one, because although the barbarous fish of the Sporades insist on only the simplest of diets they also insist that it should be scrupulously fresh. Occasionally Grigor muttered something about Vangeli's incapability of judging time, his inconsideration for others, to all of which he received only a few snorts of derision from the unrepentant helmsman who continued to hum happily to himself as he steered us on.

As we came out of the straits and made for Kyra Panayia, the high purple massif of Iura towering behind it, we decided to pay a visit to the little monastery on the east coast of the island before us, and perhaps beg some supper from the monks there, before sheltering for the night in Planidhi, in the north.

It was nearly dusk when we turned into the indentation in the cliffs that marks the monastery's only landing place. An anchor out to the centre and a warp to the rocks was sufficient for the short stay we intended; Vangeli reminded me that this was not a good anchorage, and certainly it was clear that any wind, except from the west, would roll in a dangerous sea.

Steps had been cut long ago in the cliffside. We took a torch and climbed in single file, emerging some hundreds of feet higher at the gate of the monastery. Vangeli battered at the door and called out to the monks by name. For several minutes there was no reply, and we waited while the fading sunset flared up once more under a line of clouds massing beyond Iura. A light wind sighed in the branches of a fig-tree beside us, sending the leaves in dancing silhouette against the crimson sky. For a moment we listened, all three in silence, to the leaves in the wind while the night swept up out of the east across the sea, engulfing Piperi, washing in waves of gathering darkness at the foot of the cliffs upon which we stood.

Vangeli threw himself against the door once more, and at last there was the sound of footsteps and the clank of bolts being withdrawn. A whiskered face poked through a crack that had opened between the double doors; in a moment they were flung wide. Vangeli had been recognized and with a shout was dragged inside by a small dark-gowned figure and embraced. We followed into a courtyard and up wooden stairs, along a balcony where the scent of flowers was strong in the darkness, and entered a long room lit by a single oil lamp.

The inmates of the monastery, one priest and one monk, were in the middle of their evening meal. The priest, black-bearded and broad-shouldered, sat at the head of the table and the monk who had led us in, a little fellow with pointed nose and ears, humorous darting brown eyes and streaks of greasy hair falling over his pale cheeks, sat at his right hand. Vangeli knew the monk well, and they joked with each other throughout the meal, while the priest kept refilling our glasses. They had few visitors on this remote cliff-top, and they seemed glad of our company.

A wind had sprung up during our supper, rattling the wooden shutters of the monastery windows, rustling the vines across the courtyard. As we stumbled down the outer stairs from the upstairs room, pleasantly full of the monastery's heavy wine, we were somewhat sobered to feel the strength in the wind's gusts and to see the clouds as they rode in high columns across the moon. Good-byes were hurried. The monastery gates were shut behind us, the flickering lantern of the little monk disappeared. The moon was not entirely obscured, and every now and then swam out from behind the clouds to throw its pale light over the cliffs and the gleaming sea far below.

I was worried that the anchor might be caught in some boulder on the sea-bottom, a common enough hazard in those waters, and so delay us still further in this unprotected cove. Grigor and I climbed aboard, and I started the motor. Vangeli took back the dinghy to free the stern anchor that he had wrapped round the rocks; there was already a heavy swell under the cliffs, a forestaste of what might be coming, and Vangeli slipped on the rocks and nearly fell. The bow anchor came up easily.

We had to make a decision: whether to go back to Ayios Petros, the bay in the south of the island, or to attempt to get into Planidhi on the northern side, facing Iura. Wind and sea were building up from the north, but as yet were nothing serious. To go to Ayios Petros would mean a late arrival at Iura the next morning, but the trouble about Planidhi was the difficulty in getting into it. The entrance is narrow, less than a hundred feet across, a winding channel between the hills. Even by day, the mouth of this 'canal' is hard to recognize, and at night the difficulties are increased by the presence of a small island called Sphika, the 'Wasp', across the entrance.

The moon was still fighting free of clouds and I brought out the Aldis lamp from the cabin, plugged it in by the mast and flashed its powerful beam round the base of the cliffs. It seemed to work perfectly, which was a pleasant surprise to me, and that combined perhaps with the good wine we had drunk and the drama of our situation – heaving under moon and racing clouds, the eerie black towers of the cliffs above us – encouraged us to make the bolder choice of Planidhi.

Unfortunately, by the time we rounded the north-east cape of Kyra Panayia, the moon had passed as if for ever behind a fast moving wall of cloud. As we turned along the north coast of the island, about half a mile off, it was only just possible to make out the outline of cliffs and headlands on our left, marked more clearly though less pleasantly by spouts of white foam from waves breaking on the rocks at their feet.

As it was unwise to move in closer to the cliffs and impossible to see where we were in the darkness, I made a calculation – speed of the boat, approximately four knots against this rising wind and sea, and the distance, about one sea-mile, before turning in towards Sphika and the entrance channel to Planidhi. Fifteen minutes later I went to the bows and hung on to the stays with the Aldis lamp ready while Vangeli, being Admiral of the Northern Sporades – an admiral too who had earned his rank I felt from practical experience rather than any automatic seniority rise – stood at the helm.

I had been into Planidhi several times before, but never at night. Sphika, like the low dark back of a submarine, surfaced dimly ahead. The beam of the lamp picked out the rocks to port and starboard, and going slow ahead and rolling we closed and slid into the channel. As we moved through and on into the main expanse of bay a rift in the clouds let out the moon, and the great smooth hills that curve steeply into this sea-lake shone like polished bones; the surface of the water was suddenly calm, wavelets ruffled by the wind glittering like a thousand eyes.

I call Planidhi 'Jason's Harbour'. It is almost certain that the Argonauts, like anyone else before or since crossing the Aegean at this point, would have used Planidhi as a last shelter before the seventy-mile hop over to Lemnos. I like to think, too, that they put into Panormos the night before, but it might just as well have been Skiathos, and more likely still, Staphylos – in order to pick up the hero who had given his name to the settlement he had founded on the south coast of Skopelos. With Staphylos was also his brother Phanos, both sons of Ariadne and Dionysos, who joined the expedition together.

Planidhi is perhaps the most perfect and most sheltered natural harbour in the Aegean. The most violent storms cannot make even an impression within, so narrow is the entrance and so fortunate the obstruction of Sphika across its mouth. Even by day a stranger, once he is well inside, looking back for the channel he came in by, will have difficulty in pointing it out. The tall hills sweep down on all sides, bare for the most part except for a few wild olives and the usual scrub and low bushes of the Sporades. The harbour is divided into two bays, the most westerly having a sandy beach at its head, and it is these I imagine the *Argo* must have been drawn up while the heroes built their fire and sacrificed to the gods, now that the first and easiest stage of their journey was over.

Probably, too, they stole a few goats to roast on their fire. Goats are still kept on Kyra Panayia: a family from Alonnisos camps there during the summer in a tumbledown stone-and-wood shack by the beach, and in the early mornings and evenings the slopes around the bay come alive with scattered pairs of horns and dappled bodies gathering to the sound of innumerable bells and the hoarse cries of a woman in a red shawl, the whistles of the goatherd in his broad straw hat and ragged leather leggings.

We dropped anchor in the easterly bay, because there is less wind there. In the darkness another caique loomed up, tied to the rocks ahead, and we recognized *Theodoráki*, the caique of Kosta of Vassiliko, on a fishing expedition as usual. Kosta must have been asleep as we came in, but woke up, if not because of the engine at least from Vangeli's repeated shouts across the water. We exchanged a few hails and compared personal weather forecasts for the next day before fixing the anchor light and stretching out below to sleep.

Planidhi is not the most beautiful bay of the Sporades. The water is hardly ever clear, being of a strange milky colour. The shapes of the bare gigantic hills give the place a certain grandeur, especially at night and in stormy weather, but the atmosphere after a couple of days locked up there grows oppressive; like waiting at the bottom of a volcanic crater – safe enough, but one wants to get out.

I have not discovered any ancient remains at Planidhi, though a fisherman from Patatiri, who knows these outer islands well, found some years ago a number of coins at the bay's entrance, opposite the island of Sphika. Finding that he could buy nothing with them, he threw them away; and unfortunately he cannot remember any details of their design or stamp, except that they appear to have been silver.

K

Very different is the bay of Ayios Petros in the south-west of Kyra Panayia. At the head of one of the many inlets that indent the bay, behind a tiny island called Melissa, 'the Bee', is a beach covered with fragments of ancient pottery. The sherds have fallen from a bank, neatly cross-sectioned by the weather, and in the bank itself there are many more of these broken clay pieces, some of them painted with black though most quite rough work – all of them from a foot to three feet below the present surface of the earth. Near by is the remains of some masonry, the curved part of a wall, a well perhaps, the blocks large and well-fitted.

At Ayios Petros you may stand upon crumbling pottery and look south across the dazzling blue inlets of the bay, out past the headlands to the tall purple bluffs of Alonnisos towering over the sea. People lived here, once; one thousand, two thousand years ago. Even the sadness of such lonely places, the conventional though still effective plaint of a solitary bird in this four dimensional silence, even these are offset by the brilliance of the light and sea, the wind rushing out of the blue depths of sky. The sense of desolation in Greek ruins, as at Ayios Petros, is often overlaid, for me, with some other feeling – a sort of triumph perhaps. 'Once,' the ruins say, 'we lived'. It is enough.

I was woken at the dark and outrageous hour of four in the morning. Vangeli was already making coffee, and threatening to start the engine. I have long realized that to do anything, go anywhere with Vangeli means that I get very little sleep. There is always, in Vangeli's company, a feeling of continual emergency. I suspect that one reason why no one is allowed to sleep much is because Vangeli himself sometimes suffers from insomnia, though this he denies strongly. No, there are always good reasons why we must start so early – the weather, for instance, or there's so much to do when we get to wherever we're going, or simply that it is so much *better* to travel before sunrise, more beautiful, more satisfactory in every way; and usually, once I am up, I have grudgingly to admit that he is right.

And so it was on that morning, as with cups of coffee in our hands we nosed out of Planidhi in the slow red dawn, and taking advantage of the much abated northerly still blowing, set sail for Iura.

The caique-load of goat-hunters arrived at Megalovalla, one of the island's few landing places, a little before us, and most of them were already scattered and out of sight among the rock paths over the cliffs. *Astarte* was to collect hunters and their trophies wherever necessary from the shore; and Vangeli and Grigor were there especially to fish, and this we did, sailing up the west coast of the island picking capes and deep inlets where I would stay in charge of the boat, while they floated about in the dinghy.

The sea around Iura is very deep – sometimes two or three hundred feet close under the cliffs. On a clear day the water is of a fine ultramarine colour, shading away to turquoise and green over the backs of great white boulders that rise up like towers from the sea-bottom and yet still fathoms below the surface, their foundations lost in a blue-black void that even the slanting antennae of the sun's rays can never penetrate.

There is a place called Platania some way up the coast, shelves of grey rock over the sea with a few plane trees above, and as usual where there are planes there is water – a fine spring of ice-cold water with a modern inscription by the benefactor from Alonnisos who built a drinking trough for the wild goats and a bronze spout for the fishermen. An archaeologist has identified in the rough rock platforms the base of an ancient temple, probably of Poseidon, though to the casual and unscholarly traveller like myself there is little to be seen that might encourage such a belief. The spring and the rock shelves are used now by fishermen who sometimes spend weeks from their homes cruising about these waters famous for their abundance of fish.

Pliny and others called Iura by the name of 'Gerontia', which in classical Greek means 'old men'. Why the island should have been so named is something of a mystery. Was it because of the goats, white-bearded as they are, that flourished even in that age? Or, as a friend, a classical scholar, suggested once when we were exploring the coast in *Astarte*: people may have been more sensible and more ruthless in those days, and may have exiled their elders to the island when they became senile and a menace to society. Indeed the name may have a double derivation: a place of exile for old men who behave like old goats. . . . *Old goat.* One's instincts revolt at such an appellation being ever applied to oneself, yet the eventuality cannot be altogether discounted. Maybe I should look ahead a little and rent from the monks of Athos, who own Iura, a place under one of those plane trees where one day I can rest my old, rebellious bones and only goats, fish and eagles, who are tolerant of such things, can observe my antics.

We found a fishing boat at Platania when we anchored there to eat at midday. Two young men, blackened by the sun and a week's growth of beard, had lit a fire and were cooking *kakaviá*, fish soup, and invited us to join them.

The deck of *Astarte* was by now covered with rather sad-looking and bloody carcases of once magnificent specimens of wild ram. I had heard and seen very little of the shooting. Occasionally the distant echoes of a shot would rebound from the crags, and down the steep ravines that now and then split the coastline of cliffs would stagger a man bowed under the weight of an enormous dead goat; he would hail us, and get his prize transferred first to the dinghy and then to *Astarte*. The bodies were now covered with pieces of canvas, because of the flies and the increasing heat. That evening when everyone collected again at Megalovalla it was decided to continue the shoot the next day, and since the weather remained steady we anchored in the inlet, and both Grigor and Vangeli were able to demonstrate the art of grilling fish over an open fire, boiling green *hórta* and frying potatoes.

The dead goats were transferred to the caique and the following afternoon when we set sail for Skopelos again I had to face an uneasy paradox in my feelings: I was glad that the nightmare for the Iura goats was over, and hoped too that the slaughter (of about twenty-five) was really for the good of those remaining, and I also looked forward to the contents of those great copper dishes that would be coming out of the ovens, for days on end, in Skopelos town.

Tourist Salad Days

Towards the end of June there is a stirring in the Sporades, a feeling of expectancy: the tourist season is about to begin.

The little hotels on Skiathos and Skopelos have had their new coats of paint; now they are ready and waiting. In private houses all over Skiathos village families are drawing closer together, as far as living-space is concerned, contracting like concertinas: Every family that has or can find a spare room in the house is busy spring-cleaning it, turning mattresses and laying out white linen, while self-styled plumbers have a busy time putting in order those strangely indispensable modern appliances to which they know foreigners attach so much importance – the lavatory, and if such a luxury exists, the shower.

The 'night-club' in Skiathos is about to open. The new juke-box which has been sitting in Taki's smart café on the front, seeming all these warm early summer evenings to have gone mad with shaking power, blasting out a dozen times over and over again tunes that were popular once last year and that now set the bones of their unwilling listeners rattling with fury – this monster is about to be moved. . . .

Gerry and I have been playing chess these otherwise peaceful evenings, and surely, if it hadn't been for the juke-box roaring at my ear, I would have won at least one game. Now I shall have my opportunity. They are carrying it up to Bourtsi, six men under it, a grinning, bejewelled idol of the machine mass-media age, receiving a treatment worthy of its exalted status, for there before it run and dance the children while the porters in slow step sway and stagger, and behind and on every side a small crowd is gathering to escort the chromium god across the sandy causeway, up past the statue of Papadiamandis, between the pines and by the red-roofed school to the site of its new temple. The late afternoon sun strikes a last flash from phony chryselephantine armour; the procession moves up out of sight between the trees. Gerry is pondering a move that may cause my downfall. It does, and I resign. But how can I concentrate in this silence. . . .

Along the quay are lined the tripper caiques, boats with rows of wooden seats, long awnings, ready to ply a rapid passenger service to the beaches of Lalária and Koukounariés, round-the-island tours, to Kastro and Akladiés. In a few weeks, at about nine every morning, the harbour will look like the scene of some medieval sea-battle. Most of the caiques have exhaust pipes the size of cannon that stick out horizontally at deck level on each side. When they start their engines together, puffs of smoke belching from the mouth of every cylinder, it seems exactly as if they are delivering broadsides into each other at point-blank range.

The tavernas of both islands, too, are gearing themselves for the rush, hiring waiters from Volos for the season, black-coated professionals skilled at juggling with plates and orders, who will be on their feet fourteen hours in twenty-four, while the taverna owner himself will be lucky to close his eyes for two. Skiathos is ready. And even now some tourists are arriving, just off the *Paskhális*, led with exquisite politeness to rooms or tables, while the fishermen and locals turn from their conversations to eye these shy newcomers with a novel interest soon to be dulled if not extinguished altogether by familiarity and the sheer volume of those about to come.

In Skopelos preparations echo those in Skiathos, but here the evidence is not so clear, and the feverish atmosphere so apparent on her sister isle is absent. George Kaliantzis is getting ready to step up production of his marvellous chocolate cakes, the *baklavá*, *kataifi*, and the rest. His small white-coated figure is becoming a familiar sight now, skipping under the plane trees with his morning tray of *tirópidhes* (flake-pastry triangles stuffed with hot cheese), and people have already begun to estimate, in whispers, as they do every year, the staggering profits he is likely to make again this season.

Over by Yiórgo's workshop Mad Yiannis is mustering the female members of his family, his aunt, mother, wife, and if only she could walk, his grandmother, drilling them to their tasks behind the counter and among the copper cooking pans and pots, and sitting down between whiles to shake his white head in hopeless desperation. . . . No wonder Yiannis is worried with all those women chattering round him. Yiannis too has hired a waiter from Volos this summer, a burly young man called Stephanos, already popular because of his sense of humour, and there are two little boys, Spyraki and Onouphri, so small that when they scamper towards you with a pile of dishes in their arms you cannot but wonder whether you are a victim of some cartoon hallucination and being attacked by an army of plates with legs. All this assistance is just as well.

'It's not going to be like last year, oh no!' says Yiannis to me with a sudden attempt at firmness as I sip the glass of wine he has offered me. Last year he tried to do everything himself, helped only by one boy who, when the pressure became too great one evening, simply ran away. But by that time customers had become so furious with waiting for their dinners that Yiannis was forced to retire behind the safe ramparts of his smoking stoves, and that gentle, vague expression came to his face, with only the eyes rolling wildly to betray the true state of his emotions, and in the face of hungry diners-out leaving their tables to storm his kitchen, merely stood speechlessly, waving his hands with feeble abandon, like some beetle turned helplessly on its back.

Yiannis is not really mad at all, only rather vague. He is not really cut out to run a high powered restaurant, to cope with over twenty tables set out under the planes and mulberry trees by the waterside and filled with ravenous tourists, as in the summer he tries to do. Yet in spite of the delays and breakdowns people who know him always eat there, and if one has often to go and collect one's own food from the kitchen and sometimes knives and forks as well, at least there is kept a pleasant informality about the place – lacking in the larger and slightly more efficient establishment that mushrooms out farther down the quay.

Violent scenes in his kitchen at the peak hours of the evening meal are frequent. People are jostling to grab plates of his *moussaká* or *stifádo*, all ordering and demanding at once while Yiannis stands looking helplessly from one to the other. He insists on doing the actual serving from the counter himself. His wife may pile the plates with food but Yiannis must hand them over. Once, when the pressure had mounted to more than usual heights and Yiannis seemed to have abdicated – standing amid all the uproar quite silent, and remote, ruminating it appeared on higher things – his wife had the temerity to pass over a plate of *kebáb* to an impatient customer. Yiannis came to life. With a cry of indignation he laid hands on the plate. For a whole minute there ensued a furious but silent struggle: three people were pulling at the plate – the customer, grimly holding on, Yiannis, and his wife. The plate did not, as I feared, split in three. Yiannis won. As the other two let go he staggered back, victorious. For a moment he did not know what to do, and then, by way of a consolation prize, seized a handful of fried potatoes, threw them on the plate, and presented it back to the astounded customer.

High summer does not suit Yiannis and his taverna. He is at his best when there are fewer people and there is plenty of time: in the early spring, in autumn and winter when there is a cold wind blowing outside, and the salt spray is dashing at his windows, and inside among the half-dozen tables the atmosphere is warm and friendly and full of appetizing smells. Then Yiannis comes into his own, telling his stories to the laughter of his guests, sitting with them at their tables, treating them to the extra half-litre of wine, talking, smiling, listening.

Last winter his chimney caught fire. Flames and smoke belched out of the roof-top and there was a panic among the neighbours for fear of the upper storey catching light. An excited crowd gathered and for a couple of hours there was a scene of fearful activity: everyone was shouting, calling out advice to each other at the tops of their voices, carrying buckets of water from the harbour and pouring them over the taverna, cannoning into each other as they ran back for more; everyone, that is, except Yiannis. Yiannis was stretched out on the quay. He had fainted.

There were rumours, too, of Grigor and the modern-style tourist 'pavilion' built by the government near the beach. It was said that the place was at last opening as a restaurant, and Grigor assisted by his wife was to be manager. I had confirmation of this from Grigor himself, suddenly transformed into a man overpowered with work and worry and the responsibilities of the new venture. 'Sure,' he said breathlessly as I caught him hurrying under the plane trees to his new restaurant, 'we open about two weeks. Maybe. Fishing? No time now. Work, work. You're going to eat real well soon, you see! Real high-class food!' He chuckled happily as he sped on.

Vangeli backed his friend's assertions. 'Yes,' he said loyally, 'Grigor is quite a good cook. I've been giving him lessons.'

Lately there had been much activity at the quay under the castle, near where I tie up *Astarte*. George Limonis, agent for the *Kyknos*, is branching out further into the tourist business – he already owns the hotel near Grigor's tourist pavilion. He has bought an old high-prowed caique and shipwrights are working all day on the hull, installing cabins and even, it is rumoured, a lavatory. They have painted the mast yellow. The plan is to charter her, of course, but so much time has been wasted already that it is doubtful whether she will be ready for this season. And who's going to captain her? Next year, perhaps.

Mitsos came into Skopelos harbour today, with his extraordinary looking forty-foot motor boat with rows of old bus seats inside, painted a bright blue and white and called the *Dóxa* ('Thanks'). In the spring *Dóxa* was alongside *Astarte* on the beach at Vassiliko. While I was covering *Astarte*'s keel and myself with anti-fouling paint Mitsos was laying long strips of what looked like, and was, cardboard across his long cabin roof, and painting the low rails at the stern a dazzling white. Like many of the Greeks of the Sporades Mitsos is fair, with blue eyes. He has an engaging grin and a generous nature, and since that embarrassing incident in which he towed *Astarte* with the Nomarch and party on board into Skopelos harbour, we have become firm friends. He has announced that from now on I am going to teach him English.

Mitsos has been having some trouble with his boat. He had built her in Alonnisos, and installed an enormously powerful second-hand German diesel engine, so heavy that when it was bedded in the stern the bows tilted sharply up in the air, giving her a somewhat unusual appearance which certain people, not least Vangeli, had been quick to point out. Since last summer the position of the eingine had been changed, but unfortunately it had this time been placed too far forward, and the resulting dip in the bows was still the subject of much ribald comment. This imbalance, however, did not prevent her from charging along at over nine knots, making *Dóxa* the fastest boat for her size in the Sporades. She could take about thirty people sitting in some comfort, providing the sea was calm. I had noticed that Mitsos was encouraging the use of the term 'pullman' in collo-quial reference to his boat – in the islands this word possesses mys-terious but romantic connotations of modern luxury and speed – and it is as a sort of fast marine bus that he intends to use her in the coming season, shuttling tourists once or even twice daily between Skopelos and Alonnisos. He also has more ambitious plans: to charter to foreigners, taking them anywhere in the Aegean, the Cyclades, Khios. . . .

Dóxa is now moored stern-on to the quay at Skopelos. All is ready. Mitsos drinks ouzo with me outside Evangelo's coffee house and is taking a brotherly interest in my general welfare. 'When is Angelina coming?' he asks. 'Not for a couple of months,' I reply.

'Ah,' he says. 'That's not good. It's bad to be without a woman. For one thing, it's unhealthy. . . .' Mitsos is married, but his wife of course remains in Alonnisos. During the summer he is away from her for a great deal of the time, and he admits that the sight of so many attractive young women decked out in bikinis and sun-tans disturbs him. Life, he told me, can become difficult, complicated. 'You must be careful,' he warns me. 'Just because it's so easy here in the summer, that's no good reason. . . .'

I agree with him, but Mitsos is not satisfied. A bevy of pretty girls, probably from Saloniki, trips by our table. Mitsos lays his hand on my arm, and I start guiltily. 'You were looking at them,' he says in an accusing tone of voice.

'I was only counting them,' I reply uneasily.

'Don't,' says Mitsos firmly. 'Don't count them. It only makes it worse.'

Instead we concentrate on the two little tripper boats newly painted and with smart blue and yellow cushions on the seats, tied up next to *Dóxa*. Notices, painfully inscribed on little boards, advertise the fact that they are for hire. One is called *Andrómytos*, the 'Undaunted', another '*Brave Captain Yiórgo*'. Bunches of flowers are set in plastic vases on each side of the bows, and on the stern seat of one of the boats is fixed a large photograph framed in old silver of a woman in a long dress and white hair. The photograph looks as if it was taken in about 1900.

'Who could that be?' I ask Mitsos. Mitsos is willing to do anything to distract me and together we get up and have a closer look. A greyhaired old man is sitting in the boat shining up the brass. It is brave Captain Yiórgo himself, having named his boat, as often happens, after himself. He looks up when we speak to him. 'That's my mother,' he says proudly, and when I murmur something appreciative he leans forward to give the glass another polish. . . .

In a house with a courtyard just across the river-bed – dry in summer – that cuts the shore by the bamboos edging the bay, lives an elderly gentleman called Vasilis Ródios. He is a skilled potter, as was his father before him, and he can be found most days at work at his bench shaping the moist red clay spinning under his firm hand. Ródios is something of a philosopher, with a manner as calm and gentle as the expression on his deeply lined face. He is an educated man and has an inexhaustible fund of knowledge of Skopelot folklore, legends and customs, and those of his friends who feel sad or depressed often drop in to sit quietly in his workshop to talk and to listen, watching the miracle of creation take place between his sensitive fingers, soothed by the soft whirr of his potter's wheel. Ródios loves to make fine copies of the ancient classical pots, black-glazed almost all of them, perfume bottles, cups, urns, oil-lamps, and has the reputation for being the best craftsman of his kind in Greece, and his work, which is always simple and unadorned with the hideous paintings that spoil most modern copies of classical design, is sold in Athens and in several European cities.

Now the summer is here Ródios is bringing some of the things he has made to be put on show in the window of the barber's shop on the front, and Ródios himself will be ready with his shy smile to welcome visitors in his workshop, show them his stock and allow them to try their hands at the wheel, and present them courteously when they leave – whether they buy anything or not – with a flower or a sprig of basil.

Back in Skiathos I have coffee with Gus by the harbour side and together we consider the prospect of the coming season. 'More people than ever, I guess,' says Gus. But Gus is not too happy. He likes to help out tourists, especially English and Americans: he likes to talk to them. Sometimes, however, tourists suspect him of wanting to get something out of them, though this does not prevent them using him whenever they feel the need. Anyone who wants to find a room in Skiathos, to hire a boat, to find the way to Kastro, will be told – 'ask Gus,' and Gus will oblige, very often going to endless trouble bargaining with the house-owner, the boatman, making sure that the foreigner gets a reasonable price, and often if it is a question of making an expedition across the island Gus will not only find the mules but will sometimes go along as a guide.

For these services Gus has never asked for any reward. He has a farm in the hills, as well as a house in the village. He has no need to make money out of tourists, yet, as he says, when people take up his time for a whole day, or sometimes as some of the English have done for days at a time, he would be glad of some recognition even if it was only recognition as a friend, the offer of a drink or a coffee – not because he cannot afford these things himself but simply because of the spirit implied in such an invitation, the friendliness which he has so willingly offered being returned.

There is a plan that Gus is toying with, and which I enthusiastically support, that would make him a kind of official interpreter for tourists on the island. Certainly someone who speaks English and has the local knowledge that tourists need would be a great advantage. The idea is to rent a little office next to Jimmy Delhiyanni's chandler's shop – Jimmy is the official tourist representative on Skiathos – with a large notice outside: *Interpreter*. Any opposition to this scheme is likely to come from Jimmy himself. It will be necessary, he said, to get permission from Athens. It will take a long time.

Jimmy was more interested in my opinion of his latest tourist bait: what did I think of his amphorae? He was very excited about them. 'Come and see,' he said proudly, 'real antiques, thousands of years old!'

I went to have a look. He had bought a number off the trawlers who occasionally fetch them up in their nets and they were now set on the floor by the counter, some of them three feet high, ready for the tourists and offered for sale at huge prices. Most of them were beautifully shaped and were encrusted with convolutions of embedded marine growth, but I was startled to see that on some of them Jimmy had clearly added a number of shells, carefully stuck on with glue.

'Well?' he said, stepping back triumphantly, 'fine, aren't they?'

'Yes,' I said, 'but what about these extra shells?'

'What about them?'

I tried to point out that such obvious additions were likely to shake the confidence of the most gullible tourist, but Jimmy waved aside my possibly naïve objection with impatience. 'No, no. You don't understand. You see – they can have whatever they like, they can choose: ones with shells, or ones without!'

Gus shook his head sadly, muttering, 'They'll think we're all crooks here, that's what they'll think. . . .'

There is no doubt that whatever the moral degeneration that tourists are alleged, probably quite correctly, to bring in their wake, their presence gives the islanders a great deal to do, to think and talk about, and to look at. They are interesting; and no summer passes without some unusual event connected with them. The only trouble is that in Skiathos, as in so many small communities where making money out of foreigners is becoming a habit, the islanders tend to withdraw themselves, to look upon the tourist not so much as an individual but as an object, someone to live off. In Skopelos this rather sad stage has not yet been reached: the islanders are still uncynical; they react to individual foreigners – they like them, or they don't. They have not yet had to shield themselves with indifference.

All the more astonishing to them therefore, one golden evening when the promenaders were strolling up and down the curve of the Skopelos harbour front, when a young French couple, wandering back from the beach and arriving at the War Memorial suddenly decided that they could wait no longer, and proceeded without further preliminary to copulate upon one of the benches. The performance, though observed by the islanders with great interest – an increasing crowd of them piling up at that end of the promenade – did not meet with their approval. The chief of police was disturbed, and action was demanded and taken: the French couple were banished from the island and left the next morning on the *Kyknos*. There was much hushed discussion of this extraordinary occurrence in the coffee-houses for days after. It was felt among other things, that to choose the War Memorial was in particularly bad taste.

Another rumour reached the village at about this time, that foreigners were bathing and sunbathing in the nude on the beach at Staphylos. The rumour was confirmed. Usually there is a herd of goats browsing on the slopes above Staphylos Bay, and a single goatherd. For the next week or so, as the news travelled, the area became a concentrated rendezvous for herds of goats from all over the eastern side of the island, and the green hills were dark with horns and alive with the piping of watchful herdsmen.

Nevertheless a strong puritanical feeling exists in the Sporades – and on most Greek islands that have not surrendered altogether to tourists – and it is often especially apparent among the young unmarried men.

Most of the young men on Skopelos are cheerful and well-mannered, and when they are not working – as carpenters, house-painters, or in their fathers' shops – go about together, arm in arm, drink moderately in the tavernas together, go fishing and sing a great deal, sometimes very well. A young man in Skopelos is not likely to know much about girls. If he is engaged to be married he may be allowed to see his fiancée occasionally, but otherwise there is very little opportunity for any companionship with the opposite sex. Skopelots keep their unmarried daughters under close surveillance. Their only chance is with the tourist women, Greek or foreign, but oddly enough the opportunity is rarely taken. In front of these girls the young men will flaunt themselves, show off together rather naïvely, sing more loudly but otherwise seldom do anything further. But this does not mean they are not interested and do not feel deeply; and sometimes their own passions clash too violently with the inherited prejudices of their upbringing.

I was in Sari's taverna one evening in early summer, drinking wine with *mézes* in the company of Yiórgo and Lakis and some other Greek friends. Some foreigners had arrived a day or two before and were sitting at another table. The taverna was full. There was music, popular Greek rhythms, and occasionally one of the fishermen would get up and execute the solitary steps of the *zembékiko* between the tables.

As the evening wore on Yiórgo, who had met the foreigners at his workshop that afternoon, invited them across to our table. All three of them were already quite strikingly drunk, and the heavy blond man could do nothing but rock his chair backwards and forwards roaring out a tuneless accompaniment to the music. One of them was a girl, apparently with the blond man, pretty, with long dark hair. She wore very tight black trousers.

At midnight the lights went out, and Sari brought candles. Someone fetched a portable gramophone. Most of the Skopelots left, and the taverna was less than half full. The dancing continued with increasing vigour, but most of the records were now European, and the Greeks sat back and watched.

At a table close by me, on which was the gramophone and the pile of records, sat a group of young men. A South American record was put on and the girl danced, at first with a partner who very soon dropped out. The girl was tipsy. She danced alone, and as the pace quickened she matched the rhythm with a growing frenzy of her swaying body. It was hot in the taverna, and dense with cigarette smoke; the girl's zip had broken. Even the blond man stopped his roaring and watched, drunkenly agape. There was not a sound in the room except for the rapid music and the girl's breathing, and the maenad drumming of her feet on the wooden floor.

The young man at my elbow sprang to his feet. He seized the table from underneath and hurled it across the floor. Gramophone and records, wine and glasses fell splintering at the dancer's feet.

In the sudden silence no one moved or spoke. Then everyone began talking at once. The girl, awoken from her trance, sank exhausted into a chair. The Greeks were startled and indignant. 'Why did he do it?' 'What do you mean by it!' 'Apologize!' To all of which the young man replied nothing, but stood where he was, very pale and trembling.

Yiórgo, outraged, addressed anyone who would listen to him. 'This sort of thing never happens here, it's terrible! In Skopelos! Breaking things, it's barbaric. What will they think of us? Say you're sorry, at least!'

The young man did not raise his eyes. 'I'm sorry,' he said, very quietly. He sat down. Several Greeks came up to me and apologized as if they, collectively, were responsible. They could not understand what had happened. But I was watching the young man. He continued to sit there, without saying a word; pale, but he had stopped shaking.

The party broke up soon afterwards, and everyone went quietly home to their beds.

12

Eremonisia

Now that the land at Panormos is ours and a builder engaged it is just a matter of waiting until the work can start, in September. But apart from the problem of plans, which seems to occupy most of my waking hours, there is the important question of cost. Pandelis, the builder, is busy making out an estimate from some rough drawings I have given him, but I want to have another opinion, and I need to talk to someone who has practical experience in these things, to discuss in detail and at leisure the various alternatives of shape, size and materials.

There is only one islander I know well enough who can help me, a friend too of Vangeli's, who lives in a remote inlet far along the shore of Alonnisos, at a place called Stenivalla, and now that it is midsummer there is no better time to leave Skopelos harbour for a while. In the evenings crowds of tourists, mostly Greek, walk the waterfront, filling the café tables that are spread now like a closely woven net the whole length of the quay, so that the hundred yards from Lefteri's to Yiórgo's workshop has become something of an obstacle course. Even the birds from the great plane trees, guardians of the harbour, have gone; and I am beginning to sympathize with the birds.

Sari has installed a juke-box in his taverna. But this is not all. The arrival on the Greek market of Japanese transistor radios, cheap and effective, has made a startling impression. Standing with my back to the door of George's cakeshop I can make out the glitter of these machines swinging at the wrists or shoulders of women and men as they stroll by the waterside; and at every other table there is one, carelessly tuned at full pitch to one of the four stations available at this otherwise peaceful sunset hour.

The tables are full. Around me grows a volume of voices, mostly Greek with snatches of English, French and German. The last light has gone from the eastern mountains that ring Skopelos bay, from

A street in the hill-top village of Alonnisos

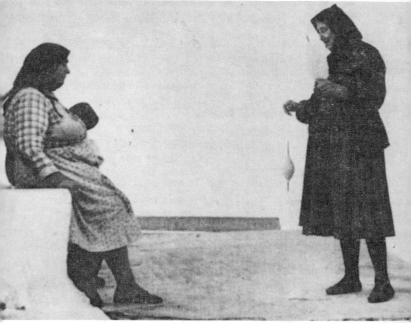

Alonnisos village
Spinning the wool, Alonnisos

the white monasteries high and inviolate upon the slopes of Mount Palouki. To the north fades the blurred craggy line of Alonnisos, pointing out and beyond to Kyra Panayia, Iura, Psathura and the rest . . . *eremonisia*, the deserted islands. And now as they fade finally in the darkness, and the harbour lights turn on, enclosing and narrowing the little world of spotlit movement, voices, music, the image of those islands comes clearer to my eye, and as noises round me fade I can hear the silence that is always there, the hoarse cry of a gull, the sound of small waves lapping among the rocks. . . .

The evening grows on, and with it my restlessness, the hardening of a decision. My chair is tilted by the table. From where I sit I can see *Astarte* moored not far away. At night, and especially on nights like this, when the *meltémi* has died, the sea gone calm, it seems that the boat is invested with a special magic, when every rope and strand of rigging, the furled sails, shrouds, warps and anchor chain all stand out floodlit in the harbour lights, the curve of the white bow pointing above a sea of black silk. From where I sit I can follow the finger of that bowsprit, out to where the harbour walls glimmer pale under the flash of red and green entrance beacons, beyond where there is nothing, an enveloping void of darkness.

The time has come. . . . Down in the cabin the music and murmur of the cafés is already partially excluded. The engine as it wakes to life cuts off the shore sounds. Take in the warps, the plank; the boat glides slowly out over the wet chain, clattering on deck; anchor in. Someone is calling my name. Now as the boat moves forward, gathering speed, I can turn to wave, vaguely, politely. We are free. Out between the harbour beacons, Skopelos town a bank of lights falling away behind, a slight swell lifting the boat now as we turn into the open sea, every beam and timber tense with power and life. Warm breaths of air from the island, no wind.

I lash the helm and sit for a time forward on the bowsprit, listening above the muffled hum of the motor to the sharp hiss of the bow wave just below, watching the phosphorescence sparking from the bow as it strains, cuts cleanly the glassy sea, riding over the swollen reflection of stars.

We swing eastward round the point. The tall hull of Ayios Yiorgios Island swims ahead, the black cliffs of Skopelos in line to the right. A strange light is flaring in the south-east, setting in darker outline the capes ahead. Now we are running through the straits.

The moon still red from the horizon haze rests on the long back of Skantzura. As it climbs, drained of colour, Alonnisos whitens to chalk, the moon track glitters where a breeze ruffles the water.

The islands are afloat. A ghostly dance begins, the white boat the central dancer, while around, conjured by the moon, the peaks and cliffs of the islands rise and fall in light and deepening shadow. We are approaching Xeró, the deserted cove in the south of the island, Peristeri: passing the headland, eyes staring in the deceptive light, round into the bay. Engine cut; drifting forward, closing towards the shallows. The anchor drops in a brilliant splash, chain rattles out, falls still; the boat swings gently, quiet at last. Heavy scent of the hills; pause, while the cicadas regaining courage begin again their throaty chorus. Nothing moves. The moon is shining through a net of olive trees that line the ridge.

I have an uneasy feeling, as I light a cigarette, that this is my last box of matches.

* * * *

I was in no hurry to get to Steniválla. For three days in Peristeri I saw no one, heard no voice; I climbed into the highlands in the centre of the island. My destination was Barba Thanassis's 'oasis' as I called it, the cold water that flowed from the mountainside near the highest peak, a place with the best view in all the Sporades, eagle-perched above the high narrow back of the island falling away below, the deep water storm-washed inlets to the south, the bay of Vassiliko to the north, and eastwards the outer islands of Kyra Panayia, Iura and Piperi, one behind the other to the distant purple of the horizon. The old woman Margalitsa welcomed me at the cottage not far below the spring, and told me that her husband was away with his boat. She offered me a glass of hot goat's milk with sugar, and some dried plums.

I take a certain pride in old Thanassis's boat, one of the oldest and most rotten-looking I have seen, nine foot long, made of heavy worm-eaten waterlogged timber about four inches thick. . . . It should have been axed up for firewood thirty years ago – or so one would have thought, and one would have been wrong. The boat floated, even sailed, with the mast that could be stepped and the patched grey lateen sail that is hoisted across it. Once in Vassiliko

Barba Thanassis found me at work on *Astarte* and asked me if I had any old paint to spare. I looked in the engine-room and dug out half a dozen tins of various colours that I had at one time or another tried unsuccessfully to mix to the shade I wanted. There was a certain amount of red, some black, half a tin of green, a few inches of yellow, blue and some old white undercoating. All these, apologetically, I handed over. I wondered, as he carried them away, what colours he would choose. I did not have to wait long for the answer: he chose them all, mixing them up in an old bucket and splashing them on the spongy hull of his boat. The result was dramatic, a garish shade of mauve, the sight of which, as I and everyone at Vassiliko could see, gave the old man a great deal of quiet pleasure and pride.

At sunrise the next morning, when I left Peristeri, coming up the coast of Alonnisos, I saw Thanassis and his wife Margalitsa sailing down from the opposite direction. We passed quite close to each other. The boat was laden with a huge pile of firewood, and a goat stood proudly in the bows. The two old people, both over seventy, sat bolt upright at the stern, Thanassis's horny hand on the sail-sheet, staring straight ahead as the wind bent the sail and sent the old hull hissing and gurgling through the waves.

From the mouth of Peristeri cove, in the channel between Skopelos and Alonnisos, can be seen the summit of the island called Ayios Yiorgios, a high cone of rock and scrub with a derelict farmhouse half-way up. There is a landing place at the bottom, among rocks in deep water, but it is a dangerous place for a boat: strong currents sweep through the straits, and an unpleasant swell gets up with the wind in a matter of minutes. There was once a chapel at the top, the hermit home of a monk in medieval times. The fact is mentioned in one of the first travel-books to be written about the Aegean, by an Italian, Buondelmonte, in 1415 '. . . *et ibi Caloierus, serviens Deo, ad solem dum dormiret, aquila . . .*' Buondelmonte tells how the hermit, sleeping out in the sun one day was sighted by an eagle who dived and tore out his eye. . . . The hermit 'infinitely grieving' prayed to God and in response Elijah appeared, and in front of all his companions, restored the missing eye.

It is interesting that it should have been Elijah, or Elias, who arrived because at the time the island was called Ayios Elias, and when the name changed to Ayios Yiorgios no one seems to know.

There are so many mountain-tops in Greece called after the prophet, and usually one on every island, that I asked in Skopelos why Elias should have become such a favourite mountain saint, and in answer to my question Yiórgo one day in his workshop put down his screwdriver and told me the following story.

Elias, it seems, was once a sailor. He sailed everywhere, and the more time he spent on the sea the more profoundly did he grow to hate it. One day, having been washed ashore after yet another wreck, he decided once and for all to have done with such an abominable element. He took the oar, which he had clung to in the sea, put it over his shoulder, and marched off inland into the hills. After some time he met a man. 'Excuse me,' said Elias politely, 'can you tell me what I'm carrying over my shoulder?' The man looked at the prophet in astonishment. 'Of course I can,' he replied, 'that's an oar!' Elias thanked him and set off again. He met someone else, asked the same question and received the same answer. Finally, after much hard climbing, half-way up a high mountain miles from the sea, he came across a farmer. 'Excuse me,' said Elias, 'I wonder if you can tell me what I've got on my shoulder?' 'Of course I can!' he said. 'That's a piece of wood for stirring porridge.' 'Thank you,' said the prophet, breathing a sigh of relief, and planting the oar firmly in the ground. 'This is where I'm going to stay.'

Not far from Peristeri, nearly opposite on the coast of Alonnisos is a place the Greeks of today call Kokkinó Kástro, 'Red Castle', where I anchored that morning on my way to Steniválla. Tall red cliffs crowned with pines ring the bay, from which a high peninsula juts out into the sea connected today by no more than a knife-edge ridge. Each year the winter rains wash patiently away at the narrow link, washing the clay down to disappear miraculously in the white sand of the beach.

Long ago the bay must have been even more sheltered by an island that now stands across it and that once was joined to the cliffs, but even without it Kokkinó Kástro was an ideal site for a small sea-settlement of pre-classical times. Traces of ancient building on the peninsula are visible quite clearly from seaward, and it is possible to land from a boat and explore more carefully the half-submerged lower courses of those massive walls.

The first time I came to Kokkinó Kástro I made there the acquaintance of an old man called Barba Iannis who lives alone three-quarters of the year in a one-roomed whitewashed stone and clay cottage by the waterside.

Barba Iannis is eighty, and looks it: every year it seems has imprinted itself with its toll of work and pain and laughter on that brown, leathery face, in the lines about the blue eyes that dance and wink under the shock of short white hair.

The old man is a resin-collector, or rather he is the guardian of the big stone and cement resin tank built beside the cottage. All around Kokkinó Kástro the hills are covered with pines. The trunk of every tree is notched, the bark stripped off, and a little tin cup set in place to catch the slowly oozing resin. Throughout the summer men make their rounds collecting the cups from each tree, pouring the contents first into large tins and then into the resin tank by the cottage.

Barba Iannis does some of this work himself, but mostly he conserves his energies for cultivating the little vegetable plot at the head of the bay. Once a month perhaps a caique will come in to moor under the cottage and the long process of loading the resin into open four-gallon cans will begin. The captains and crews of these broad caiques, as well as the resin-collectors themselves – wild, unkempt-looking men who seem shy of all human contact and flit among the trees like wood sprites in the forests that are their own kingdom, axe on shoulder, knife stuck in the wide cloth cummerbund at their waists, a bag of bread, olives and goat's cheese slung behind – these are the only people Barba Iannis may meet the whole summer through.

'It gets lonely here, you know. Eight months out of every year. I don't care for it much. But *ti na kánoume*? What can one do?' And he will leave me sitting on the low wooden stool he has set out for me in the shade of the cottage and totter off to fetch me a present of a melon or a few tomatoes or some other fruit, if there is anything, which is rare enough; and in exchange I will present him with a tin of corned beef or some other metropolitan delicacy.

Barba Iannis showed me where there should be fresh water, if a well were dug, high above the bay of the red cliffs, and spoke of the rich earth – red as blood, he said. There is a desolate, wild feeling about Kokkinó Kástro, as if the end on that closely-built peninsula came too suddenly and too terribly ever to be forgotten, a wound in that red earth that even the centuries have not healed. Or perhaps

it just needs someone to love the place again and live there, to recon-
cile the ghosts, bury them quietly.

'And where are you off to now?' Barba Iannis says to me, somewhat testily as if I shouldn't be off anywhere.

'To Steniválla.'

'Ah.' He is about to say something. His handshake is unforget-
table: his palm is the hardest I have touched, like the bark of a tree,
or a worn stone. As usual, as *Astarte* glides out of the blue bay, he is
standing by his cottage door watching me out of sight behind the
headland, vigorously waving a large white handkerchief in great
full-arm sweeps as if signalling in semaphore his message of good-bye.
In fact the old man is nearly blind and he probably stands there, just
to make sure he is not being impolite, long after *Astarte* has disappeared.

Steniválla is just two miles away to the north-east, farther along
the coast of Alonnisos. It is really no more than a narrow inlet set
back into the hills, with two tavernas built above the water's edge
and an old cottage behind; and yet Steniválla is an important place:
important to the islands because it is the only safe harbour, winter
and summer, on Alonnisos, the last station on the way north to the
outer Sporades and beyond, a final outpost before the wastes of sea
and barren rock begin, a place where fishermen may meet and talk,
eat, drink, dance and sleep and anchor their boats in the midst of
their solitary work. But to me Steniválla is important because it is the
home of Kosta Mavrikis.

If it is true that I have been fortunate enough to make three great
friends in the Sporades, then two of them are Vangeli and Yiórgo in
Skopelos, and the third is Kosta at Steniválla. It was Vangeli who
first introduced Angelina and me to the place and to Kosta, one
evening when we moored in the light of the hurricane lamp that
hangs from the vines of the taverna roof and happened to meet there
a half-dozen of Vangeli's friends. That night was spent eating and
drinking a great deal too much while Vangeli played the guitar and
the company sat and sang song after song long after the full moon had
set and the morning star was paling in the east.

I came back many times after that, partly because of the place –
the perfect little harbour with so much colour and warmth and life,
set in all that loneliness of water and bare hills, and partly because of

Kosta and his family. I used to come sometimes straight from Skopelos, but more often it was from some bay at Kyra Panayia or Xeró when the silence had become oppressive and the cliffs and hills suddenly too big for comfort, and I needed to hear voices and see expressions pass across people's faces, to listen and to speak. Coming with *Astarte* I always blew my conch shell before the last headland stood back and the tavernas and fishing boats came into view, and always Kosta was ready by the rocks to take my warps and welcome me ashore.

Kosta is small, has a snub nose set in a face that is marvellously crinkled, and his eyes slant upwards at the corners with humour and kindliness. He speaks very quietly, and all his movements are unhurried and gentle. He seldom bothers to shave, and because the hours of his day are full of work wears only the oldest of clothes. His trousers are broad-bottomed and flap around his ankles, and in summer he can be seen in an astonishingly bright shirt, sent by a friend from America, and a faded blue beret. In winter this headgear is replaced by a strange woollen hat, knitted by his wife. His hands are broad and hard, gnarled as the roots of an olive tree.

Kosta was born about fifty years ago, on the island of Ikaria, on the other side of the Aegean. He is descended·from a Byzantine family that fell into disgrace and were sent in exile to Ikaria from Constantinople. 'So they must have been a bad lot,' says Kosta rather sadly, and when I suggest that Emperors weren't always right, Kosta shakes his head. 'No, I'm sure this one was. . . .' Not that Kosta cares much about his past.

He met Angeliki, his cheerful buxom wife, during the war; married her and came to Steniválla where his wife's family owned a piece of land. The cove was used by Alonnisiot fishermen as a winter refuge even then, but except for an abandoned cottage there was nothing else there. Together they set to work. They repaired the little house by the water's side and built on a larger kitchen. Kosta is a builder by trade. He set up poles outside the cottage next to the water, grew vines overhead and filled in the spaces with ferns and brushwood. He made tables and chairs, and Angeliki began to boil coffee and cook meals for the fishermen stormbound in the little harbour. They had opened a taverna.

They planted olive trees and fruit-trees, dug a well, built a cistern for rain-water and channelled it to the trees. Now that Steniválla had shelter for men as well as boats fishermen began to use the cove more often. The *eremonisia* had always been rich in fish; the trouble was getting the catches back to Volos before they went bad. Kosta ordered ice from Volos, and it became worthwhile for the *Paskháli*s to extend her itinerary and come on past Patatiri to Steniválla. (Now, of course, he gets Vangeli's ice, direct from Skopelos.) The fishermen who began to come from as far afield as Trikeri and the Pagasitic gulf used Steniválla as a base, in the centre of their fishing grounds, and Kosta packed the fish between layers of broken ice, into wooden boxes and straight on to the *Paskháli*s. Finally Kosta made steps down to the water, and set iron mooring rings in the concrete. Steniválla had become a busy fishing station.

Kosta's and Angeliki's children are growing up. Katina is the eldest, an attractive slim girl with blue eyes. She was about to get married. Mitsos was the son, a sturdily built lad of nineteen who had become with his father an expert fisherman, and made expeditions, away among the *eremonisia*, sometimes for days at a time, using often a mask and harpoon gun to bring back fish – enough to feed the guests in the growing taverna as well as to sell on the family's own account in Volos. Youngest is Tassia, a slight, fey fifteen year old, with shy hazel eyes and long gleaming fair hair. Tassia helped in the kitchen, carried water on the donkey's back every day from the well, and like every member of the family worked from before dawn until long after dusk.

Tassia's special job was to look after the animals. In Greece it is not usual for people to care much about animals. Animals share their work, and they look after them because it is in their own interests to do so; but in Steniválla they like animals for their own sake. The place is full of cats, and with all that fish around they live well. Tassia keeps pigeons, and is sad when sometimes one is lost to a hawk or an eagle. She takes out the goats to graze, milks them and knows each one by name. A donkey foal is on the way and this is promised as a present for Angelina when the house is built at Panormos; Tassia also keeps silk-worms. There is a gull with a broken wing which Kosta and she rescued one stormy winter night; she tried to mend the wing, but it never got well enough to fly. The gull can only hop and flounder and has lived with the family for over a year now. It jumps up on the tables and makes throaty noises when it is hungry, and likes Tassia to feed it fish one by one from her hand. The cats, after some initial painful experiments, have learned to keep their distance.

Three years ago, when Kosta saw that tourists were being brought up for the day from Patatiti, he decided to expand. With Mitsos' help and another workman he made a low white building divided up into four rooms, each with two beds and a washbasin, and a long veranda in front where flowers bloom from clay pots and vines and roses trail overhead. In July and August the rooms are usually full, with Greek professional people mostly, their wives and children, lawyers or doctors from Athens or Volos; they come again and again, not only because of the place but because they have become friends of Kosta and Angeliki, and staying there is like being part of the family.

'You're coming to the wedding of course?' was the first question I was asked by Kosta when I stepped ashore from *Astarte*. I certainly was. We had received a fine printed invitation card months before. 'But what about Angelina? Can't you tell her to come from England in time?'

They were in good spirits that evening. Preparations for the wedding – it was to take place at Patatiri – were going well, and Kosta sat bemused at a table under the vines, his spectacles balanced on the end of his snub nose, a pencil poised in mid air, going over the figures once more: a hundred and fifty guests – how many people to one roast kid? How many loaves of bread? Onions, beans, potatoes, salad, oil . . . and wine – 'I hope there's going to be enough to drink, Kosta?' Kosta grins broadly. 'Don't worry, there'll be enough wine to float the *Paskhális*! At least, I hope so' – and an extra crease of concentration appears on his forehead as he bends to his accounts once more.

Niko was the prospective bridegroom, a tall dark young man who lived at Patatiri and owned a long boat with an engine, in which he carries tourists around during the summer. The engagement had been a long one, as usual. Kosta had a house ready in Patatiri as part of the dowry.

Like the girls at Vassiliko who knew the distinctive beat of their father's engine long before his caique came into sight, so Katina knew the sound of Niko's boat. 'He's coming!' She hurriedly adjusted the white shawl round her head and stepped down to the rocks with a lantern in her hand.

Her brother Mitsos was sitting against the wall of the taverna, preparing the *paragádi* lines for the night's fishing. He winked at me. 'I can't hear anything, can you? Can you hear anything, Father?'

Kosta raised his eyes gravely and cocked his head. 'Nothing,' he said firmly.

Angeliki came out of the kitchen with a plate of fish for me. 'They keep teasing her. But you better be careful,' she added, addressing her husband and son who looked up at her innocently, 'She won't be here at all soon!'

'That will be terrible,' said Mitsos. 'What will we do?' He called down to Katina who refused to be drawn. 'Niko will be just in time to help me with this —' he held up the pieces of squid bait he was attaching to each hook.

Katina turned. 'Oh, no, not tonight! We've got things to talk about.'

Mitsos chuckled and murmured something into his fishing-basket. Kosta paused from his calculations and looked down at his daughter's slim figure by the waterside. 'You have children, and then they grow up, and leave you. That's what God intended, I suppose. . . .' He lit a cigarette. 'Vangeli's coming? He said he was.'

'Yes,' I replied. 'We'll probably come together on *Astarte* or *Makhi*. We're not likely to forget.'

*   *   *   *

A wedding on Alonnisos was supposed to be something very special. People got married on other islands and on the mainland, this was generally admitted, but on Alonnisos – ah, there it was different. The Alonnisiot wedding tradition, though it often cruelly strained the resources of the parents-in-law was one, in everybody else's opinion, well worth keeping up.

On the morning of the great day when we left Skopelos harbour for Alonnisos and Katina's wedding it was fortunately calm. About six of us climbed on board *Astarte*: Vangeli and Alexandra, Kosta the harbour-master, myself and two or three others. There was some delay at the quayside – we were waiting for a huge plate of snails to be sent down from the house. At the last moment Makhi and Eleni came running down to the harbour balancing the big hot dish between them; we took it on board and were off.

Long before we passed the straits of Ayios Yiorgios the snails, superbly cooked in garlic, herbs and oil, were finished. As part of the boat's standing equipment I carry a reserve stock of ouzo and *tsipuro* in two-gallon flasks protected with wicker-work which I try to keep full, but as it was a beautiful morning and we were going to a wedding, with shoals of fish flying in the sunlight above the waves and a dolphin twisting in our wake, it was only natural that the flasks should be broached. We came into Patatiri at high speed, narrowly avoiding the anchor lines of numerous small boats and caiques moored at the jetty and with difficulty and some confusion manœuvred to our berth.

'Am I not the Admiral of the Northern Sporades?' cried Vangeli, standing unsteadily at the helm. 'What are all these caiques doing here, blocking the quay?' A small crowd welcomed us – we were late – took our warps and hauled us with much cheerful shouting onto the jetty.

In the cabin Vangeli sat down and put his hand over his eyes. '*Po-po-po!* So much ouzo. . . . Why so much?' As if it was my fault.

We had brought suits to change into. Thoughtlessly I had left my only suit in Athens, and had borrowed one from Vangeli: double-breasted, dark blue and with a white pin-stripe. The trousers were very broad and were much too short for me. As I stepped ashore I had the feeling they finished just below my knees.

Kosta was dancing impatiently on the quay. '*Ach, Vangéli mou*, what are you doing to us? Quickly!'

'Lead on, my brave Kosta – we are ready!'

It was already an hour after midday, and the church service was supposed to start at two; before then we should pay our respects to the bride and groom.

We joined the mill of people outside one of the little houses that line the steep streets of the village. Children and young women were handing round trays of cakes, *loukoumi*, and glasses of powerfully-scented ouzo. All the men were dressed in suits and dazzling white shirts; their hair was carefully brushed and everyone had shaved. The women were the most brightly arrayed, and with their gay head-shawls, brocaded jackets and full embroidered dresses looked like so many exotic butterflies fluttering their new wings in the sun. I forced my way up the stairs to where Katina was being made ready for the church. About forty people, mostly women, were crowded into the stifling room. Katina in white satin, pale and tense, sat like a princess with her ladies-in-waiting busy around her putting the finishing touches to her make-up, her hair, preparing the flowers and sewing the last stitches on her veil. More cakes, *loukoumi*, ouzo. . . . Tassia was in close attendance on her sister, with numerous aunts and female relatives, and her three cousins from Vassiliko, the granddaughters of Lycúrgos.

Down in the courtyard again I met Vangeli who hurried me up the streets to another house where the groom was already dressed in his dark suit and shining tie, his shoes polished to a gloss matched only by his hair. There was the sound of music coming up the lane, and Niko braced himself. They had come to take him, the musicians and a cheerful crowd of friends and relatives filling the outside staircase and the balcony to his room. Violin, *bouzouki*, clarinet and accordion – the musicians were fresh and the rhythm lively. Out he came, Niko, shy now, reserved and unsmiling, his jaw set. His mother, a small stout woman, led the gay procession down the winding street, dancing ahead of them all, a grave circular swinging of her heavy skirts, arms raised, round and round. . . . A dance of abdication, the passing of a woman's thrall, one to another? But this was also a cheerful dance, and as she saw Vangeli in the press of people leading her down she took his arm and together they swung round with much laughter down the steps.

A rain of flower petals. Niko had come down to the bride's house and was calling for her in the courtyard. But they did not meet. Again he was led away, this time on the long uphill pathway to the church, high above the houses through the olive groves and vineyards while the sun burned down on the long procession and at the rear, with the biggest retinue, walked the bride.

The church service lasted only half an hour. After the *koumbáros* had switched the wreaths over the couple's heads, we trooped in line to kiss the bride and groom.

I joined Vangeli and Alexandra once more down at the harbour. 'Sleep!' said Vangeli sternly. 'One hour's sleep, it is very necessary!' In the end it was I who slept, locking myself in the fo'c's'le, stretched out on a bunk. Vangeli knew too many people. He found himself caught up with playing cards, *távli*, singing . . . none of which he could ever resist. When I woke at sunset to the sounds of music and dancing on the shore, Vangeli reproached me for his not having slept. 'No sleep,' he groaned. 'Terrible, my head!'

The dancing had begun in the afternoon as soon as the church ceremony was over. Now as the lamps were lit, carried out and set in the trees outside the tavernas, the dancers gathered for a renewed effort, linked hands in a great circle and set their feet moving to the *syrtó*.

Vangeli was talking to the bridegroom's father, an amusing character whom I had met before. He was tall, thin and grey-haired. He spoke very quickly and always with great fervour, tumbling his words over each other. When I'd seen him last in Patatiri it was the night of the full moon; he was going home, up to the village on the heights, and though it was nearly as light as day, he was carrying a lantern.

'Do you see the lamp he has?' Vangeli had said to me. 'He's very superstitious. He's afraid of the dark. Look, we'll ask him why —' He called him over and offered him a drink.

The old man sat down with us, but most unwillingly. He kept asking the time. 'It's late, you know, very late! I ought to be going.'

'Seen any devils lately?' Vangeli asked him casually.

He glanced quickly to each side. 'Shh! What a question!' He lowered his voice and bent closer to us across the table. 'And on a night like this!' He shivered, and crossed himself. 'May the saints protect me, they're everywhere. Too many of them.'

It was not difficult to encourage him to talk. Apparently on Alonnisos people see devils as frequently as on other islands they see tourists. Niko's father, however, was a devil specialist. He had an eye for devils. According to him they come out at nights and wail and screech and dance especially around churches. There was one church on the top of Alonnisos where the devils actually appeared in broad daylight, flying around the top of the ikon screen during the services. He had spoken to the priest about it several times, but the priest had done nothing. One night, some years ago, he was forced to beach his caique at Agnonda on the west coast of Skopelos because two devils were persistently following behind his boat. He hoped to elude them on the shore but they kept after him, 'shrieking horribly,' he said. He was so frightened that he ran all the way across the island to Skopelos village. It was a particularly arduous journey because in order to avoid being overpowered by the devils he had been forced to run the whole way with his arms stretched out horizontally, like a bird. This of course made his body in the shape of a cross, an infallible protective sign against those emissaries of the underworld.

Another time he had been playing cards at a friend's house, up in Alonnisos village, and in spite of meaning to leave early he forgot how late it was: nearly midnight. Now, in order to reach his own house it was necessary to pass a stretch of cobbled lane beside a church which was a notorious devil sanctuary.

'I waited for a long time for someone else to come along, so that we could pass down that street together. But no one did. Everyone was asleep. So I took off my shoes and put them in a hole in the wall. I could collect them, you see, in the morning, and I didn't want to make any noise to wake up the —' He shuddered. 'Well, I had to do it. I closed my eyes and ran full tilt down the street . . .' Such an incident would have been so commonplace as not to merit any particular interest had it not been for another Alonnisiot, in roughly the same fearful predicament, who was approaching also at a break-neck run, from the opposite direction. The two of them collided head-on round the corner of the church, crashing into each other in a terrified fury of flying fists. The other man came off worst: his head was badly cut and had to be stitched up by the doctor. The whole village had been woken by the frantic shouting.

His latest devil experience had been at sea. One dawn only a few weeks ago, approaching Iura from the south he had seen a colossal white figure standing on the high cliffs of the island.

'So what did you do?' asked Vangeli.

'Well, I turned back of course – what do you think?'

'A white figure, though. Couldn't it have been an angel?'

Niko's father shook his head decisively. 'That was only a disguise, a trick. Someone like you would have walked straight into a trap like that. No, no it was a devil all right. You can't see angels, they're too good to be seen. . . .'

It was time for the wedding feast. The long room of the taverna had been laid with tables round each wall, with a space big enough for dancing in the middle. The musicians were seated at one end. Plates piled high with roast kid, potatoes and salad and fried fish were rapidly served by Kosta and the rest of the family, and jugs of deep red Alonnisos wine were distributed down the long tables. The musicians struck up, and as the debris from the tables were gradually cleared away, and toasts drunk to the bride and groom and the guests, Niko's mother took the floor, singled out an old uncle of hers, a man who must have been over eighty, and romped with him round the room. They were followed by Niko and Katina with much cheering from the guests. Katina would be on her feet the whole night, Alexandra told me – she was obliged to dance with every man who asked her, and most of the men present would be asking her at some time during the evening. Fourteen hours continuous dancing – 'She'll be half dead by the morning, poor thing; but it's only one night in her life. . . .'

From then on the floor was never empty, the big circle of the *syrtó* wound and stamped round the room. The dancing spread out of the taverna, into the little square by the quay, and other men with their own musical instruments played in the taverna opposite, and young men put their arms on each other's shoulders and danced in line to their own reflections in the starlit water.

By the time I went to bed at about three o'clock, the scene had not altered: if anything it seemed that the evening was just beginning to warm up. Kosta, hot, tired but grinning released me unwillingly. 'Not going so early?' 'A fine wedding,' I said, 'Congratulations.' It had gone well, and would be remembered and talked about by the islanders for months after; and it was something of a triumph for Kosta Mavrikis, who had left his own island with nothing, so many years before; and it was a vindication, too, of Steniválla itself.

* * * *

It is in spring and autumn that Steniválla can be seen as it really is, a working place, a fishing station, a last human frontier post against the rocks and the sea.

In bad weather when the north winds are wailing through the pines and clouds race over the mountain-tops, and the narrow straits between each of the Sporades are truly the 'gates of the wind', white with flying spray, the cove of Steniválla maintains a quiet and a stillness in its sheltered water, with only a slight swell rocking the caiques at anchor. At times like this there may be twenty craft or more in the harbour, from big cargo caiques piled with firewood or grain, to the little twelve or twenty-foot fishing boats from Patatiri or Trikeri on the mainland. The smaller boats tie up along the rocks under the taverna, the bigger anchored fore and aft with warps ashore, four abreast and sometimes five lines deep, filling the entire head of the cove. The men come ashore, crowding the taverna with their salt-soaked bodies, with tired unshaven faces, quick to laugh and quick sometimes to quarrel, sipping coffee or *tsipuro* before the fire, or if it is not raining sitting against the wall outside, their bare toes hooked in the nets they are mending.

In the evenings if the day has been fine enough for fishing, the boats come back and gulls follow them screaming and diving to hover above the taverna chimneys and the masts of the caiques, as the catches are dragged ashore, the nets spread out and the long work of disentangling the fish and sorting them begins and may continue far into the night.

In Steniválla there is no special time for sleep. People rest when they can, and that is not very often or for long. At dusk Kosta lights the pressure lamp and hangs it from the wooden struts under the vines. Oil lamps flicker in the kitchen and the fishermen sit around in the cold starlight repairing their gear, ready to drop exhausted into their boats or onto the warm carpeted benches of the taverna for an hour or two's snatched sleep if they are lucky, before dawn when they must be on the move again. Bad weather may have kept them idle for days on end : when it is fine they must make the best of every moment.

Work at Steniválla never stops. If it isn't the fish, or the ice, or cooking or baking, over which Angeliki tirelessly presides, it is the olives. I have found Kosta and Angeliki before sunrise sitting quietly together splitting black olives by the light of an oil lamp, slowly filling up the huge baskets before them. They have been working there since two in the morning. There is so much work at Steniválla that I have found it tiring simply to watch it all, even to think about it ; and if it's not the olives, or the plum-picking, or the fig-drying, then it is charcoal, the building of the *kaminé* – at Steniválla one of the main events of the autumn.

Kosta is proud of his charcoal burning and claims to produce as fine a quality of charcoal as is humanly possible ; a claim which may give him great satisfaction but which seems hardly sufficient justification – considering also the infinitesimal financial reward – for such a back-breaking labour.

I was interested to see how it was done. For the last few weeks

The resin collectors'
cottage and the site
chosen for the
house, Panormos

The house nearing
completion

Panormos and the view from the house towards the entrance of the bay, with *Astarte* at the half built jetty

Tassia, helped occasionally by Mitsos or Kosta, had been bringing in the cut branches and tough short roots of the *koúmara*, the low ever-green bush that flourishes on the surrounding hills. These twisted shoots of hard wood, dropped from innumerable donkey loads, now littered a great space at the head of the inlet, like a graveyard of silent dark limbs, drying in the autumn wind and sun.

The building of the *kaminé* begins. The wood is piled in a tall mound about eight feet high and twice as broad. The wood is lit, and begins slowly to burn. Immediately, from heaps previously collected around the fire, a six-inch layer of earth-mould, leaves and ferns is carefully laid on until the entire pyramid is covered. This is a tricky part of the work as the fire inside must not burn too quickly while the ferns and leaves are spread on top of it, nor must it be allowed to go out, or the whole construction of the *kaminé* must be started over again.

Having built the *kaminé*, Kosta, I thought, had done with it. There it was, this great mound, gently smoking away. But the work had just begun. For five consecutive days and nights someone had to tend the *kaminé*, to be always on the alert, watching for the fire to break through the outer layer and repair the damage. A ladder rested against the side of it, which could be laid wherever it was needed, and Kosta had to climb this ladder with his tin of earth-mould and ferns and with a spade or by hand sift this material over every new smoking gap. It is important that the fire deep inside burns slowly and with a great heat: hence the care in bandaging the wounds as they appear.

As Tassia and Mitsos, sometimes their aunt who lived in the cottage behind, helped in the building of the *kaminé*, so Angeliki helped Kosta in the tending of it. At nights they slept together on a blanket under a tree by the side of their work, taking alternate watches, ready every couple of hours to jump up and set to with shovel and tin. After the first few days this part of the work became even more strenuous: as the *koúmara* roots inside burned and hard-ened into charcoal so they broke, contracted, and the fire constantly fell in, and Kosta had to work continuously thrusting in new wood, spreading again the poultice of ferns. . . . In the mornings I'd see him walking slowly back from the fire, black from head to foot from his night's labours, exhausted, coming for a cup of coffee and a cigarette before the rest of the day's work began.

When he had judged sufficient carbonization had taken place he would dismantle the mound, spreading the charred pieces to smoke and cool over the hillside. Later they would be packed into sacks and sent to Volos; and when the first lot was done he'd start the whole process again, building two or sometimes three *kaminés* each autumn. . . .

Sometimes I wondered what would happen if one of the family ever became seriously ill, though it seemed to me that the mere idea of illness at Steniválla was so dangerous that it had been permanently exorcized, like some criminal heresy. Once when I shamefully succumbed to bronchitis and a high temperature there, and went to bed for a few days in one of Kosta's guest-rooms, Angeliki had appeared with a tray, six large tumblers, a bottle of methylated spirits and a kind of home-made torch – wire and cotton waste. She held each glass upside down, thrust the lighted torch inside and then quickly pressed down the glasses one by one on my back, the vacuum causing the flesh to be sucked up into lumps the size of an orange. '*Vendouzes*,' she said. I had been 'cupped'.

I can imagine that cupping might be of some medical use, but on another occasion when Angelina had a headache Katina produced a glass of water, sprinkled a few drops of olive-oil in it – taken from the little lamp that burns religiously day and night above the kitchen fireplace – and then began to mutter a repetitive mixture of prayers and spells over it, maintaining as she offered it, that this was an infallible remedy. Perhaps it is just as well that all the Mavrikis family are by nature extremely healthy.

I sat with Kosta as we talked out the problems of the house at Panormos, discussed the possible expenses. Stone walls, so many cubic metres of rock; cement; the cost of wooden ceilings. . . . The plan? I brought out my drawings, made new ones, while Kosta put on his spectacles, cocked his head on one side and made calculations in pencil on the back of his cigarette packet.

'I wish I could build it for you,' he said. 'But all this —' He waved his hand. 'You must tell me how it gets on. You can always telephone us, you know.' He grinned. 'Give me a ring!'

The telephone! I had almost forgotten its existence, and the family's excitement and anxious speculation earlier in the year when the first poles began to be set up in line northwards from Patatiri, through the pines and over the hills, in the direction of Steniválla. There had been a problem: where was it to be installed? For there was another cottage next to Kosta's by the sea, owned by an active old man called Vassilis. In the last few years Vassilis had turned his place also into a kind of taverna, originally to take the overflow from Kosta, but now a house established in its own right. Vassilis, it was rumoured, had friends in Patatiri; the telephone, a symbol of prestige as much as being an object of some slight practical value, might well go to him. Kosta refused to discuss the subject, considering such petty jealousy beneath his dignity, but Mitsos confided in me with indignation the outrageous possibility of such an injustice being done. 'It isn't *right*,' he said bitterly. 'Do they even *need* a telephone over there?'

'Certainly not,' I said.

But there was no need to worry. Kosta, who had his own friends, won, and when I arrived at Steniválla on that summer flight from Skopelos, the telephone had just been put in.

It stood in the kitchen, near the fireplace, just behind the head of the table where Kosta usually sat. The novelty of its use had by no means worn off. To make a call one had to wind a handle. When it rang once, the call was for Patatiri; twice, for Votsi; three times, for Steniválla. Whenever it rang there was an immediate hush in the kitchen. Everyone looked away, avoiding each other's eyes, pretending not to care too much. It rang once; twice – tension visibly mounting; *three times*! With exaggerated slowness Kosta turned and lifted the receiver, clamping it to his ear. 'Hallo, hallo. Steniválla! Mavrikis speaking. What? Speak up, I can't hear a word! Ah, Adoni. *Yeiásou*, Adoni, how are you? . . .' I looked round the faces of the family – Angeliki a slight flush of pleasure on her cheeks, over-vigorously polishing a plate, Mitsos looking absently down at his feet with a selfconscious smile, Tassia already beginning to giggle.

Kosta put down the receiver with a flourish.

'What was that about?' I asked.

'Oh, just Andoni, asking how we were. . . . I told him we were fine. Hey, Mitsos – give our guest a drink! And I think I'll have a little one myself. . . .'

We drank first to the telephone – long may it ring – and then to Panormos and the house. The time for the building was drawing near, and the whole family at Steniválla was taking an interest in the plans. 'But will you ever come and see us, when you've a fine house in Panormos?' asked Angeliki.

'Of course they will,' said Kosta. 'They won't forget us.'

'I know one thing you've forgotten,' said Tassia, holding up the drawings.

'What?'

'Angelina's baby donkey, of course. Where is it going to live – in the kitchen?'

13

A Balcony Over the Sea

The date that I had agreed with Pandelis the builder to start work on the site was September 5th. 'Please, Pandelis,' I had said, 'I don't mean the 15th or the 30th, I mean the 5th!' And Pandelis had grinned broadly and replied, 'I know that you are an English gentleman, and the English say what they mean; and I, Pandelis Kefalonitis,' drawing himself up to his full five feet five inches, 'am a Greek, and Greeks don't always do what they say they will – *but*, I have promised the 5th and the 5th it will be!'

He was as good as his word. On the 4th he came, riding across the hills from Skopelos village on his pony, and together we marked out the ground plan with sticks of wood and lengths of taut string. On the morning of the 5th, as the sun climbed over the pines, I was woken by the steady rhythmic thud of pick-axes on earth and rock, echoing across the water. I rowed ashore and found lame Iannis Patsis, Andrikos, and Spyro Karaiophilis striking bravely at the slope among the almond trees. With them was a boy, also called Spyro, who helped clear away the earth as the diggers advanced deeper into the hillside.

I had been working out plans for the house, with Angelina, the preceding winter, and all that summer. The house had started very small, and gradually got bigger; I suppose that was inevitable. We must have space we said, lots of light. It was difficult to imagine internal distances, and Greeks whose houses I had been in lately were startled to see me pace their rooms, measure the height of their ceilings: I had never owned a house before, let alone built one, and I was very much aware of the difficulties; I hoped to make up for lack of experience with what I liked to call 'imaginative forethought', and hoped it would be enough. At least we had an ally, which I determined should play a vital part right from the beginning: Panormos, the site itself.

The key to the site was the cliff, about fifteen feet of grey rock.

Over this, obviously, there must hang a balcony of wooden beams and floor, with wooden columns supporting the tiled roof overhead. It wasn't much to start with, but it was something. It was also important to have some kind of courtyard, with the two nearest olive trees in the middle of it. A three-sided building would be too big, so it had to be a **⌐** with the toe-end of the foot resting on the low cliff top and the longest side running north, set back, parallel with the water. The inner cove of Panormos Bay ran north and south; our land was on the eastern, or right-hand side of the cove. From the cliff-face overlooking the sea the building withdrew inland – long living-room, and then turned north, with bathroom in the corner, kitchen and bedroom. Over the living-room, but set well back from the cliff, must be the study (shading the courtyard from the south), with a veranda opening westward from it, over the cove. The angle made by the two sides then faced north-west across the water towards the entrance of the bay. The island of Daseiá was in view, the far headland of Skiathos and beyond through the opening in the hills across the open sea the hazy ramparts of Mount Pelion. The bedroom faced west, with a broad veranda in front of it, supported by wooden columns. The kitchen was to be open in the summer – an idea taken from Vangeli's house up the valley – with doors and windows easily fixed across in winter.

The important thing, I decided, was to get a picture of the house as an absolute, an ideal, and work from there. Gradually the pieces fitted together. With the balcony over the cliff, and the study set back over it, it would have something of the look of an Athonite monastery. But Athos was only seventy miles to the north, and wooden columns and balconies were also a feature of Skopelos architecture. Against the background of pines and Skopelos mountains it would look perfect.

In fact the more I thought of it the more perfect it appeared. It was the most beautiful, the most splendid house that, probably, had ever been built; except of course it had not yet been built. There were various problems, even at this early stage. One was the sloping hillside: a solution was to raise the long side of the house, make a step in the living-room; perhaps with a few wooden columns across it.

'Are you sure we haven't too many wooden columns?' Angelina asked doubtfully. 'There are four in front of the bedroom, seven on the cliff balcony —' 'Nine,' I interrupted her, 'because the balcony goes on round the south side —' 'All right, nine, and four more in front of the study on top, and now some more in the living-room . . .'

'Once you start with wooden columns,' I said, 'you have to go on. You can't have too many. Now, on Mount Athos they weren't worried about having too many —'

'One thing though,' she said. 'How are you going to get up to your study? A ladder?'

It was a somewhat important oversight. Somewhere there had to be stairs. We decided to have them inside at first, and then half-way through the building Angelina had a vision, and as a result we moved them out: an outside stone staircase, itself a common feature of Aegean island building. When it rained anyone climbing the stairs would get wet, but in one way this was an advantage: it gave a feeling of isolation to the study, cut it off from the rest of the house. With sudden changes in midstream like this, it was a good thing that Pandelis was a talented improviser: it was one of the reasons why we had chosen him.

Vangeli recommended Pandelis, and his recommendation was heartily supported by Vangeli's great friend George Agorópoulos, the senior architect-engineer of the Nomarchy in Volos. He had come to Panormos in the summer, looked at my plans and inspected the site. Not long afterwards he sent back the plans, professionally drawn, so that Pandelis could work from them. 'It's got to be strong,' he said, 'because of possible earth-tremors. Pandelis is just the man for you. He won't mind if you make changes suddenly. He's clever, and with that cliff you'll need a clever builder. Above all, Pandelis loves building. . . .'

It was the most important thing of all. Pandelis was fifty, small and wiry and full of energy, with a crinkled sunburnt face and blue eyes always ready to light up in a smile. He usually wore a large tweed cap. He had built many houses in Skopelos, and a school, and was always chosen by the Volos Nomarchy for anything difficult or important, like harbour works or public buildings. Vangeli described him as 'the best builder in the Northern Sporades'. The house at Panormos was a challenge to him. Apart from the unusual cliff-top design, there were going to be big problems in the transport of materials: the road was not yet open, and not likely to be until next summer, and everything must come either by caique or by mule, a journey in both cases of over two and a half hours from Skopelos village.

I wanted the house to be made of stone. Pandelis warned me that brick would be cheaper, even though the bricks would come by caique. But to me the whole idea of stone was important: stone walls at least half a metre thick – built of brick the house would lose most of the character I had imagined for it even before it had begun.

There were some cliffs farther up the main Panormos valley: it was good rock, and had been quarried in ancient times – the remains of the old city, the ruins at the top of Kastro, were all of stone taken from the same place. Pandelis and I called on the owner of the land that included the quarries and he generously allowed us to take whatever we needed. Two or three men with mules and crowbars set to work and began hewing out the rock, loading it on to their animals and carrying it over to the site. The journey from quarry to cliffs was about twenty minutes, less than a mile.

'What about the cock?' Pandelis asked me with a grin. The levelling was done and the diggers had attacked the foundations; tomorrow they would be ready. The usual practice, he said, was at this stage to take a cock, cut its throat and spill the blood in the foundations. The workmen would then eat it for lunch. It was a very old custom, Pandelis said, for 'good luck', though he couldn't tell me what it really meant, and no one seemed to know the origin of the rite.

I told him that if Angelina discovered that a cock was to be ritually murdered under her house she would not be happy. Pandelis roared with laughter. 'You mean, it's like the cats, with Angelina?' Over the last year or so she had rescued several kittens from starvation or disease. They now kept me company and lived happily enough on *Astarte*. 'Yes,' I said, 'it's something like that.' Would the diggers and masons mind, I went on, if we missed out the cock and I brought some ouzo instead. Pandelis shook his head, still laughing – ouzo was fine.

'One more thing,' he said. 'Will you be wanting a priest?'

'A priest?'

'Yes, to bless the ground. You know how it is . . .'

We discussed the matter. I didn't want to cause offence. I pointed out that as neither of us were Greek Orthodox perhaps the priest wouldn't care to come along anyway; besides it would hardly be proper, in the circumstances. . . . Pandelis agreed. It wouldn't make any difference, he said: the house was going to be a good one, priest or no priest – wasn't he building it? I was not to worry about anything.

'Anything else?' I asked him, anxiously. I was beginning to wonder if I should have to put out a bowl of goat's milk to propitiate the ghost of the Panormos dragon that Ayios Rhiginos had driven to its death sixteen centuries ago. Pandelis looked at me for a moment, and then slapped his thigh, doubling up with laughter. 'No! Nothing else. Tomorrow the masons come, and we start the building. . . .'

I was relieved. Having robbed the old gods of a cock undoubtedly their due, it was just possible that I had made amends by not having a priest. At least, I hoped so. A pantheist would have a wonderful time in Panormos, a godhead plain in every element, earth and water, trees and sky. It was difficult not to tread on anyone's toes, and if I had sensed, as it were out of the corner of my eye, the god Pan dancing in bawdy triumph on the Christian ruins of Ayia Sophia – itself at one time almost certainly a temple – just behind the house, I would like to have warned him that his jubilation was premature: Vangeli intended one day to rebuild the chapel, and I would help him. It was an age of tolerance, for Panormos at least: the old gods and the new must learn to live together. To the old I was prepared to libate generously with wine and spirits, but there was to be no more blood. I hoped they would understand.

I heard the masons arriving the next morning, the jingle of bells on their mules, ponies and donkeys, the barking of their dogs. The cats on board *Astarte* came on deck, sat on the mainsail gaff and bristled at the sound. There were four masons, Panayióti and another Pandelis, and Pandezis and Nikos. These last two were great friends and extremely good builders. They were both tall men, Pandezis white-haired and blue-eyed, Nikos dark with a long swarthy face and a black mongrel dog that he called oddly enough 'dog', though it sounded more like 'dock'. They used to go fishing together in the rowing boat Nikos kept in a stone and brushwood boathouse that was half a cave, near the retsina barn. Usually they fished at night, for squid or octopus. All these four lived with their wives and families in cottages they had built themselves about half an hour's climb above the bay, across a grassy plateau on the slopes of which they grew vines and fruit trees and olives. We were following Vangeli's wise advice – employing as far as possible those who were going to be our neighbours.

The caique with the cement from Volos was late. It should have arrived two days ago; but that morning we heard the sound of an engine from behind Daseiá. I rowed across to the caique as she came in and told the captain where to anchor – at the head of the cove by Vangeli's barn, where the cement was to be stored. There were two hundred and fifty sacks: twelve and a quarter tons, the first instalment; and with the cement a great deal of other material.

About this time Pandelis introduced me to a person who was to prove most important to the building of the house, a man generally known as Captain Ilias. He owned and worked a heavy rowing boat about twenty feet long, that also stepped a mast and a lateen sail. His main job was bringing sand and pebbles for the house, to mix with the cement, but he and his boat were also useful in ferrying materials from the various caiques that now began to put in to Panormos to the beach under the house.

Captain Ilias was fifty-eight, with a large red nose, a straggling moustache and watery pink-rimmed blue eyes. Wisps of grey hair hung deceptively from under the oversized cloth cap he wore low down over his ears – deceptively, because on the rare occasions that he took his cap off it showed that he had no other hair at all. His high domed head was bald as an electric-light bulb. He was difficult at first to get to know, because he was rather shy, but eventually we became good friends.

He had been doing this particular work, he told me, in his deep throaty voice that reminded me of a preacher fulminating from a pulpit, for thirty-five years. This was his third boat. He carried sand for most of the buildings in Skopelos, and Pandelis, he said, had a very high opinion of him – 'That's why I always work for him. He trusts me. He knows I won't cheat him, because every boatload I bring is a full one!' He was paid by the boatload. 'And do you know what I *could* do?'

'What?'

'Well, I could go and get the easiest sand, sand right next to the sea, and full of salt. But do I? No! I go and get it from the back of the beaches, good clean sand, and fine! Washed by the winter rain. . . . Look—', and he took up a handful and let it fall through his fingers. 'Want to taste it?'

There was no doubt it was exhausting work, to row over a mile to one of the big beaches north of Panormos, run his boat on to the sand and start shouldering cans of pebbles and sand from high up the shore. Each boatload weighed a ton, and for each load he was paid the equivalent of £1.

'Why don't you get someone to help you?' I asked him.

'I'm waiting for Yiórgo to come. That's my son. Then we can make two journeys a day. But Yiórgo doesn't like this work so much, it's too hard for him. . . .' There was another reason I discovered. The last job the pair of them had been on was carrying sand from the north coast of the island into Skopelos harbour. A wind had got up suddenly, and a sea, and the heavily loaded boat had sunk just as they rounded in between the harbour lights. Yiórgo, although an experienced sailor as I found out later, could not swim; the experience of nearly drowning because, as he said, his father insisted on filling up the boat too high, had rather put him off such work.

'But he's coming all right,' said Captain Ilias. 'He'll be here any day now. He's my son, isn't he?'

Yiórgo was thirty-five and nearly as bald as his father. He was the eldest of Captain Ilias' six children, four of whom were girls. During the war Captain Ilias took eight escaping Englishmen from Glysteri cove on the north coast of Skopelos to Vassiliko. When the fighting was over he was summoned to Volos and paid for this feat, and others like it, the sum of £30. He had been interrogated, he says, by the Italians, who broke his leg: they pushed him over the sea-wall by the castle. Another more popular version is that he was drunk, and fell.

Not that Captain Ilias is exactly an alcoholic; but it's true that he likes a drink, or several, every so often, and he can be found most evenings when he is not working drinking in his favourite taverna under the old castle wall. Occasionally there, when the mood takes him and he finds it necessary to relieve his feelings, he will break a few chairs; in the morning he returns to pay for the damage. When he is working, however, he prefers *tsipuro*, and whenever I saw him at Panormos there was always a little bottle of that fiery spirit concealed somewhere in the boat.

We would see him coming from a long way off, rounding the point into Panormos Bay, his great blue boat loaded to the gunnels with sand, nearly awash, propelled with slow oarstrokes across the water; and the builders would rest for a moment, grin and say, 'Ah – there's

Captain Ilias!' And when he had arrived, pushing his boat up against the temporary wooden jetty we had made under the house, they'd call down to him, 'Ho there, Captain Ilias! How are things going?' To which his invariable reply was, 'Badly, friends! Badly. . . .'

However he would then usually shout, 'Maiko, Maiko!' (one version of my name) and when I'd gone down to the beach, he would dig under a layer or two of sacking and pull out a bottle. 'Try some of this – it'll do you good.' Again the builders would call down: 'Hey, Captain Ilias!'

'Yes? I'm listening.'

'How can you do any work with all that *tsipuro*?'

'How can I do any work without it?'

The work was going well. A mountain of sand had grown up on the beach. A pit had been dug near by and a caique had brought a load of limestone that was set to boil and hiss, pouring its white liquid into the pit.

Spyro and Iannis Patsis said that years ago when they were boys and worked for the old man, Alexandra's father, there used to be a well with good water which they used for the tile-making. They remembered the place roughly, well inside our plot of land, and I checked the position with Alexandra's father who gladly pointed it out. We dug and found water. It had a slightly salty flavour, but oddly enough the streams flowing in, which were clearly visible, came not from the direction of the sea but from inland. Some of the workmen drank it, and claimed it possessed excellent digestive powers; certainly it would be fine for watering trees and plants, and was good enough for building. Pandelis was delighted. We got on well with him, and I think he liked us nearly as much as we liked him. As the autumn drew on and the days shortened, rain sometimes stopped work; storms blew up from the north-west, clouds massed over distant Pelion and rolled with thunder across the sea, and Panormos became a cauldron of white frothing water, raked with violent gusts hurtling down from the hills on every side.

Caiques put into Panormos for shelter on days like these, great crimson and orange half-moons of ships, loaded with salt or wheat or wood, paint peeling from drenched, heavy timbers, their captains shouting orders against the scream of the wind as the rusty chain rattled through the anchor ports, and the proud steep bows swung round against the storm.

The bad weather never lasted long. It was the beginning of November but still warm enough to swim. Skopelos came out in her autumn colours with heather purpling the hills, and Panormos became a green paradise of rich grass and myriad flowers; steam rose like smoke between the pines and cypresses, and the olives swelling and darkening on the trees began to fall. It was a good crop that year.

Pandelis and his assistant, a young man whom he was training, slept at nights in part of Vangeli's retsina barn. The place had first been used by Ilias and his son Yiórgo, when the nights became too cold to sleep out in their boat. Captain Ilias was glad of company because he was afraid of the *pondikia*, the mice or rats that lived in the hay. 'I have to sleep with my stick beside me,' he complained to me, 'you can't imagine it! Rustle, rustle! The rats! Bang, I go with my stick, and they scamper all over my legs. . . . I can't sleep a wink. Is it right for a man like me, to have to sleep with mice, like that?'

'I don't know about the mice,' said Pandelis, 'but certainly I can't sleep with Captain Ilias beating me with his stick every hour or so. . . .'

Stephanos, Pandelis's son, arrived from Athens for a time, and often we asked them on board for supper, with Ilias and Yiórgo; Angelina cooked huge spaghettis and *Astarte*'s wine reserves were put to good use. Pandelis spent hours poring over the plans that were now permanently laid out on the chart table, calculating the amounts of various materials the house would be needing, especially wood, and roof tiles. I'd made a scale model of the house in cardboard, mainly to see what the roofs with their many different slopes would look like, which Pandelis enjoyed looking at. As he got to know us better he told us something of his life.

His father had been poor, and Pandelis left school very early, having learnt however to read and write and do simple sums. He started as a builder's help, just like any of the boys now working on the house. He determined to learn every part of the trade, bricklaying, masonry, carpentry and the mysteries of reinforced concrete. He became a craftsman, a *mástoras* himself, saved money, and when he was twenty undertook his first building on his own account. From then on he never stopped, gradually earning a reputation for honesty, hard work and intelligence. He was very proud of the things he had built, and especially of the harbour beacons that flash red and green at the end of the mole at Skopelos. He'd got the contract by putting in a lower estimate than anyone else, and then, in spite of popular scepticism proceeded to build and finish the lights before the winter gales. The beacons there before had been repeatedly washed away, destroyed by the sea.

'They're strong, and they look beautiful too – don't you think? But when the first big gale came from the north I was very anxious – if they'd gone down after all the arguments and battles I'd fought about building them, I knew I'd be finished. I used to stand by the cafés in the wind and rain shivering as I watched the waves come crashing over the mole, the beacons disappear in white foam . . . and what a sea that was, too. But they held, and they've held ever since, and that was years ago. . . .' Pandelis had also invented a useful and ingenious method of laying concrete under water: he had made a ten-foot long iron funnel – the mixture was poured in at the top, and because it was contained in the cylinder the cement powder did not float away in a cloud when it hit the bottom.

Having lacked any real education himself, he was determined that his son should have the best. (Besides Stephanos there were three other children, two girls in their early teens and a small boy.) Stephanos was sent to Athens to become an architect, and for seven years Pandelis paid out in fees what was by island standards enough to keep a large family. Stephanos was a slim, good-looking young man, twenty-one years old, with a sensitive face and excellent manners. He helped a lot with the plans as the house progressed and worked with his father on the walls and in laying the concrete beams across the doors and windows. 'If he's to be a good architect,' Pandelis said, 'he's got to be a good builder first. He must learn everything there is to learn. . . .'

The relationship of fathers and sons in Greece, especially in the islands and the remoter parts of the country, is governed by strict convention. It is a rule for instance that a son never smokes in front of his father. Yiórgo, the son of Captain Ilias, although thirty-five years old, would never dream of lighting up if his father was in sight. Sometimes when they were together I have without thinking offered Yiórgo a cigarette which he has quietly refused with that reverse nod, upward movement of the head that is the Greek negative, with an explanatory sideways glance at the old man puffing away at his cigarette a few yards away.

The convention has its amusing side, too, when the relationship of father and son is a close one. In the cabin of *Astarte* at night after supper, Stephanos might suddenly get up and muttering something about a breath of fresh air climb out by the companion-steps. Pandelis gives me a slight, embarrassed grin, and goes on with what he is saying, while behind him on deck there is the brief flare of a match. This is part of accepted practice. Yet the son would never over-embarrass his father by announcing his intention of going out to smoke, and a considerate father is careful to allow a decent lapse of time before calling him, or going out himself, to allow him the enjoyment of his cigarette in peace. Pandelis has only to turn his head to catch his son in the act; but this is exactly what he does not do. When Pandelis runs out of cigarettes at Panormos he will think nothing illogical in borrowing a packet or two from Stephanos, who is usually much better stocked.

*   *   *   *

The concrete ceiling of the living-room was laid. The long room set back from the top of the rocks was now seen to possess a most unusual acute angle at one corner; this was because the line of the cliff face was by no means square with the rest of the building, and I insisted that the outer wall, where there would be the overhanging balcony, should follow the rock summit as closely as possible. 'Are you quite sure that's how you want it?' Pandelis asked me dubiously. 'I've never seen, much less built anything like that before. . . .' 'Yes,' I replied firmly, 'that's how it must be. . . .'

'*Kyknos!*' the builders said, referring to the sharp high prow of the island steamer. The corner certainly looked like the bows of a ship, from the base of the rocks to the roof of the living-room about twenty-five feet high. 'It won't look so odd,' I said, 'when the balcony comes out of it, with the tiles over . . .' At this stage, I told myself, there must be no faltering. Gazing up at it from the beach the house looked like some medieval fortress; but there was one effect that the masons had managed perfectly: the house seemed part of the rocks, to grow up out of them.

There were moments of searching doubt. For one thing the house appeared to be much bigger now that the walls were up than I had imagined it would be. My plans and sketches on pieces of paper and the cardboard model, had seemed to me easily understood. Setting the builders to translate the pencil lines to solid stone and mortar, three-dimensional, had let loose something that once started had gone in a way beyond my control. It was like a poem, or a book: it suddenly became a separate thing, apart from its creator. Staring up at it I felt it no longer belonged to me as it had before, that it no longer even recognized me; and standing now in the shadow of its walls I felt a peculiar moment of loneliness.

Still, if it was to be a good house it was right that it should have a character of its own; and that it certainly had. I kept reminding myself that as long as the house looked part of the rock, then because the rock was part of Panormos, the house must belong too, if not to any person then at least to the place where it stood.

Over the cliff face the scaffolding seemed particularly high and dangerous, but no one fell off. Angelina became popular ministering to the wounds caused by those small accidents common to building— Andrikos got lime in his eye, one of the boys cut his thumb badly, and Yiórgo son of Ilias while wading ashore with a can of sand on his back trod on some rare poisonous fish or shell, so that his leg became swollen.

That week we laid up *Astarte* in Vassiliko, leaving the boat in the care of the three granddaughters of Lycúrgos. Back in Skopelos again we returned to Panormos by the rough mule-track over the hills. Vangeli leant us Takis the donkey, on whom we loaded stores for a week and the warmer clothes we would be needing. We were going to stay in the family cottage on the slopes of Panormos valley, so as to be near the building.

Vangeli was busier than usual just then. It was the time of the olive harvest, and besides arranging for the collection of his own crop, he was supervising the olive-pressing in his big barn on the outskirts of the village. There are only two olive-presses on Skopelos, and Vangeli owns one of them: it is, he says, one of the most financially rewarding of businesses because everyone on the island must have his olives pressed somewhere and though the press only takes a small percentage, usually paid in oil, the amount adds up.

Before we left for Panormos I went to see how it was done. I was surprised to find that, although the ice-making had temporarily reduced the noise in the great building, the general appearance of confusion and activity had doubled. The old engines were still thunderously at work, power from them being shifted by overhead fan belts to the giant millstones revolving in their huge iron trough. About twenty people were in the barn, six or seven employed at the machines and working at the olives, the rest standing by either as spectators, or queueing up with tall baskets loaded to the brim with olives, waiting for their turn.

'Very automatic, everything,' shouted Vangeli above the din. 'I will show you all. Notice, please, that in the beginning the olives are washed —' He took me round to the back of the barn and we climbed some steps to look over into the grinding-trough. A conveyor belt brought up the olives through a stream of running water and tipped them into the mill where the two broad granite discs, each four feet in diameter and half as thick, ponderously rotated, grinding the olives, stones, skin and all into a brown sticky pulp. 'Better not to fall in, here,' Vangeli advised me.

At the bottom stood a man working against time to keep up with the flow of crushed olives that oozed out of a wide spout at the base of the mill. Beside him was a pile of brown flat bags or sacks, big as doormats, and made out of the same rough material, into which he shovelled the pulp, spreading it thinly inside. As he completed each one it was seized by another man who swung it across to yet a third who stacked the sacks in a column, one on top of the other, in the jaws of the presser.

When the pile was as high as his head he kicked a lever and the upper platform began to descend. The first pressing was beautiful to watch: bright beads of fine oil began to appear along the edges of every sack and as the pressure increased turned into a richly running stream, glittering in the harsh electric light of the barn like liquid gold. Each column of sacks was pressed three times, the third after every one had been opened and a can of hot water, heated in the furnace behind, had been thrown in.

The liquid drained from the press, a mixture of oil and hot water, was channelled in a pipe across the barn and drawn up by pumps into a machine that spun the oil and water in a drum, separating the two (oil being lighter than water) so that the water was discharged as waste at the bottom and the pure oil ran out of a spout at the top, from here it was put into big cans, marked, numbered and stored away. Later Vangeli would do a few tests with the little chemical apparatus he keeps in his house to decide the quality and grading of each volume of oil. Nothing is wasted. Even the dessicated brown pulp that is thrown out of the sacks once they have been pressed is put to some use : either as fertilizer on the island or sent away to a factory in Khalkis where a further amount of oil juice is extracted to make soap.

Vangeli made pieces of toast over the fire and held them for a moment under the fine stream of warm oil as it came out of the separator. I have never tasted oil so good, though when I first came to Greece I didn't like olive oil in the least. (It reminded me of an evening sometime before, having supper with the Hannas family : the subject of olive oil came up and the family were appalled to learn that no olives grew in England. Vangeli of course knew the awful secret. 'They only use it to put on their heads!' he said, amid a roar of laughter. 'But what do the English use for cooking, then?' the grandmother asked me. 'Butter,' I said, noting the expressions of glum consternation round the table. 'And other fats, lard —' 'But surely not on meat, and vegetables?' 'Yes.' '*No oil*,' they kept murmuring, as if such a natural misfortune were hardly imaginable. No wonder, they seemed to be thinking, the poor English liked coming to Greece . . .)

The olive gathering and the pressing goes on through the autumn and into the winter. Most of the olives being pressed were green – the only difference between green and black olives is that the latter have been allowed to ripen longer on the trees. In Greece black olives are usually kept for separate eating – stored away first in great barrels of salted water, split open, soaked, and after some time ready to eat. In Panormos where we stayed for a couple of weeks Alexandra assisted by two women were daily going the rounds of the olive groves, collecting the olives from the ground and sometimes shaking the upper branches of the trees with long sticks, heaping the olives into panniers and on to the backs of Takis and Foola.

The weather was changeable, and it rained more frequently. Upstairs in Vangeli's house there is a long seven foot wide 'shelf' stretching and filling one end of the room. This is a bed ; not by any means the only bed in the room – there are three others – but certainly the most interesting one. It was covered with thin straw mattresses, cushions and bright, heavy island-woven blankets. At one end of it slept Angelina and I, and at the other end the two grey-haired women – who came every year to help the family with the fruit and olive harvests. But there was plenty of room : the bed, fifteen feet broad, had often slept, according to Alexandra, seven people at a time.

The building was getting slower and slower. Every morning we went down the valley to the cove, collecting mushrooms on the way, to see how many workmen and masons had turned up. It wasn't only the weather that delayed us now. Every one of the men working on the house had his own plot of land somewhere in the hills: the olives needed picking, and the fruit, the vines pruning. . . . It was a bad time for other kinds of work, like building, and first things came first. . . . Pandelis was in despair. Often, with the boy who helped him, he was the only person at the site. But at least the roof-tiles had arrived, the curved 'Byzantine' kind that I particularly loved, brought by caique from Khalkis, and now that the walls were finished Pandelis was busy setting up the beams and angled joists for the roof. He had arranged with the captain of the *Katerina* to change his route one day and land at Panormos from Volos most of the wood for the roofs and balconies. Included in this load were the twenty-one columns the house would be needing, of chestnut wood from Mount Athos. The passengers of course were not informed of this change in the caique's itinerary, and the *Katerina* was four hours late when she finally arrived in Skopelos harbour.

At least the living-room was dry, and with its own ceiling, and the wood was stored inside; but there were no doors or windows yet. The wind whined through the shell of the house, eddying scraps of paper and dust in the corners, amid the debris of wood and cement, heaped stones and crumbling brick. Sometimes the place looked more like an abandoned ruin than a house being built. It was three weeks to Christmas, and clear that not much more work would be done now before the spring. Captain Ilias sat in his boat at the jetty, clutching his *tsipuro* bottle and waving it menacingly at the wind. 'A heavy winter we'll have this year!' he cried. 'I can smell it in the air – storms, cold, snow. . . . Listen to that wind, Maiko, listen. . . .'

14

Elections for Mayor: Vangeli Stands

Captain Ilias was right. The winter in Skopelos that year was the worst within living memory. Continuous storms battered the Sporades, snow fell, and even on the shores of the islands lay for a week. The temperature dropped below freezing point and frost 'burnt' many olive trees. Worse than the cold however was a series of earth tremors that shook the island – leaving Skiathos and Alonnisos untouched. No one was hurt, but most of the older houses, built without cement, suffered some damage: walls cracked and buckled, roofs shifted, and the little village of Klima which clings to the steep west coast of the island actually slipped a short way down the hillside. The houses were abandoned, and now the plan is to rebuild the village down by the sea, near the beach called Eleos, 'Mercy', where Ayios Rhiginos landed long ago.

We returned to Skopelos at the end of March, driving out from England in a second-hand Land-Rover I had bought on Vangeli's behalf. The vehicle was useful to us for the carrying of all the things we needed for the house, and Vangeli had always wanted one, to transport his olives, wood, resin and fruit, and for general work in his estate at Panormos, now that the road was at least passable and would soon be open even for the bus. It was the first private vehicle, owned by an islander, to land on Skopelos, and its possession gave Vangeli, who in any case was greatly respected by the majority of Skopelots, a certain added prestige.

Earth tremors could still be felt on the island, once or twice a day, but most of them were slight, and as the worst of the architectural shake-down was over, there was no more serious damage.

In Panormos the old resin-collectors' cottage that had once been a customs-house, was badly damaged and was clearly unsafe to live in. Even worse, Vangeli's house up the valley was rendered uninhabitable, with a broad crack visible across the whole of one wall. The old retsina barn, oddly enough, was untouched. The family was in mourning when we arrived. Vangeli had written me the sad news during the winter: his father-in-law was dead. Alexandra and her mother wore black – they would continue to do so for a year, and Vangeli wore a black tie and arm-band. We missed the old man's kindly face at the kitchen table, his seat in the corner against the wall.

Nothing had happened to our house – 'it's on a rock,' said Pandelis, 'and strong as a castle. All of Skopelos would have to fall before it was harmed. . . .' I said I hoped it would never be put to such a test and Pandelis wholeheartedly agreed, crossing himself quickly.

Not much in the way of building had taken· place during our absence, partly because of the difficulty in crossing the island in the snow and bad weather, and also because all the builders were busy repairing their own houses. Pandelis was still putting the roof up in April.

One warm night at the beginning of May, we were about to go to sleep on *Astarte*'s cabin top. There was no moon, and everything was very still. A curious, low, booming thunder began suddenly to roll round the hills, gradually increasing in strength and volume until we were both sitting up staring fearfully into the darkness around us. The boat shuddered and a glass crashed off the table in the cabin; the anchor chain grated harshly on the sea-bottom. It lasted only six or seven seconds but it was long enough. In the ensuing silence I could hear tiles falling from the retsina barn opposite and stones clattering on rocks. Hundreds of birds – I never knew there were so many in Panormos – got up from the trees, twittering uneasily. Dogs barked in the valley and the shouts of men and women rang out, calling across to each other from their cottages in the hills.

The islanders had not been slow to fix the blame for these manifestations of chthonic displeasure: if it was not the hydrogen bomb tests of the Russians or Americans then it was the work of the Communist 'underground'. . . . More specifically was singled out a foreign woman known on the island as Kyria Litsa who had with government permission repaired and renovated an old monastery in the rich valley behind Skopelos village and kept it to house, in youth-hostel fashion, batches of French students throughout the summer. Such blasphemy – considering also the rumoured 'immoral' behaviour of the young French within the monastery walls – clearly marked out the island for a demonstration of divine wrath.

It was a time too of political change. By the general election of last autumn the conservative E.R.E. party of Karamanlis had after many years' rule been dislodged from power. Soldiers had come to the Sporades to ensure a free vote and prevent the scandals of previous Greek elections. No one had been allowed to carry arms during that time, and travelling on the big day was forbidden. Voting was compulsory. All the coffee-houses were closed, the sale of alcohol prohibited. The voting passed off without incident in Skopelos and the *Kendro* or 'Centre' party under the leadership of Papandreou formed the new government. A second election in the early part of the year, while we were still in England, returned Papandreou to power with an increased majority. In June there were to be held, in every town and city throughout Greece, the mayoral elections, and in Skopelos Vangeli had decided to stand for mayor.

Elections for mayor in Skopelos did not usually excite much attention, even among the islanders themselves. At the last moment a candidate could weigh the general feeling in the island, and if it was clear that his chances of success were slim, he would stand down. The present mayor was a stout, patriarchal, white-haired gentleman called Doulidis. He had been mayor of Skopelos several times before. Vangeli had defeated him eight years ago – mayors were elected for a term of four years – and it was said that Doulidis was so upset at his defeat that he locked himself up in his house for a month, seeing nobody, and finally slipped out and went to live in Athens for a time.

At the end of Vangeli's term Doulidis stood for election again, and Vangeli, gauging the situation as not being in his favour, did not oppose him. Mayoral elections are not supposed to be connected with national politics but it was inevitable that they should be influenced in some respects. It was felt that a mayor not of the same party as the government of the time was not likely to obtain a sufficiently sympathetic hearing from the government ministries upon whose goodwill often depended the allocation of funds for roads, schools, etc. Doulidis was a Karamanlis man; Vangeli supported the new order as represented by Papandreou and the 'Centre' party now in power.

This time also there was much more at stake. The new govern-

ment had introduced a number of sweeping reforms : besides creating
a new and welcome atmosphere of greater political freedom, with the
removal of those fascist undertones that had come to be associated
with the last government, there were new laws making education
free for everyone, and a free health service was to be introduced all
over Greece.

This last was of special significance in Skopelos : local self-government in Greece keeps to itself much power, and the two doctors on
the island, cousins of Vangeli, opposed the introduction of the health
scheme and began to canvass for the election of Doulidis the conservative candidate. In a country where family ties are strong and
taken very seriously this defection, betrayal – as Vangeli saw it – of
the doctors, drove him into furious indignation and hardened his
determination to win. It was expected that at the last moment
Doulidis would stand down. He was said to be over seventy, and it
seemed that all the signs were against him ; but he didn't : Vangeli
came across to Panormos and told me the news. We stood on the
balcony that Pandelis had just finished, overhanging the low cliff.
'Politics is a terrible thing,' Vangeli said, staring over the sea. 'I do
not like them, they can be so much bad . . . besides I have my own
life, my family. I know what it is to be mayor, for four years – no
time except for arguing, talking, work. . . . But now I cannot stand
by. I have a responsibility for my island – isn't it so? No, I must fight
this election.' He struck the open palm of one hand with his fist. 'It
will be difficult, but *I shall win.*'

The electioneering campaign was conducted on both sides with
considerable passion. The whole island was divided, and even
families were split, making the contest peculiarly bitter. Skopelots
are on the whole conservative in nature, being mostly small land-
holders and shopkeepers, and Vangeli was standing for a new order,
a more democratic, socialistic régime echoing the change of government in Athens, and his political platform did not appeal to everyone. But if anyone could be called a 'man of the people' it was
Vangeli. As an old peasant said to me one evening in Skopelos, 'You
can talk to Vangeli, go up to him and say what you feel. He *listens*;
and you know he *understands*. He's one of us.' Almost everybody could
say the same thing, and in a strange way it would be true for them
all.

Each party was now drawing up its list of prospective councillors,

whose names would appear on the two ballot papers, and for whom
every man and woman must register a vote. Speeches in front of the
coffee–houses down at the harbour became frequent and noisy. The
only microphone and loud-speaker system was held by the present
mayor and corporation : Doulidis spoke into it to good effect from a
balcony overlooking the cafés, and withheld its use from his opponent. When Vangeli spoke – a party of schoolchildren were organized
to clap and chant and try and drown his voice – he made up for lack
of volume with the force of his oration and the violence of his
gestures. It began to look as if the two parties were fairly evenly
opposed : it was going to be a very close thing, and no one could say
for certain what would be the outcome.

As election day drew nearer, tension mounted. The sound of fierce
argument and much beating of table-tops could be heard issuing
from every coffee-house and taverna, and under the plane trees by
the sea friends passed each other without saying good morning, and
sat in groups whispering and glowering at their neighbours at the
next table. Of Vangeli's dozen or more prospective councillors I
knew several quite well : one was my barber, one a shopkeeper who
sold me paint, nails and other things, another a carpenter who was
supposed to be making the doors and windows for the house (he was
already a month late with them) and a taverna-owner who supplied
me with my wine and ouzo.

There was no question as to with whom my own sympathies lay.
Besides not knowing Doulidis at all, I liked the sound of the new
Papandreou government and everything it stood for; but of course
most important of all was the fact that Vangeli was a great friend,
and if he wanted to be mayor I wished him every success. Still, I was
a foreigner, and Greek politics was none of my business. Nevertheless,
as it turned out, I did find myself indirectly playing a small part.

*   *   *   *

It was Makhi who was sent to look for me on the morning before
election day and found me having lunch with Rolf and Barbara,
who were still having difficulties over the building of their hotel.
'Please come to our home quickly – my father says it is very important.' When I arrived there was a small crowd outside the door and
the hall was full of people. Alexandra said : 'Vangeli is in the

study —' and bustled me up past those lining the stairs and into the room. Vangeli was at his desk, and eight or nine of his would-be councillors sat round the walls, expressions of tense anxiety on their faces.

Vangeli greeted me and asked me if I would do something for him. He explained to me rapidly what he wanted me to do: drive with him across the island as quickly as possible to Panormos, and sail *Astarte* over to Skiathos. I was to take two others with me, Mikhális Tchoukalas, the captain of the *Pródromos*, and another man. It was a matter of vital urgency he said, and concerned the hundred Skopelots working in Athens, who were now waiting at Pefki on Evvia to come across to Skopelos and vote. . . . There were many questions which I would have liked to ask, but clearly this was not the time.

Vangeli said: 'Is *Astarte* in a state of readiness for sea?'

'Of course,' I replied, not really knowing whether she was or not, and already beginning to feel like one of those cool characters in a badly written thriller. The dialogue seemed just right.

'How many minutes before she can leave?'

'Ten.'

'From Panormos to Skiathos?'

'An hour and twenty minutes.'

'And twenty-five minutes in the Land-Rover —' He looked at his watch. Everybody checked their watches. There was a murmur of approval. It seemed that whatever it was they wanted done might just be managed in time.

I already had the ignition keys in my pocket. I went down to the harbour-front and started the engine. Vangeli joined me and we drove quickly to the ice factory to refuel. A moment later Mikhális arrived, followed almost immediately by the second passenger I was to take across to Skiathos: a man I had never seen before, stocky, unshaven and with light blue eyes. He seemed to be behaving as if he didn't want anyone to see him – he came slinking along the white walls of the narrow street and now dived for the protection of the cab. I was beginning to understand why they had arranged to meet here, rather than down by the cafés.

I rode behind to allow the three of them to talk and finish making their plans. As we drove out of Skopelos across the Old Bridge we saw the bus coming towards us. Instead of simply drawing in to one side, Vangeli turned the car right off the road down by the river-bed. As the bus jolted by the second passenger, whom clearly I ought to call Z, raised his arms to shield his face from being recognized. Vangeli turned to me through the rear window. 'We are like gangsters!' He seemed to be enjoying himself.

We drove now like madmen, the Land-Rover leaping like a stag over the innumerable pot-holes of the earth road, only occasionally it seemed making some grinding contact with the surface, changing gears on the steep up-gradients, swinging round the cliff bends with wheels whining on the edge of the gravel. Dust billowed out behind. I held on with difficulty.

As we came down to Agnonda the usual holiday-makers were sitting round the tables under the giant planes. The second passenger, Z, ducked and crouched down behind the dashboard as we rattled past. It seemed to be getting better and better. My only regret, as we hurtled up the twisting road through the pines, was that the time had been badly chosen – how much more dramatic at midnight instead of midday, with lanterns winking from the shore, muffled oars, to slip out of Panormos as the moon went down, secretly and without lights. . . . Still, perhaps I wasn't taking the situation as seriously as it deserved.

Vangeli stopped the car on the road above the house. We ran down to the cove. I pushed out the dinghy lying ashore under the balconies, and Vangeli launched his from the retsina barn. He was not coming with us but would remain in Skopelos at the centre of events. He rowed Captain Mikhális and Z out to *Astarte* and helped us cast off the moorings. I had gathered so far that my mission was simply to proceed to Skiathos, drop off the other two, and come back immediately. A certain Vervéris, captain of a large caique – I knew him : he was the arthritic gentleman who had brought my cement from Volos – was supposed to be in Skiathos harbour, and with luck and a little persuasion would set off immediately to Pefki and pick up the Athenians. But this explained only the main outlines of our journey – the secrecy and extreme urgency, the almost sinister presence of Z, were matters about which I was greatly curious. I would have an excellent opportunity, I decided, to question my passengers on the voyage, for I was glad to see that the north-westerly that had been blowing with violence the last two days and nights had dropped considerably, and the weather promised a fair passage.

Fortunately the engine started at once. Vangeli in his dinghy had some difficulty working with the mooring ropes and at the same time keeping himself afloat. The boat had been lying dry in the sun and the timbers were open; the water was already up to his knees and rising fast. My last view of him as we rounded Arapi Point, heading for Daseiá, was bailing frantically, water pouring like a cataract from his rapidly working bucket.

Settling down at the tiller I began to ask my questions. . . . The voters from Athens, who had come up by coach, bus, motorcycle and every available transport, were expecting to be picked up by the *Katerina* on her way from Volos that afternoon. They were all supporters of Vangeli. It had been carefully arranged, and, it was supposed, secretly, because it was well known that the opposition party would do everything in its power to prevent their arrival. The *Katerina* was to have landed her valuable cargo on Saturday (today) evening; they would be well in time to join their families and vote the next morning. (Polling stations were open from sunrise and closed at sunset.) Unfortunately this apparently foolproof plan had been discovered by Vangeli's opponents and at the last moment successfully sabotaged.

The captain of the *Katerina*, only two hours before, had made a frantic telephone call from Volos to Skopelos with the astounding news that the harbour authorities had categorically forbidden him to put into Pefki and take on board the Athenians. The reason urged for such an unprecedented order was that Pefki was not on the *Katerina's* regular itinerary, and for this voyage at least she was not to stray a yard from her scheduled course. . . . As so often in Greece it had been a question of who had friends where.

The timing of the prohibition, from the point of view of Vangeli's opponents, had been perfect. It had been left, cunningly, so late that the *Paskhális* which might have been able to do the job, as the place was legitimately on her normal itinerary, had already left Pefki and was now on her way to Skiathos. The reason that the *Katerina* was chosen in the first place was because her captain was one of Vangeli's còuncillors to be, and could be relied on to see that all hundred Athenians were safely embarked; the owner of the *Paskhális*, however; though a friend of Vangeli, lived in Skiathos and was therefore more difficult to include in such complex and necessarily secret plans. In the face of the Volos port embargo the *Katerina's* captain was powerless : as a piece in this complicated political chess game he and his ship were right off the board. His telephone call had been the last before the telephone offices closed down for the long afternoon siesta : five hours in which Vangeli and his councillors could do nothing, while the valuable time slipped by. It was indeed a masterly, if somewhat unscrupulous, move in the game.

The problem that faced Vangeli and his friends gathered that midday so solemnly at his house was how and with what to counter such a devastating blow. Their confidence in Vangeli's election on the morrow was high, but it depended on the presence of the Athenian contingent. According to the latest records of the canvassers, as Mikhális told me that afternoon on *Astarte*, out of a total electorate of 1,760 Vangeli could count 480 votes for certain : this figure, doubled because it did not include the men's wives, and in Greece women usually vote as their husbands tell them, made 960, giving him a narrow but sufficient majority at the polls. However, counted in this 480 were the 100 Athenians now stranded at Pefki : unless a means were rapidly devised to get them across the sea the cause, as Captain Mikhális put it, munching nervously at the remains of his cucumber, was lost. . . .

Of the craft moored just then in Skopelos harbour only one, the *Pródromos*, Mikhális's ship, was big enough and fast enough to undertake such a mission, but unfortunately various vital parts of her engine were lying scattered about Yiórgo's workbench. . . . A caique therefore had to be found in Skiathos, either Vervéris' boat, or the *Korfini* – in any case, as it was impossible to use the telephone, someone had to get to Skiathos immediately, and make what arrangements he could, at the earliest moment. One way was to send one of the small fishing boats, *venzinas*, then in the harbour, but the sea was still running high at Cape Gourouni, and the journey that way round would take several hours. Panormos, on the comparatively sheltered west coast of the island, facing Skiathos, was the obvious choice, with *Astarte* lying conveniently at anchor in the bay.

'Make the sail, if it is possible!' Vangeli had shouted after me as we left, but the wind was practically head on, and only as we came within a mile or so of Répi lighthouse could I raise the staysail. But what about Z? Why was it so important that no one should see him leave Skopelos village and cross the island?

The answer, as they told me, was fairly simple. Z was well-known as the representative and organizer of his fellow-islanders working in Athens. The opposition, having put the *Katerina* out of action, were no doubt congratulating themselves in the belief that the men coming from Athens would never arrive in time to vote. If they saw Z speeding across the island with Vangeli to Panormos they would realize why. There might be time to put pressure on the harbour-master at Skiathos – Doulidis, after all, was still mayor, even though it might be his last day – and so prevent any caique from sailing to Pefki. I had gathered, by this time, that the majority of those waiting on Evvia were, politically speaking, of the extreme left.

'Communist' is a loaded term anywhere in the world these days, but nowhere more so than in Greece. Here the memories of the civil war, only fifteen years past, are still fresh in the mind, and the memories are bitter. The Communist Party is outlawed in Greece, but as long as it does not call itself communist it may exist in one form or another, and in Greece the party calls itself E.D.A., although it is certain that the kind of communism it preaches has changed in one important respect: it is now more national, rather than inter-national. Of course there is still the hard core of fanatics devoted to the principle of world communism, looking naturally to Russia for support and leadership; there are also the so-called idealists, the born revolutionaries who conceal beneath an avowed selflessness in the cause of others quite the opposite sentiment, containing in their egotism a grudge against themselves and against their fellow beings. But it is believed that of those who voted for E.D.A. in the last general elections the majority belonged to that mixed grouping of people – mostly the very poor, the uneducated, some sincere if muddle-headed, others merely envious who see in the easy slogans of the working man's party a quick road to a utopia in which everyone can be rich. In Greece, where extremes of rich and poor live side by side and in noticeable contrast, there is much to explain such an ambition. It is, therefore, fairer to call those of the extreme left by the name many of themselves quite honestly prefer: not communists, but socialists.

There have been two main theories as to the best method of deal-ing with the threat of communism in Greece: the old method, of exclusion, imprisonment, discrimination in the ordinary means of living – as practised by the last government under Karamanlis. The second, made easier by time and the raising of general living standards in the country, could be called one of absorption rather than exclusion. This is the one favoured by the present government of Papandreou's party of the Centre, *Kendro*, and it is an attitude in which Vangeli believes passionately. 'If you hit these people *there* and *there*' – his arm striking the air – 'they will remain to hate you! It is necessary to bring them with you, to go together. That is the only way. Men are not donkeys to be beaten because they think different things to you!' Even Doulidis tried to enlist the support of the extreme left in his own election campaign. He failed where Vangeli succeeded. Vangeli is not afraid, should he be elected mayor, of having a few leftists in his council – the carpenter, for one, who is supposed to be making my doors: 'communist' his enemies call him, and of course he may well be. But this would be the test of Vangeli's attitude, the theory applied.

As we approached Répi, one of the islands that ring Skiathos Bay, I asked Z if he belonged to E.D.A. 'I am a socialist,' he said, evading the question. I then asked him what exactly was the difference between E.D.A. and *Kendro*.

'*Kendro*,' he said, 'is democratic and socialist, but only a little. In *Kendro* there are mostly the rich. They give to the poor, just a little,' he leaned forward, 'a little and only when they like. But E.D.A.,' and his voice rose, 'E.D.A. wants to give not a little but *everything* to the poor! No, E.D.A. is not communist but truly socialist!'

Mikhális, I noticed, of a more gentle nature, was embarrassed by his companion's outburst, and he changed the subject. 'Are your navigation lights working?' he asked.

I knew what was coming. They had been anxiously discussing what they should do if they couldn't find a suitable caique in Skiathos willing to transport a hundred voters from Evvia to Skopelos. The plan now, should all else fail, was for *Astarte* to take on board as many as she could safely carry in a calm sea – the wind was dying and the night promised, as so often in the Aegean, to be flat calm – and perhaps towing others in a large rowing boat behind make two or three journeys, landing the Athenians at Agnonda. It would take all night, but it was possible. Mikhális spread his hands wide, his kindly face creased with anxiety – what else could we do?

I agreed, but not without some serious misgivings. It was not that the doing of it worried me: the idea of ferrying voters from one island to another, at dead of night, appealed to me. But I was aware that such an action might possibly be interpreted as an unjustifiable interference in local politics, and I knew that foreigners could be expelled from Greece fairly easily : it depended on how many enemies you had been stupid enough to make, and how highly placed they were. I was no longer simply a tourist on holiday, a bird of passage. The land at Panormos, and the house, were stake enough, indeed to me they seemed almost everything.

On the other hand, I was not *interfering* in politics : I was merely helping voters who had a right to vote, who wanted to vote, to vote. I was doing (surely) what any public-spirited person should gladly do. It then occurred to me that if, after all this, Vangeli lost the election, then life for me on Skopelos might become somewhat hazardous : fortune favours the victorious – lose, and not only are you wrong, but also rather bad. A primitive law, but like all primitive laws one that dies hard. My real motive was personal, and concerned Vangeli, but whatever my reasons I reflected as we came between the island of Marango and Skiathos, turning slightly with the pines of Bourtsi on our left, I had in a sense come full circle. The freedom from all ties, from involvement, that I had boasted two years ago and had been so wary of losing, was now lost for ever. Perhaps it was inevitable. Oddly enough, now that it had happened, crept up behind and overtaken me, I no longer seemed to mind.

We avoided the main quay and headed for the lagoon. Mikhális had seen the *Korfini* at anchor in the bay, and at this stage they did not want to draw the attention of the harbour master to *Astarte*. We flung a rope to the *Korfini* and tied up to her, swinging at her stern. Captain Mikhális and Z climbed aboard off the bowsprit and I watched anxiously as they argued with the captain. By their long faces I could see that here at least they had no success : the caique had just come off the slip and was not yet ready for sea. Mikhális and Z were rowed rapidly ashore. Mikhális shouted to me to wait, but keep ready.

It was three-thirty in the afternoon, and Skiathos was deep in siesta. Only a few people sat under the café awnings. A ceaseless trilling of cicadas carried to me across from the Bourtsi pines. Beyond the neck of the peninsula and the sleeping harbour the mountains of Evvia shimmered palely in the heat. I settled down to repairing a new fitting for the jib, a roller-reefing gear, that had broken a few days ago.

I did not have to wait long. It must have been twenty minutes later, when I was just finishing, that I heard a hail from the shore and turned to see Mikhális standing in a boat that a small boy was rowing vigorously towards *Astarte*. 'Start the engine! Quickly, we're leaving!'

Captain Mikhális climbed aboard, breathing heavily, we cast off and headed once more for the open sea. With an effort Mikhális calmed himself. 'We have to catch the *Paskhális* – if we can! Perhaps it is too late!'

An entirely new set of circumstances had arisen. There was no caique in Skiathos big enough for the work in hand. But they had gone to the owner of the *Paskhális*, and he had agreed in principle to his ship being used – but the *Paskhális* had left Skiathos a few minutes before we had come in. She was making due east for Glossa, and by now might even have arrived there, and from Glossa she would go up the west coast of Skopelos, round Cape Gourouni and so to Skopelos harbour; and from there she would continue to Alonnisos and Steniválla, returning by the same route the next day. The owner had agreed that if the *Paskhális* could be stopped, her passengers and cargo could be transferred to *Astarte* – this part of the plan startled me a good deal – we would go on with them to Skopelos while she raced back to Pefki to embark the hundred Athenians. . . .

The scheme sounded feasible, but there was at least one important drawback. Could we stop her in time? The *Paskhális* is a fine caique, the pride of the Sporades, and her top and cruising speed (in the Aegean this is the same thing) is nine knots. The telephone office in Skiathos was still closed. Z was staying behind to try and rout out the operator and open it up, but finding the man might be difficult, and it would be too late to contact the agent in Loutráki (the harbour below Glossa) before the *Paskhális* left; it was up to *Astarte* with her maximum speed of six knots to catch her.

It was impossible to catch the *Paskhális* in Loutráki. As we came out into the open sea, the seven mile strait between Skiathos and Skopelos, she was nowhere to be seen, and therefore must already be behind the Loutráki breakwater. The only chance now, and a slim one, depending on how much loading and unloading she had to do there, was to head *Astarte* for a point just south of Gourouni, and try to intercept her before she rounded the cape.

Mikhális was not optimistic. 'We'll never do it,' he groaned.

'We'll be too late!' And then, a moment later, 'Maybe, if we're lucky. . . .' I turned the engine to its maximum revolutions. The sails were ready, but at present there was no wind.

But why, I asked him, couldn't the *Paskháli* be allowed to go on to Skopelos and receive her new sailing orders from there? She would lose at the most four hours, and by that time the telephone offices would have been open and she could go back to Pefki from Skopelos, returning with the voters on Sunday morning.

Mikhális looked at me darkly. 'Don't you know,' he said, 'who the agent of the *Paskháli* is in Skopelos?' I didn't, but no more needed to be said. He turned to me again. 'Even more important, there is the question of time! *The women* . . .'

Ah, the women. This was just one more new and for me unforeseen complication. Most of the women, it appeared – the wives, sisters, grandmothers and daughters – of those hundred key Skopelots waiting at Pefki remained behind in Skopelos. It was the usual practise for Greek women – in the Sporades at least – to vote first thing in the morning, soon after the polling stations were open at sunrise, probably because with all their housework to do they preferred to discharge their political obligations as early in the day as possible.

Now the doctors – the backbone of the Doulidis faction, who had been doing everything they could to prevent Vangeli's election – had, it was said, been making the rounds of the houses in Skopelos village, giving special attention to those homes where the husband was away working in Athens. . . . The influence that doctors have over ordinary people, especially women, is well known if deplorable. Vangeli's party had reason to suspect that the doctors were using their influence to persuade the women to vote for Doulidis, and it was generally felt that those wives whose husbands were absent were very likely to act on the doctors' advice: unless the menfolk arrived well in time to beat some sense into their women some seventy or more vital votes, cast in the early morning, would be lost.

It seemed that the situation was desperate. There was still no sign of the *Paskháli*, but as we strained our eyes in the direction of Glossa, easily making out now the cluster of houses at the foot of the green mountains, the thin white line of the breakwater from behind which at any moment the *Paskháli* must emerge, we prayed the caique should be delayed – just another ten minutes, fifteen – by

which time we would be in a fair position to cut her off on her northward course to Gourouni.

'If she comes out now,' said Mikhális, 'we can't do it —'

We were midway between the two islands. Five more minutes was
all we needed now – and then we saw her, first the tall mast and
superstructure, sliding it seemed along the top of the distant breakwater, then the white hull, still hardly more than a speck, two miles
away, turning out past the rocks and swinging north. Mikhális
swore.

I could see wind coming, gusting down the mountain-sides from
the south-east, dark patches sweeping across the sea. The gusts
steadied, small waves began to smack against the side of the boat; I
put up the staysail, then the jib.

The distance between the two boats was closing rapidly. There was
still a chance. The wind was freshening and *Astarte* heeled under her
two foresails. I could not help thinking what a splendid sight she
must be making when immediately the reefing-gear snapped loose
from the end of the bowsprit sending the entire jib streaming like a
fabulous red banner from the masthead. At least, I thought, this now
rather extraordinary if not so splendid sight would draw the attention of the people on board the great caique which could now be
clearly distinguished, with her white bow-wave building under the
prow. I collected the jib with difficulty, and brought up from the
cabin a large white sheet. This Mikhális proceeded to use like a
gigantic whip, lashing it from side to side in enormous sweeps as if he
were driving a racing chariot towards the finishing post with a dozen
horses galloping before.

One of *Astarte*'s treasures is a conch shell, given to me by a friend
called Petros who so sadly died in Skiathos the previous winter. This
shell, more than a foot long, is a rare and wonderful thing. Once the
art of blowing it has been mastered, and this is not easy, it is possible
to produce a profound, hoarse, flesh-tingling booming note the
potency of which lies not so much in its apparent loudness but in its
thorough penetrating power, carrying effortlessly across miles of
water, plumbing with its barbaric cough the depths of the sea, the
buried hearts of mountains. I put it to my lips, took a deep breath, and
began to blow.

What with the repeated and shattering blasts from the shell, and
Mikhális's sheet flailing from the stern, it was impossible for Captain

Eli of the *Paskháli* not to take the most immediate notice. If ever there was a clear case of one vessel urgently signalling to another to heave-to, it was this; and sure enough we watched, triumphantly, the big caique's bow wave subside, the *Paskháli* slow to a rolling halt.

I hauled down the staysail, and we came up round the caique's stern. The rails were lined with startled faces. While Mikhális shouted out his message to the captain, and we edged in alongside, I began to worry about the next stage in this somewhat unusual series of events. How many passengers were there on board? And how much cargo – was I expected to take it all? I had never met the owner of the *Paskháli* in Skiathos, and probably he had never seen *Astarte*. I suspected that Mikhális, in persuading him to countermand the sailing orders of his ship, had given him the impression that a large and fast luxury yacht would take off his passengers and their belongings and waft them on to Skopelos. *Astarte*, though possessing other inestimable qualities, was neither large, fast nor luxurious. I dreaded a descent of, say, fifty people from the high decks of the *Paskháli*, under whose packed weight *Astarte* would sink immediately to the bottom.

The problem was also of concern to Mikhális, as he repeatedly cried out asking how many passengers there were, and when we heard 'about thirty' we exchanged glances of relief. The transference began. Lashed loosely alongside each other in a still considerable swell the two vessels rolled heavily together, and it was a wonder that no damage was done. More surprising was the docility with which Captain Eli, scowling down at us from the wheelhouse, had accepted his unexpected new orders, and surprising too was the way in which the passengers bravely stepped, or rather lunged across and down to *Astarte*'s deck, a forest of arms outstretched to propel and receive them, heavy peasant women in bright shawls and yards of skirting, babies and children, men in city suits, and with them the luggage. . . . This rained down in an unceasing stream, suitcases tied with string, painted tin boxes, a covey of screeching chickens, feathers flying, and baskets, innumerable baskets filled with fruit, tomatoes, cheese, eggs . . . these were tied in a fantastic pyramid upon the cabin top; and all this with the maximum of noise, orders, counterorders, screams of fright, cries of encouragement and consolation, until at last it was done and we were making astern to get free of the *Paskhális*'s swinging superstructure which threatened as we drifted broadside to the swell to smash *Astarte*'s rigging.

There were twenty-seven passengers in all, crowded on the deck, except for the seven women and six children, most of whom were down below in the cabin. Included also were two young Englishmen who had observed the Red Ensign at the stern. (I discovered, later, they were architects.) They sat watching everything carefully and commenting in low voices to each other on this strange occurrence, very properly restraining their curiosity, but beginning to wonder, I felt, whether they were not the victims of some audacious act of piracy on the high seas. As we began a slow but steady progress northward to Cape Gourouni I turned to watch the *Paskhális*, already disappearing in the distance, the white wake boiling from her propeller, her course set firm for Pefki.

The rest of the journey was fortunately uneventful. There was a slight swell round the Cape – slight but more than sufficient to induce, as always among the female travellers in the Aegean, all the over-publicized pangs of seasickness. When Greeks, especially their womenfolk, begin to feel seasick they seek out the most airless and hottest part of any ship unfortunate enough to be carrying them, preferably a place where there is also a strong smell of diesel fumes, and having found it they proceed to be sick, without troubling to move from their positions, groaning and wailing, and calling hopelessly upon the Panayia. I realize that this description is both unsympathetic and even cruel, but it is not really intended to be : but I had more than once begged the sufferers to climb up and get some fresh air. Once I had stepped across the bodies on deck to look down into the cabin. . . . I decided I could not bear to look in again, until the two and a half hour voyage was over. I called silently on Vangeli's name and wondered if this, even for the sake of friendship, was not going almost too far.

Our entry into Skopelos harbour preceded that of the *Kyknos* by about ten minutes. It was Saturday evening, about seven o'clock, the day before the election, and the water-front cafés were crowded. There were also gathered on the quay those waiting for the steamer, and those who had already been waiting for at least an hour for the arrival of the *Paskhális*.

As *Astarte* came in between the harbour beacons, making for that part of the quay where the *Paskhális* normally docks, there was a general and concerted movement along the whole harbour front towards her. People at the café tables stood up to crane their heads, and a crowd converged at the water's side. Although I was in no position to see her, being intimately involved in the attempt to prepare fenders and warps for coming alongside, it seems that *Astarte* made a somewhat curious picture. She was packed with bodies from stem to stern, and was lying very low in the water, but apparently most astonishing of all was the huge heap of luggage, mostly baskets, piled high over the cabin top and completely enveloping it, giving her the appearance, as one friend crudely put it, of a foundering camel.

The disembarkation of the twenty-seven passengers took place without mishap, and it was with some relief that at last we made fast to Vangeli's permanent mooring in the centre of the harbour. The clearing up of the cabin was done quickly and silently, mostly by Mikhális and with the help also of Yiórgo, son of Captain Ilias, who had come with a rowing boat to take us ashore. That night I slept aboard early. At 3.30 in the morning I was woken by the sound of engines: the *Paskhális*, sweeping in from Pefki and the open sea, ablaze with lights and judging by the noise coming from between the decks heavily loaded. I learned later that she put off on the quay at Skopelos no less than one hundred and five people. Half an hour later I left with *Astarte*, sailing round to Panormos and her own moorings, and came in to Skopelos again at noon of the great day by bus.

The election results would not be known until nine or ten o'clock in the evening. It was dark when Rolf and I joined the groups of excited people that were gathered anxiously waiting on the street leading up to the school which was one of the two polling stations. They were counting the votes, and as they did so messages came down, passed hurriedly by word of mouth – Vangeli was leading by so much, no – by some other figure; he wasn't leading at all. . . . We went up to the school where the press of people was greater. We found Vangeli on the steps, surrounded by his friends. He hadn't slept for days and had eaten practically nothing, using up his reserves of nervous energy until one had wondered how he could go on. He was calm and confident. 'I'm going to win,' he said. 'Don't worry.'

It seemed to be true. As the results came out of the school-house we heard he was leading by some sixty votes. But this was the men's polling station – the women, farther down the hill – they might have a different verdict. . . . It was going to be close.

Down at the harbour front, at the café tables under the planes, there was an air of despondency – but here were gathered most of the opposition, sitting gloomily, anxiously whispering. Heavy-hearted Doubdis had shut himself up in his house.

Someone let off a firework, some dynamite. A church bell began to toll. There was the sound of confused cheering. A procession, chanting victoriously, swept down the narrow main street, Vangeli marched in the front rank and people stepped out to wring his hand, kiss him on both cheeks, slap him on the back. He had won, by twenty-six votes.

Up at the Hannás house a large crowd of several hundred jammed the three streets that converged upon the tall house at the corner. They kept up a continuous chant of 'Down with the plutocrats! Down with the swindlers! Long live democracy! . . . socialism! . . . freedom! . . . Greece! . . . Skopelos! . . . Vangeli! *We – want – Vangeli*!'

Vangeli appeared briefly at a window with Alexandra, and waved. Makhi and Eleni and other helpers were circulating outside in the packed street with trays of *loukoumi* and ouzo, replenished as fast as they were emptied. Elected councillors embraced, fell on each other's necks and congratulated each other and every one else within range. The kitchen and downstairs rooms were full of people, drinking endless toasts to the new mayor and each other. Alexandra was excited and calm at the same time: hadn't she known, all along, who would win?

The crowd outside stayed to chant and cheer until the early hours. As *Astarte* was in Panormos I was staying the night with the family. Long after everyone had dispersed and we had gone to bed, I looked out of the window of my room over the old tiled rooftops of the village, stars shining on the mountains across the bay, on the jungle array of chimney pots, white walls. The tavernas seemed to have opened up again – after all it was another day – and people still walked arm in arm in the streets singing. Their jubilant cries carried up through the warm night air . . . 'Long live the Mayor!'

15

Harbour of Silence

The summer was drawing out. At Panormos the house was nearly finished, the roof on long ago, the floors cemented in. Even the doors and windows had arrived, the slatted shutters; I would paint them myself – blue, perhaps. The choice of the colour could wait: decisions of such importance must not be hurried, I needed time to think. . . . The balconies were done, the chestnut columns from Mount Athos in place. I had put oil on them. The grained smoothness of the wood was good to touch. It was good, too, to lean on the crossed balustrade over the low cliff and stare across the cove to the pines on the peninsula that trembled slightly in the heat, and watch the changing shadows and reflections of trees and hills on water as the sun moved round.

Inside it was cool. The white-washers had come, mixed the lime and splashed two coats over the walls, inside and out. Two cane chairs and a table had arrived from Volos; there were only two other pieces of furniture as yet, made by the carpenter on the workbench he had set up in the courtyard: a large double bed, and my desk, made of cypress wood and fitted into a corner of the study upstairs.

Even the jetty is finished. A sponge-diver from Lemnos is marrying a girl from Skopelos, and so now the island can boast the embryo of a sponging fleet – one rather battered caique. The diver came round to Panormos and helped to put down the concrete bases for the jetty, which is overlaid with wood. *Astarte* is tied to the end, and also to a massive and ancient 200 lb. anchor that Vangeli and others helped me to lay out as a permanent mooring. From the study veranda I can look down on her deck: the synthesis of land and sea.

Digging in the grove of cypresses next to the house we found water, and only a few feet below the surface of the earth a crumbling and rather mysterious skeleton. This is now the main well, and the water is better than that of the first one by the beach. Yiórgo comes over on his new motor cycle, shutting up for the day his workshop in

Skopelos, and is busy rigging up pipes and a pump to take up the water to the tank under the roof.

There are two large rain-water cisterns under the house. At the moment they are dry, and we shall have to wait for the first autumn rains to fill them. Spyro, and sometimes Iannis Patsis come every other day with drinking water from the spring in the valley tied in cans or curved clay jars to the back of a mule or donkey. They are still advising me on the kind of trees I should plant, and where: oranges, lemons, and of course there must be vines; but not until the autumn, or better still the early spring. They even suggested that they cut down the olive tree in the courtyard and put up a vine trellis in its place, and were surprised at my indignant refusal: after all, to a Greek, what is a single olive tree? The almonds on the nine almond trees, the olives on the five olive trees are ripening well. This fact seems to surprise no one, but to me it is somehow a miracle. 'Don't you think it's a good crop?' I say to Spyro. '*Veváios*,' he replies, with a grin. 'Of course. Why not?'

Pandelis is anxious to finish the bathroom before Angelina arrives in a week or two, and is at work putting up blue tiles round the walls. He has got over his disappointment at being defeated at the elections (he wanted to be a councillor): he has his building, and indeed he wishes to wind up the work at Panormos as quickly as possible because there are so many contracts waiting for him in Skopelos. A few days ago some friends of his and their wives and children came on the bus to attend a *panayiri* up the valley, and having drunk a good deal of wine, came down to see the house. They brought more wine with them and invited Pandelis to join them. I was woken from my afternoon sleep by the sound of music and the stamping of dancers' feet on the kitchen floor. Not being in the mood to join these festivities I contented myself with a fixed smile and polite conversation while the dancers drank toasts to the 'good rootedness' of the house, and I tried to make myself coffee. When they left, and I came downstairs some time later, I found Pandelis curled up asleep in the bath, still wearing his large tweed cap and with the last blue tile clutched in his fingers.

Stammatis has taken over the driving of the Skopelos bus, to the general satisfaction of the islanders. The bus rumbles past on the road above the house once in the morning and once again in the evening, coming back from Glossa. When there is bread and other food, bought for me in Skopelos, Stammatis blows his horn and leaves the basket by the roadside for me to collect.

Rolf and Barbara came across the island to see me. Their hotel, too, is nearly finished and it will soon be opened. It has taken Rolf two years. The obstructions and misfortunes that he had overcome, and that had nearly overcome him, starting from that ill-fated discovery of a temple of Asklepios in his foundations, had been almost incredible. I told him that he had aged considerably since he first came to Skopelos. 'Not two years,' he said, 'but two hundred.' Nevertheless he still has his sense of humour and a fine hotel as well, a long graceful white building among the bamboos and olive groves on the edge of the sea, with a view of Skopelos village mounting in its white half circle above the bay, and behind a river of olive trees climbing into the hills. We had been to Steniválla together, and he and Barbara and the Mavrikis family have become friends. They so much liked the home-made bread that Angeliki bakes that when the hotel opens there will be a regular order by caique every day.

The last time I was in Skiathos harbour I had no time to go ashore. But I saw little Kosta in Skopelos one day – he had found himself a job on the *Korfini* as a deck boy. Perhaps he will be a sailor after all. He tells me that Gus and Panayioti are well and send their greetings. Kosta is wondering whether I will go across with *Astarte* and bring him and Paraskevoúla back to Panormos to see the house. There must be some odd jobs for him to do, he says. . . . We shall see about it when Angelina arrives.

In spite of his mayoral duties Vangeli occasionally finds time to come to Panormos. 'Ah, Michael, if I could be finished with all my works, and live like you in Panormos – I will be the happiest man in the world!'

The resin-collectors' cottage, destroyed in the earth-tremors, has been pulled down and Vangeli is now rebuilding it, on a slightly larger scale, and is making it, as he says, very strong. Until the family house up the valley is rebuilt this will be somewhere for him and Alexandra and the children to come and stay. At present Vangeli stays either with me or in the retsina barn where is also packed all the furniture, cutlery and bedding from the cottage in the hills. He has brought *Makhi* round to the bay, and propping up the caique by the shore spends much time, wearing two days' growth of beard, his pale green undershorts, a filthy shirt and a red straw hat, scrubbing the underside of the hull. Sometimes I wish some stranger would pass and I could start pointing out some of the more prominent features of the view. 'There's Daseiá,' I'd say, 'and Skiathos in the distance, and beyond, Mount Pelion. Oh, and d'you see that person up to his knees in the sea? That's the mayor. . . .' However, nobody passes, and that is just as well.

The other day Alexandra and Makhi arrived and we all went squid fishing in the rowing boat Iannis Patsis has just bought. The night was as it should be for this kind of fishing, dark, with a moon setting early. There were five of us, and Iannis and Vangeli rowed. The boat is in fact a very old one, but seaworthy enough and specially fitted out for catching squid. An old rusty frying-pan grew out of the side, over the water, and in it were placed wood shavings, a lump or two of resin which was then lit with a match. We rowed out on the calm black water with this fire like a torch blazing at our elbows, smoke drifting across our heads obscuring the stars. Past Arapi Point, not far from the shore, with the lights of Skiathos sparkling on the horizon and the lamps of the *gri-gri* boats strung out in the distance, we began to fish. It was very simple. Lines with a strange hook, unbaited, made of needles bound together in the shape of a shuttle-cock, are let down deep into the sea. Either the squid are there, or they are not. If not, we change our position, closer to the rocks or farther away. Phosphorescence gleams from the oar-blades and Iannis nods his grey head, cocking an eye at the moon which is red now, sinking over Evvia. There is a tug at Makhi's line. The little girl gives a cry of excitement, 'Vangeli – I've got one! The first, the first!'

Up it comes, and as it flies up out of the sea discharges a sackful of water in the air. The squid is a beautiful amber colour; as it dies the colour drains away, the shining skin fading to white, soft ivory.

I have one now, and Vangeli; Alexandra is pulling them in as quickly as she can unhook them on the deck. The air is full of jets of sea-water that descend from the sky and drench us. In an hour we have caught about thirty pounds, and there will be squid fried, boiled, stewed, enough to keep us all for days. . . .

Sometimes in the evenings when Vangeli comes alone to Panormos we play *tavli*, either on the study veranda or at a low table brought out under the carob tree by the retsina barn, a lantern at our side. Vangeli has been winning again. 'What do you expect?' he says,

'Am I not the Admiral of the Northern Sporades, the Mayor, the best cook, squid-fisher and *tavli*-player in the Balkans?' It is no good arguing with him.

At sunset when the workmen leave there is no one at Panormos, and I sit out high above the water as the reds and golds withdraw across the sea, and the tops of the pines and cypresses stand out dark and feathery against the sky. The trees grow taller as the light fades, and blacker, closing in upon the smooth clear water. A goat-bell jingles in the olives, is silent. Somewhere far up the valley a dog barks. I am waiting for the ghosts of ships and men to loom across the sea: a trireme, oars flashing silently upon the unruffled water, bellied sails of a galleon where there is no wind. Sometime I know, if I wait long enough I shall see them, coming in to Panormos the 'all-harbour' as once they used to do. And the ancient marble column, when I set it up as I must, crowned with its worn capital, somewhere on the rocks – perhaps if I listen, that too will speak, and the ruined chapel behind me deliver up its secrets.

For a moment I had thought that finishing the house was too much the end of something; but the house will never be finished, in one sense: it is only the beginning of living in it. The islands I have hardly begun to know; they are nearer now than they have ever been, yet still elusive. I have touched only their outer rim, blinked at the vague silhouette of fishing boats, mountains, men. The wind-gates of the Sporades have opened wide enough to let me in; perhaps in time they will allow me to pass through.